Table of Contents

Chapter 1: Introduction to Visual Studio Code...20

1.1 The Evolution of Code Editors: A Brief History 20

1.2 Visual Studio Code: An Overview...21

    1.2.1 Cross-Platform Support..21

    1.2.2 Lightweight and Fast 21

    1.2.3 Extensibility..21

    1.2.4 Integrated Development Environment (IDE) Features 21

    1.2.5 IntelliSense and Code Completion 21

    1.2.6 Integrated Terminal...22

    1.2.7 Git Integration..22

    1.2.8 Theming and Customization...22

    1.2.9 Accessibility Features...22

    1.2.10 Active Development and Community Support 22

1.3 Key Features That Set Visual Studio Code Apart...23

    1.3.1 Versatile Language Support..23

    1.3.2 Powerful Extension Ecosystem 23

    1.3.3 IntelliSense and Code Navigation...23

    1.3.4 Integrated Git Version Control 23

    1.3.5 Debugging Made Simple 24

    1.3.6 Integrated Terminal...24

    1.3.7 Customizable Themes and UI..24

    1.3.8 Extensive Documentation and Community Support...24

    1.3.9 Cross-Platform Compatibility 24

1.4 The User Interface: A Tour...25

    1.4.1 Editor Area 25

    1.4.2 Sidebar 25

    1.4.3 Status Bar..25

    1.4.4 Activity Bar..26

    1.4.5 Panel and Terminal 26

    1.4.6 Command Palette 26

    1.4.7 Customization and Themes...26

    1.4.8 Zen Mode..26

1.5 Installing and Setting Up Visual Studio Code 27

    1.5.1 Installation 27

    1.5.2 First Launch 28

    1.5.3 Basic Configuration 28

    1.5.4 Extensions 28

    1.5.5 Workspace Configuration 28

    1.5.6 Key Takeaways 29

Chapter 2: Customizing Your Workspace 30

2.1 Personalizing Themes and Colors 30

    2.1.1 Themes vs. Color Schemes 30

    2.1.2 Changing the Theme 30

    2.1.3 Installing Additional Themes 30

    2.1.4 Customizing Themes 31

    2.1.5 Popular Themes 31

    2.1.6 Key Takeaways 31

2.2 Managing Workspaces and Folders 32

    2.2.1 Workspaces vs. Folders 32

    2.2.2 Creating a Workspace 32

    2.2.3 Adding Folders to a Workspace 33

    2.2.4 Switching Between Workspaces 33

    2.2.5 Workspace Settings 33

    2.2.6 Workspaces for Multi-Project Management 33

    2.2.7 Key Takeaways 33

2.3 Keyboard Shortcuts and Efficiency Tips 34

    2.3.1 Basic Navigation Shortcuts 34

    2.3.2 Code Editing Shortcuts 34

    2.3.3 Multi-Cursor and Selection Shortcuts 35

    2.3.4 Search and Replace Shortcuts 35

    2.3.5 Integrated Terminal Shortcuts 35

    2.3.6 Customizing Keyboard Shortcuts 35

    2.3.7 Key Takeaways 36

2.4 Extensions and Plugins: Enhancing Functionality 36

    2.4.1 What Are Extensions? 36

    2.4.2 Installing Extensions 36

2.4.3 Popular Extension Categories...37

2.4.4 Managing Extensions..37

2.4.5 Creating Your Own Extensions..38

2.4.6 Key Takeaways...38

2.5 Setting Up User and Workspace Settings....................................38

2.5.1 User Settings vs. Workspace Settings......................................39

2.5.2 User Settings...39

2.5.3 Workspace Settings...39

2.5.4 Common Configuration Settings..39

2.5.5 Syncing Settings..40

2.5.6 Key Takeaways...40

Chapter 3: Coding Efficiently in Visual Studio Code..........................41

3.1 Intelligent Code Completion..41

3.1.1 Getting Started with Code Completion.....................................41

3.1.2 Context-Aware Suggestions...41

3.1.3 Triggering Code Completion Manually.....................................41

3.1.4 Snippets and Emmet Abbreviations...41

3.1.5 Customizing Code Completion...42

3.1.6 Code Completion with Extensions...42

3.1.7 Key Takeaways...42

3.2 Code Navigation and Refactoring Tools.....................................43

3.2.1 Go to Definition and Peek Definition.......................................43

3.2.2 Find All References...43

3.2.3 Renaming Symbols...43

3.2.4 Code Refactoring..44

3.2.5 Keyboard Shortcuts for Navigation and Refactoring................44

3.2.6 Extensions for Advanced Refactoring.....................................44

3.2.7 Key Takeaways...44

3.3 Debugging Made Simple..45

3.3.1 Setting Up Debugging Environments..45

3.3.2 Debugging Features..45

3.3.3 Remote Debugging Capabilities..47

3.3.4 Debugging Configuration Options..47

3.3.5 Debugging Extensions..47

3.3.6 Debugging Tips..47

3.3.7 Key Takeaways..47

3.4 Integrated Terminal Usage..48

3.4.1 Accessing the Integrated Terminal...48

3.4.2 Customizing the Terminal..48

3.4.3 Running Commands..48

3.4.4 Multiple Terminals...49

3.4.5 Terminal Split View..49

3.4.6 Debugging in the Terminal...49

3.4.7 Running Tasks...49

3.4.8 Key Takeaways..50

3.5 Version Control Integration..50

3.5.1 Initializing a Repository..50

3.5.2 Cloning a Repository..50

3.5.3 Git Integration...51

3.5.4 Version Control Providers..51

3.5.5 Visual Studio Code GitLens Extension...51

3.5.6 Key Takeaways..52

Chapter 4: Extensions and the Marketplace..53

4.1 Navigating the Extension Marketplace...53

4.1.1 Accessing the Extension Marketplace..53

4.1.2 Browsing Extensions..53

4.1.3 Extension Details...53

4.1.4 Installing Extensions..53

4.1.5 Managing Installed Extensions...54

4.1.6 Extension Recommendations...54

4.1.7 Keeping Extensions Updated..54

4.1.8 Installing Extensions from the Command Line...54

4.1.9 Managing Extensions Remotely..54

4.1.10 Key Takeaways...54

4.2 Must-Have Extensions for Developers...55

4.2.1 ESLint...55

4.2.2 Prettier - Code Formatter...55

4.2.3 GitLens...56

4.2.4 Bracket Pair Colorizer 2 56

4.2.5 Live Server...56

4.2.6 Docker 56

4.2.7 Visual Studio IntelliCode..56

4.2.8 Remote - SSH 56

4.2.9 REST Client...56

4.2.10 Live Share..57

4.2.11 Code Spell Checker..57

4.2.12 Jupyter 57

4.2.13 Docker Compose 57

4.2.14 Code Runner 57

4.2.15 Rainbow Brackets...57

4.2.16 CodeTime 58

4.2.17 Bookmarks..58

4.2.18 Git History 58

4.2.19 Quokka.js 58

4.2.20 CodeTour 58

4.3 Creating Your Own Extensions 58

4.3.1 Why Create Your Own Extension? 59

4.3.2 Extension Components 59

4.3.3 Getting Started..59

4.3.4 Extension API 60

4.3.5 Extension Development Resources 61

4.4 Community Contributions and Support..61

4.4.1 The Power of Community 61

4.4.2 Engaging with the VS Code Community 62

4.4.3 Supporting the VS Code Project 62

4.4.4 Recognizing Contributors..63

4.5 Keeping Extensions Updated 63

4.5.1 The Importance of Extension Updates...64

4.5.2 Managing Extension Updates...64

4.5.3 Best Practices for Extension Updates 65

Chapter 5: Languages and Frameworks..67

5.1 Support for Major Programming Languages 67

5.1.1 Language Server Protocol...67

5.1.2 Built-in Language Features 67

5.1.3 IntelliSense and Autocompletion 67

5.1.4 Debugging Support...68

5.1.5 Language Extensions 68

5.1.6 Polyglot Development...68

5.1.7 Custom Language Support 68

5.2 Tailoring Visual Studio Code for JavaScript...69

5.2.1 JavaScript Language Features..69

5.2.2 JavaScript Extensions 69

5.2.3 Customization for JavaScript...70

5.2.4 Node.js Development..70

5.2.5 JavaScript Frameworks...70

5.2.6 Debugging in the Browser 70

5.2.7 Collaboration and Version Control 71

5.3 Python Development in Visual Studio Code...71

5.3.1 Python Language Features...71

5.3.2 Python Extensions 72

5.3.3 Customization for Python...72

5.3.4 Python Web Development...72

5.3.5 Data Science and Machine Learning..73

5.3.6 Python Version Control 73

5.3.7 Collaboration and Remote Development..73

5.4 Exploring C# and .NET Capabilities 73

5.4.1 C# Language Features..73

5.4.2 .NET Core and .NET 5+ Development..74

5.4.3 C# Extensions..74

5.4.4 Customization for C 74

5.4.5 .NET Core and ASP.NET Core Development 75

5.4.6 Entity Framework Core 75

5.4.7 Collaboration and Version Control 75

5.4.8 Unity Game Development...75

5.5 Other Languages: From PHP to Go 75

5.5.1 PHP Development 75

5.5.2 Ruby and Ruby on Rails...76

5.5.3 Java Development 76

5.5.4 Rust Programming..76

5.5.5 Go Programming...76

5.5.6 TypeScript and Front-End Development 76

5.5.7 Swift and iOS Development..76

5.5.8 Dart and Flutter..76

5.5.9 Web Development with HTML and CSS..76

5.5.10 Shell Scripting and DevOps 77

5.5.11 LaTeX and Technical Writing 77

Chapter 6: Source Control Integration 81

6.1. Understanding Git Integration 81

6.2. Committing and Pushing Changes...82

Committing Changes 82

Pushing Changes 83

Commit and Push Best Practices 83

6.3. Branch Management and Merging 84

What Are Branches?..84

Creating a Branch 84

Switching Between Branches 85

Merging Branches..85

Handling Merge Conflicts...85

Branch Management Best Practices 86

6.4. Resolving Merge Conflicts...86

Identifying Merge Conflicts 87

Steps to Resolve Merge Conflicts..87

Using VS Code's Built-in Merge Conflict Resolution 87

Additional Tips for Conflict Resolution...88

6.5. Advanced Git Features and Extensions 88

1. GitLens Extension 88

2. Git Graph Extension 89

3. Git History Extension 89

4. Gitignore Support 89

5. Git Stash 90

6. Git Workspaces 90

7.1. Setting Up Debugging Environment 91

1. Installing the Necessary Extensions 91

2. Creating a Launch Configuration 91

3. Setting Breakpoints 92

4. Starting the Debugger 92

5. Debugging Actions 92

6. Inspecting Variables 92

7. Debugging Console 92

7.2. Breakpoints and Watchers 93

Setting Breakpoints 93

Working with Breakpoints 93

Adding Watchers 94

Conditional Breakpoints 94

Data Tips..94

7.3. Inspecting Variables and Stack Traces 95

Inspecting Variables...95

Navigating Stack Traces...95

Exception Handling...96

7.4. Remote Debugging Capabilities..96

Setting Up Remote Debugging 96

Remote Development Scenarios 97

Troubleshooting Remote Debugging 98

7.5. Solving Common Debugging Issues 98

1. Debugging Information Not Visible:..98

2. Breakpoints Not Hitting:...99

3. Code Not Pausing at Breakpoints: 99

4. Debugging Slow or Unresponsive: 99

5. Exception Handling:..99

6. Misconfigured Debugging Environment: 99

7. Dependencies and Environment:..99

8. Outdated Debugging Extensions:...99

9. Network-Related Issues:..100

10. Inconsistent Debugging Environment: 100

8

11. Memory and Resource Issues: 100

12. IDE-Specific Issues: 100

Chapter 8: Testing Your Code 101

8.1. Introduction to Testing in Visual Studio Code 101

Why Testing Matters 101

Types of Testing 101

Testing Frameworks and Libraries 102

Writing Your First Test 102

8.2. Setting Up Testing Frameworks 103

JavaScript and Node.js 103

Python 105

8.3. Writing and Running Tests 105

Choosing a Testing Framework 105

Setting Up Your Testing Environment 106

Running Tests in Visual Studio Code 106

8.4. Test Coverage and Reporting 107

Understanding Test Coverage 107

Setting Up Test Coverage 108

Visualizing Coverage Reports 108

Interpreting Coverage Reports 108

8.5. Automated Testing and Continuous Integration 109

Automated Testing 109

Continuous Integration (CI) 110

Benefits of Automated Testing and CI 110

9.1. Multi-Cursor and Snippets 111

Multi-Cursor Editing 111

Code Snippets 112

Benefits of Multi-Cursor Editing and Snippets 112

9.2. Code Folding and Regions 113

Code Folding 113

Code Regions 113

Benefits of Code Folding and Regions 114

9.3. Regular Expression in Search and Replace 114

Using Regular Expressions in Search 114

Using Regular Expressions in Replace..115

Tips for Using Regular Expressions..115

9.4. File Comparisons and Merging..116

Comparing Files..116

Merging Changes..116

Extensions for Enhanced Merge Conflict Resolution 117

Visual Studio Code as a Git Merge Tool 117

Conclusion..117

9.5. Advanced Formatting and Beautification Tools 117

1. Auto-Formatting on Save..117

2. Built-in Formatters...118

3. EditorConfig Support...118

4. Custom Code Styling with Settings...118

5. Using ESLint and Prettier 118

6. Custom Code Snippets 119

7. Extensions for Code Formatting..119

Conclusion..119

10.1. Improving Startup Time and Efficiency..120

1. Update to the Latest Version...120

2. Optimize Extensions 120

3. Custom Workspace Configuration...120

4. Use Workspaces and Folders...120

5. Limit Large Files and Folders 121

6. Adjust Git History...121

7. Clear Workspace State 121

8. Reduce Telemetry and Error Reporting 121

9. Optimize Hardware..121

10. Troubleshooting and Profiling 121

10.2. Managing Memory and CPU Usage 122

1. Limiting Concurrent Processes..122

2. Extension Profiling...122

3. Customize Search Behavior 122

4. Extension Recommendations 122

5. Increase Heap Memory..123

    6. Manage Large Workspace Folders 123

    7. Monitor Task Manager 123

    8. Close Unused Tabs and Editors 123

  10.3. Troubleshooting Performance Issues 124

    1. Slow Startup 124

    2. High CPU and Memory Usage 124

    3. Unresponsive Behavior 125

    4. Inefficient Search and Indexing 125

    5. Visual Studio Code Updates 125

    6. Editor and Workspace Settings 125

    7. External Factors 126

    8. Feedback and Reporting 126

  10.4. Best Practices for High-Performance Coding 126

    1. Use Proper Data Structures and Algorithms 126

    2. Avoid Nested Loops 127

    3. Optimize Database Queries 127

    4. Minimize I/O Operations 127

    5. Avoid Global Variables 127

    6. Use Lazy Loading 128

    7. Profile and Benchmark Your Code 128

    8. Optimize Memory Usage 128

    9. Keep Code Modular and DRY 128

    10. Regularly Update Dependencies 128

  10.5. Leveraging Hardware Resources 129

    1. Parallelism and Concurrency 129

    2. GPU Acceleration 129

    3. Memory Management 130

    4. Caching and Prefetching 130

    5. Load Balancing 130

    6. Energy Efficiency 131

    7. Profiling and Monitoring 131

Chapter 11: Customizing the Look and Feel 134

  Section 11.1: Themes and Icon Packs 134

    Themes 134

Icon Packs...134

Section 11.2: Customizing Font and Display Settings 135

Changing the Font..135

Line Spacing and More 136

Section 11.3: Accessibility Features 137

1. Screen Reader Support..137

2. High Contrast Themes..137

3. Keyboard Navigation..137

4. Other Accessibility Settings 138

Section 11.4: Personalizing the Sidebar and Panels..138

1. Sidebar Customization...138

2. Panel Customization 139

3. Customizing Appearance 139

Section 11.5: Creating a Comfortable Coding Environment.....................................140

1. Workspace Layout..140

2. Customizing Themes 141

3. Font and Typography...141

4. Comfortable Shortcuts...141

5. Accessibility Features 141

6. Version Control Integration...142

7. Extending Functionality 142

8. Personalization is Key..142

Chapter 12: Collaboration and Remote Development...143

Section 12.1: Pair Programming with Live Share..143

What is Live Share?...143

Setting Up Live Share 143

Features of Live Share 143

Tips for Effective Live Share Sessions...144

Section 12.2: Remote Development Extensions..144

Remote - SSH...144

Remote - Containers 145

Remote - WSL (Windows Subsystem for Linux) 145

Remote Development Tips 145

Section 12.3: Collaborating Across Different Platforms 146

Multi-Platform Collaboration 146

Live Share..146

GitHub Integration 147

Collaborative Development Workflows................................147

Section 12.4: Code Reviews and Pull Requests.................148

Setting Up Code Review Environments................................148

Managing Pull Requests..148

Code Review Extensions..149

Best Practices for Code Reviews 149

Section 12.5: Managing Projects and Teams.....................150

Project Management Extensions..150

Team Collaboration and Communication 150

Version Control and Teamwork 151

Chapter 13: The Command Palette and Shortcuts 152

Section 13.1: Mastering the Command Palette.................152

What is the Command Palette?...152

Opening the Command Palette 152

Using the Command Palette 152

Customizing the Command Palette 153

Section 13.2: Essential Keyboard Shortcuts.....................153

Keyboard Shortcut Basics 153

Essential Keyboard Shortcuts 154

Section 13.3: Customizing Shortcuts.................................155

Accessing Keyboard Shortcuts..155

Viewing and Searching Keyboard Shortcuts......................155

Customizing Keyboard Shortcuts 156

Resetting Customized Shortcuts 156

Exporting and Importing Keybindings.................................156

Advanced Customization..156

Section 13.4: Command Line Integration...........................157

Opening the Integrated Terminal 157

Customizing the Integrated Terminal..................................157

Running Commands in the Integrated Terminal 158

Output and Debugging...159

Section 13.5: Efficiency Tips and Tricks 159

1. Multiple Cursors and Selections 159

2. Emmet Abbreviations 160

3. Fuzzy Search in Command Palette 160

4. Snippets...160

5. Zen Mode 160

6. Peek Definition and Go to Definition 160

7. Code Folding...160

8. Custom Keybindings..160

9. Automatic Code Formatting 161

10. Version Control Integration..161

11. Explore Extensions 161

12. Intelligent Code Suggestions 161

13. Customizing Themes and Fonts..161

Chapter 14: Integrating with Other Tools and Services 162

Section 14.1: Connecting with Cloud Services 162

Azure Cloud Integration..162

AWS Integration 162

Google Cloud Platform (GCP) Integration 162

Other Cloud Services 162

Cloud-Based IDEs...163

Key Benefits of Cloud Service Integration...163

Section 14.2: Using Docker in Visual Studio Code 163

Docker Extension 164

Container Management...164

Docker Compose Support..164

Debugging Containers...164

Container Registry Integration 164

Key Benefits of Docker Integration 164

Section 14.3: Integration with Database Tools...165

Database Extensions...165

Connection Management...165

Query Execution 166

Schema Exploration 166

14

IntelliSense and Code Assistance 166

Version Control Integration 166

Database-specific Features 166

Section 14.4: Working with REST APIs and Postman 167

REST Client Extension 167

Request Syntax 167

Response Inspection 167

Collections and Environments 168

Debugging and Testing 168

Integration with Postman 168

Version Control and Collaboration 168

Section 14.5: Combining with Other Development Tools 168

Shell Integration 169

Git and Version Control 169

Docker Integration 169

Database Tools 169

Cloud Services 170

Collaboration Tools 170

Chapter 15: Mobile and Web Development 171

Section 15.1: Setting Up for Web Development 171

Installing Node.js and npm 171

Setting Up a Code Editor 171

Installing Extensions 171

Creating a Workspace 172

Conclusion 172

Section 15.2: Mobile Development with React Native and Flutter 173

React Native 173

Flutter 174

Conclusion 174

Section 15.3: Responsive Design and Cross-Browser Testing 175

Understanding Responsive Design 175

Visual Studio Code for Responsive Design 175

Cross-Browser Testing 176

Conclusion 176

Section 15.4: JavaScript Frameworks: Angular, Vue.js, and More.............................176

   The Importance of JavaScript Frameworks.............................176

   Angular.............................177

   Vue.js.............................177

   React and Other Frameworks.............................178

   Conclusion.............................178

Section 15.5: Building Progressive Web Apps.............................178

   What Are Progressive Web Apps (PWAs)?.............................179

   Building PWAs with Visual Studio Code.............................179

   Conclusion.............................180

Chapter 16: Scripting and Automation.............................181

Section 16.1: Automating Repetitive Tasks.............................181

Section 16.2: Building and Running Scripts.............................182

Chapter 16: Scripting and Automation.............................184

Section 16.1: Automating Repetitive Tasks.............................184

Section 16.2: Building and Running Scripts.............................185

Section 16.3: Task Runners and Build Tools.............................188

Section 16.4: Custom Automation Workflows.............................190

Section 16.5: Using Visual Studio Code for DevOps.............................191

Section 17.1: Setting Up for Data Science Workflows.............................194

Section 17.2: Python and R Integration.............................195

Section 17.3: Working with Jupyter Notebooks.............................197

Section 17.4: Visualization Tools and Libraries.............................199

Section 17.5: Machine Learning Model Development.............................201

   Setting Up Your ML Environment.............................201

   Exploratory Data Analysis (EDA).............................201

   Model Development and Training.............................202

   Model Evaluation and Hyperparameter Tuning.............................202

   Model Deployment and Serving.............................203

Chapter 18: Security and Version Control.............................204

Section 18.1: Ensuring Code Security.............................204

   Code Analysis and Linting.............................204

   Static Code Analysis.............................204

   Dependency Scanning.............................204

Code Reviews and Collaboration 204

Secure Coding Guidelines 204

Security Testing and Vulnerability Scanning...............................205

Encryption and Authentication 205

Compliance and Security Standards 205

Continuous Security Monitoring 205

Section 18.2: Managing Dependencies and Security Updates.............205

Dependency Management Tools 205

Dependency Scanning Extensions 206

Automating Dependency Updates 206

Security Notifications...206

Security Best Practices 206

Section 18.3: Working with Version Control Systems.......................207

Initializing a Repository...207

Cloning a Repository 208

Tracking Changes..208

Branching and Merging..208

Resolving Merge Conflicts..209

Working with Remote Repositories 209

Commit History and Diffs 209

VCS Extensions...209

Section 18.4: Best Practices for Secure Coding..............................210

1. Keep Software Up-to-Date 210

2. Use Secure Extensions 210

3. Configure Security Settings...210

4. Secure Your Development Environment...................................210

5. Avoid Storing Sensitive Data...210

6. Implement Proper Authentication and Authorization 210

7. Regularly Test for Vulnerabilities...211

8. Follow the Principle of Least Privilege 211

9. Encrypt Data in Transit and at Rest..211

10. Handle Errors Securely..211

11. Keep an Eye on Security Advisories.......................................211

12. Educate Your Development Team...211

Section 18.5: Handling Sensitive Data and Credentials 211

1. Use Environment Variables 212

2. Use a Secrets Manager 212

3. Secure Credential Storage 212

4. Encrypt Sensitive Data...212

5. Implement Access Controls 212

6. Audit and Monitor Access...213

7. Regularly Rotate Credentials 213

8. Educate Your Team 213

9. Use Encryption Libraries 213

Chapter 19: Tailoring Visual Studio Code for Enterprise Use 213

Section 19.1: Large-Scale Deployment Strategies 213

Section 19.2: Managing Licenses and Compliance 215

Section 19.3: Enterprise-Level Customizations..216

Section 19.4: Security in an Enterprise Environment..218

Section 19.5: Training and Support for Teams 220

Chapter 20: The Future of Visual Studio Code...222

Section 20.1: Emerging Trends in Development..222

Section 20.2: Visual Studio Code in the Next Decade 223

Section 20.3: Community and Open Source Contributions 225

Open Source Foundation 225

The Extension Marketplace..226

Collaboration Beyond Borders...226

A Culture of Giving Back 227

The Future of Community and Open Source...227

Section 20.4: Integrating AI and Machine Learning Tools...227

AI-Powered Code Assistance 228

ML-Powered Predictive Analysis...228

AI-Enhanced Testing 229

Future Possibilities 230

Section 20.5: Staying Ahead with Visual Studio Code..230

1. Keep VS Code Updated..230

2. Explore New Extensions 230

3. Join the Community 231

4. Attend Webinars and Conferences 231

5. Learn Keyboard Shortcuts 231

6. Explore Insider Builds..231

7. Embrace AI-Powered Tools 231

8. Experiment with Remote Development...231

9. Contribute to Open Source...231

10. Explore Emerging Trends..231

Chapter 1: Introduction to Visual Studio Code

1.1 The Evolution of Code Editors: A Brief History

Code editors have come a long way since the early days of computing. In the early years, programmers had to use rudimentary tools to write code, often relying on paper and punch cards. As computers evolved, so did the tools used for coding.

The first text editors were simple command-line tools that allowed programmers to input code using a keyboard. These early editors lacked many of the features we take for granted today, such as syntax highlighting, code completion, and version control integration. Programmers had to manually manage every aspect of their code, from formatting to debugging.

One of the notable early text editors was the Unix-based "ed" editor, which was a line-oriented editor that required users to specify line numbers for editing operations. While "ed" was a powerful tool, it was not user-friendly and required a steep learning curve.

The advent of graphical user interfaces (GUIs) brought about a significant shift in code editing. Integrated Development Environments (IDEs) started to emerge, offering more advanced features and a more user-friendly experience. IDEs like Borland Turbo C++ and Microsoft Visual Studio became popular among developers.

However, IDEs were often heavyweight and resource-intensive, making them less suitable for some programming tasks. In response to this, lightweight code editors began to gain popularity. These editors focused on providing essential features for coding without the bloat of a full-fledged IDE.

The introduction of open-source software and collaborative development platforms further fueled the evolution of code editors. Developers from around the world started contributing to projects like Emacs, Vim, and Sublime Text, enhancing their functionality and making them highly customizable.

In recent years, Visual Studio Code (VS Code) has emerged as a standout in the world of code editors. Developed by Microsoft, VS Code combines the best of both worlds: the simplicity and speed of lightweight editors with the power and extensibility of IDEs. It has quickly gained a massive following in the developer community and has become the go-to choice for many programmers.

In this chapter, we will delve deeper into the evolution of code editors, leading up to the introduction of Visual Studio Code. We'll explore how VS Code has redefined the landscape of code editing and what sets it apart from other editors and IDEs. Additionally, we'll take a tour of the user interface and guide you through the process of installing and setting up Visual Studio Code on your system.

Whether you're a seasoned developer or just starting on your coding journey, understanding the history and capabilities of code editors like Visual Studio Code is essential for maximizing your productivity and making the most of your coding experience. So, let's begin our exploration of the world of code editors and the exciting journey of using Visual Studio Code.

1.2 Visual Studio Code: An Overview

Visual Studio Code, often abbreviated as VS Code, is a free, open-source code editor developed by Microsoft. It has gained immense popularity among developers for its versatility, speed, and extensive ecosystem of extensions. In this section, we'll provide you with an overview of Visual Studio Code and its core features.

1.2.1 Cross-Platform Support

One of the standout features of VS Code is its cross-platform compatibility. It is available for Windows, macOS, and Linux, making it a versatile choice for developers working on different operating systems. This cross-platform support ensures a consistent development experience regardless of your preferred platform.

1.2.2 Lightweight and Fast

VS Code is renowned for its speed and efficiency. Unlike heavyweight IDEs, it doesn't consume excessive system resources, allowing it to launch quickly and run smoothly even on less powerful machines. This lightweight nature makes it suitable for a wide range of coding tasks, from small scripts to large-scale projects.

1.2.3 Extensibility

One of the key strengths of Visual Studio Code is its extensibility. It provides a robust extension marketplace where you can find a vast array of extensions and plugins contributed by the community. These extensions enhance the editor's functionality, adding support for various programming languages, frameworks, and tools. Whether you're a web developer, data scientist, or DevOps engineer, you'll likely find extensions that cater to your specific needs.

1.2.4 Integrated Development Environment (IDE) Features

While VS Code is a lightweight code editor at its core, it offers many IDE-like features through extensions. These features include code navigation, intelligent code completion, debugging capabilities, version control integration, and more. With the right set of extensions, you can transform VS Code into a powerful IDE tailored to your workflow.

1.2.5 IntelliSense and Code Completion

VS Code provides intelligent code completion, often referred to as IntelliSense. This feature suggests code completions, function signatures, and variable names as you type, making coding more efficient and reducing the likelihood of syntax errors. IntelliSense is language-aware and works seamlessly with a wide range of programming languages.

1.2.6 Integrated Terminal

A built-in integrated terminal is another handy feature of VS Code. You can open a terminal directly within the editor, allowing you to run commands, execute scripts, and interact with your project's files without leaving the coding environment. This integration streamlines your workflow and eliminates the need to switch between the editor and a separate terminal application.

1.2.7 Git Integration

Version control is a fundamental aspect of modern software development, and VS Code includes seamless Git integration. You can view changes, commit code, push and pull from remote repositories, and manage branches and merge conflicts—all from within the editor. This simplifies collaborative coding and ensures your project's codebase remains well-managed.

1.2.8 Theming and Customization

Visual Studio Code offers a range of themes and customization options, allowing you to tailor the editor's appearance and behavior to your preferences. Whether you prefer a dark theme, a specific font, or customized keybindings, you can configure VS Code to match your style.

1.2.9 Accessibility Features

Accessibility is a priority for the VS Code development team. The editor includes features like screen reader support and high-contrast themes to ensure that developers with different needs can comfortably use the tool.

1.2.10 Active Development and Community Support

VS Code is under active development, with regular updates and new features being introduced. The extensive community of users and contributors ensures a vibrant ecosystem of extensions, forums, and online resources. If you encounter issues or have questions, you can often find solutions and support from the VS Code community.

In summary, Visual Studio Code is a versatile and powerful code editor that combines the best aspects of lightweight editors and full-fledged IDEs. Its cross-platform support, speed, and extensive extension ecosystem make it a top choice for developers across various domains. In the following sections of this book, we will explore Visual Studio Code in greater detail, covering its features, customization options, and practical usage scenarios.

1.3 Key Features That Set Visual Studio Code Apart

Visual Studio Code (VS Code) stands out as a popular code editor due to its impressive array of features that cater to the needs of developers across various domains. In this section, we'll dive deeper into the key features that set VS Code apart from other code editors and explain why it has become a favorite among developers worldwide.

1.3.1 Versatile Language Support

One of the standout features of VS Code is its extensive language support. It offers built-in support for a wide range of programming languages, including but not limited to JavaScript, Python, Java, C++, and Ruby. This versatility makes it suitable for developers working with different languages on diverse projects. VS Code's language server protocol ensures that language support is efficient and responsive, providing features like IntelliSense, code completion, and syntax highlighting.

1.3.2 Powerful Extension Ecosystem

The strength of VS Code lies in its vast extension ecosystem. The Visual Studio Code Marketplace hosts thousands of extensions contributed by the community. These extensions enhance the editor's functionality, adding support for specific frameworks, tools, and workflows. For instance, you can find extensions for web development, data science, DevOps, and more. With the right extensions, you can tailor VS Code to suit your unique needs and workflow.

1.3.3 IntelliSense and Code Navigation

VS Code's IntelliSense feature is a game-changer for developers. It provides context-aware code suggestions, autocompletion, and documentation pop-ups as you type, significantly boosting productivity and reducing coding errors. Additionally, VS Code offers advanced code navigation tools, allowing you to quickly jump to function definitions, find references, and explore your codebase with ease.

```
// Example of IntelliSense in action
function greet(name) {
    return "Hello, " + name;
}

// As you type 'gre', IntelliSense suggests 'greet' and provides parameter in
formation.
```

1.3.4 Integrated Git Version Control

Version control is an essential part of software development, and VS Code simplifies the process with its integrated Git support. You can perform Git operations such as commit, push, pull, and branch management directly from the editor. VS Code's version control features provide a visual representation of code changes and make it easy to collaborate with team members using Git repositories.

1.3.5 Debugging Made Simple

Debugging code is a crucial aspect of the development process, and VS Code streamlines this task. It offers a built-in debugger with support for multiple programming languages. You can set breakpoints, inspect variables, and step through code execution seamlessly. Whether you're debugging a web application or a server-side script, VS Code provides an intuitive debugging experience.

```
// Example of setting a breakpoint and debugging in VS Code
function calculateSum(a, b) {
    let sum = a + b; // Set a breakpoint here
    return sum;
}
```

1.3.6 Integrated Terminal

The integrated terminal within VS Code is a valuable feature that allows you to execute shell commands, run scripts, and manage your development environment without leaving the editor. Whether you're working with package managers, running test suites, or interacting with your project's files, the integrated terminal keeps your workflow seamless.

1.3.7 Customizable Themes and UI

VS Code offers a wide selection of themes and the flexibility to customize its user interface. You can choose from a variety of themes that match your aesthetic preferences and adjust font sizes, line spacing, and color schemes. Customizing the editor's appearance ensures a comfortable and visually pleasing coding experience.

1.3.8 Extensive Documentation and Community Support

As a widely adopted code editor, VS Code benefits from a rich pool of online resources and an active community of users. You'll find extensive documentation, tutorials, forums, and Stack Overflow discussions related to VS Code. This abundance of support makes it easy to find answers to questions and solutions to common issues.

1.3.9 Cross-Platform Compatibility

VS Code's cross-platform compatibility ensures that developers can use it on Windows, macOS, and Linux systems. This versatility allows teams to work seamlessly on different platforms while maintaining a consistent development environment.

In summary, Visual Studio Code distinguishes itself with its versatile language support, a thriving extension ecosystem, powerful code editing features like IntelliSense and Git integration, and a commitment to cross-platform compatibility. These key features collectively make VS Code a top choice for developers seeking a productive and customizable coding environment. In the following sections, we'll delve deeper into using these features effectively to enhance your development workflow.

1.4 The User Interface: A Tour

Visual Studio Code (VS Code) boasts a user-friendly and intuitive user interface (UI) that contributes to its popularity among developers. In this section, we'll take you on a tour of the key elements of the VS Code UI, helping you become familiar with its layout and functionalities.

1.4.1 Editor Area

The central part of the VS Code UI is the editor area. This is where you write and edit your code. Each open file or document appears in its tab within this area, making it easy to switch between different files. The editor area provides features like syntax highlighting, code folding, and line numbers, all of which enhance code readability.

1.4.2 Sidebar

On the left side of the VS Code window, you'll find the sidebar. This sidebar provides access to various panels and functionalities:

- **Explorer**: The Explorer panel displays the files and folders within your project. You can navigate through your project's directory structure, create, delete, and rename files and folders, and perform other file management tasks.

- **Source Control**: If you're working with version control systems like Git, the Source Control panel allows you to view and manage changes, commits, and branches.

- **Extensions**: The Extensions panel lists all the installed extensions and allows you to search for and install new ones from the Visual Studio Code Marketplace.

- **Remote Explorer**: If you're working on remote development or connected to remote servers, the Remote Explorer panel provides access to remote file systems and resources.

- **Run and Debug**: This panel is used for running and debugging your code. You can configure debugging sessions, set breakpoints, and view debugging output here.

- **Extensions Marketplace**: When you're browsing for extensions to install, the Extensions Marketplace panel displays available extensions, providing detailed information and options for installation.

1.4.3 Status Bar

At the bottom of the VS Code window, you'll find the status bar. The status bar displays various pieces of information, including the name of the currently open project or workspace, the selected programming language, and the line and column number of the cursor's position. It also houses several icons and menus for quick access to features like changing the coding language mode, selecting the encoding of the file, and configuring the editor layout.

1.4.4 Activity Bar

The activity bar is located on the far left side of the window and provides access to different sections of VS Code. It includes icons for the Explorer, Source Control, Run and Debug, Extensions, and Remote Explorer panels. Clicking on these icons or using keyboard shortcuts allows you to switch between these sections quickly.

1.4.5 Panel and Terminal

VS Code includes a panel that can be accessed by clicking on the square icon in the top right corner or by using keyboard shortcuts. This panel hosts various views, such as output logs, search results, and extensions output.

Additionally, VS Code features an integrated terminal that can be accessed using the `Ctrl+`` (Backtick) keyboard shortcut. The integrated terminal allows you to execute shell commands and interact with your project directly from the editor.

1.4.6 Command Palette

The Command Palette is a powerful tool in VS Code that can be summoned using the `Ctrl+Shift+P` keyboard shortcut. It allows you to access and execute various commands and actions within the editor. You can search for commands by name and even execute them without having to remember specific keyboard shortcuts. This feature is incredibly handy for navigating and customizing the VS Code environment.

1.4.7 Customization and Themes

VS Code is highly customizable, and you can personalize it to match your preferences. You can change the color theme, adjust font sizes and line heights, and even customize keyboard shortcuts. Themes and extensions can be installed to change the appearance and functionality of the editor to suit your coding style and needs.

1.4.8 Zen Mode

For a distraction-free writing experience, VS Code offers a Zen Mode that minimizes distractions by providing a full-screen, clutter-free interface for focused coding or writing. You can enter Zen Mode by selecting it from the Command Palette.

In this brief tour, we've covered the main elements of the Visual Studio Code user interface. Familiarizing yourself with these components will help you navigate the editor effectively and make the most of its features. As you continue to explore and use VS Code, you'll discover additional customization options and shortcuts that suit your workflow.

1.5 Installing and Setting Up Visual Studio Code

In this section, we will guide you through the process of installing Visual Studio Code (VS Code) on your system and configuring it to suit your development needs. Whether you're a beginner or an experienced developer, getting VS Code up and running is a straightforward process.

1.5.1 Installation

Windows

1. Visit the VS Code website.
2. Click on the "Download for Windows" button.
3. Run the downloaded installer (.exe file).
4. Follow the installation prompts, including selecting options like adding VS Code to the system PATH for easier command-line access.
5. Once the installation is complete, you can launch VS Code from the Start menu.

macOS

1. Visit the VS Code website.
2. Click on the "Download for macOS" button.
3. Open the downloaded .dmg file.
4. Drag and drop the VS Code application into the Applications folder.
5. Launch VS Code from the Applications folder or the Dock.

Linux (Debian/Ubuntu)

1. Open a terminal window.
2. Run the following commands:

```
sudo apt update
sudo apt install software-properties-common apt-transport-https wget
wget -q https://packages.microsoft.com/keys/microsoft.asc -O- | sudo apt-key add -
sudo add-apt-repository "deb [arch=amd64] https://packages.microsoft.com/repos/vscode stable main"
sudo apt update
sudo apt install code
```

3. Once the installation is complete, you can launch VS Code from the application menu.

Linux (Red Hat/Fedora)

1. Open a terminal window.
2. Run the following commands:

```
sudo dnf install -y wget
wget https://packages.microsoft.com/config/rhel/8/prod.repo -O /etc/yum.repos.d/vscode.repo
```

```
sudo rpm --import https://packages.microsoft.com/keys/microsoft.asc
sudo dnf install code
```

3. Once the installation is complete, you can launch VS Code from the application menu.

1.5.2 First Launch

Upon launching VS Code for the first time, you'll see a welcome screen that provides several options:

- **Open a Folder**: If you already have a project folder, you can open it directly in VS Code.
- **Clone Repository**: This option allows you to clone a Git repository from a remote location.
- **Open Recent**: Shows recently opened projects and files.
- **New File**: Create a new, empty file to start working on a new project.
- **New Workspace**: Create a workspace to manage multiple related projects together.

1.5.3 Basic Configuration

Before diving into coding, you might want to configure some basic settings in VS Code:

- **Themes**: Choose a color theme that suits your taste by clicking on the gear icon in the lower right corner and selecting "Color Theme."

- **Font and Font Size**: Adjust the editor's font and font size by going to "File" > "Preferences" > "Settings" and searching for "Font."

- **Keybindings**: You can customize keyboard shortcuts or choose from predefined keymap extensions to match your preferred coding style.

1.5.4 Extensions

Extensions are a vital part of customizing VS Code to your workflow. You can explore and install extensions from the Visual Studio Code Marketplace. Common extensions include those for specific programming languages, code linters, debugging tools, and project management.

To install extensions:

1. Click on the Extensions icon in the sidebar.
2. Search for the extension you want to install.
3. Click the Install button for the desired extension.

1.5.5 Workspace Configuration

You can configure settings on a per-project basis by creating a `settings.json` file within your workspace. This file allows you to define project-specific settings, including preferences, extensions, and other configurations.

To create a `settings.json` file:

1. Open your workspace or project folder in VS Code.
2. Click on "File" > "Preferences" > "Settings."
3. In the top-right corner, click on the {} icon to open the `settings.json` file.
4. Add your custom settings within this file.

1.5.6 Key Takeaways

- Installing Visual Studio Code is a straightforward process on Windows, macOS, and Linux.

- VS Code provides a welcoming welcome screen with options to open projects, clone repositories, or create new files.

- You can customize VS Code's appearance, keybindings, and functionality through themes, font settings, and extensions.

- Workspace-specific settings can be configured by creating a `settings.json` file within your project folder.

Now that you have successfully installed and set up Visual Studio Code, you are ready to explore its powerful features and start coding in a productive environment. In the subsequent chapters, we'll delve deeper into specific aspects of using VS Code to optimize your development workflow.

Chapter 2: Customizing Your Workspace

2.1 Personalizing Themes and Colors

Visual Studio Code (VS Code) provides a range of customization options to tailor the appearance of your coding workspace. Among these options, personalizing themes and colors is one of the first steps you can take to make your coding environment visually appealing and comfortable. In this section, we'll explore how to select, install, and customize themes in VS Code.

2.1.1 Themes vs. Color Schemes

In VS Code, themes and color schemes are often used interchangeably, but they have distinct roles:

- **Themes**: Themes in VS Code encompass the entire visual appearance of the editor, including colors, fonts, icons, and UI elements. A theme can drastically change the overall look and feel of VS Code.

- **Color Schemes**: Color schemes, on the other hand, focus primarily on the syntax highlighting within your code. They define the colors used for different programming languages' keywords, variables, comments, and other code elements.

2.1.2 Changing the Theme

To change the theme in VS Code:

1. Click on the gear icon in the lower-right corner of the window to open the settings.

2. Select "Color Theme" from the dropdown menu.

3. Browse through the available themes and select the one you prefer.

4. VS Code will apply the selected theme immediately.

2.1.3 Installing Additional Themes

The default installation of VS Code comes with a few built-in themes, but you can install additional themes from the Visual Studio Code Marketplace to expand your options.

To install a new theme:

1. Click on the Extensions icon in the sidebar.

2. Search for "themes" in the Extensions Marketplace.

3. Browse through the available themes, click on the one you like, and click the "Install" button.

4. Once installed, you can activate the new theme by following the steps in the "Changing the Theme" section.

2.1.4 Customizing Themes

Many themes in VS Code offer customization options to suit your preferences. These options might include changing the color of specific code elements, adjusting font sizes, or enabling/disabling certain UI features.

To customize a theme:

1. Click on the gear icon in the lower-right corner of the window to open the settings.

2. Select "Color Theme."

3. Click on the gear icon next to the currently selected theme, and choose "Edit Color Theme."

4. A JSON file will open with various color settings. You can modify these settings to customize the theme.

5. Save your changes, and VS Code will apply the customized theme.

2.1.5 Popular Themes

There are numerous themes available in the VS Code Marketplace, catering to various preferences. Here are a few popular themes that developers often choose:

- **Dracula**: A dark theme with vibrant colors and a high contrast appearance.
- **One Dark Pro**: A popular dark theme inspired by Atom's One Dark theme.
- **Solarized Light/Dark**: A theme with soothing, balanced colors that are easy on the eyes.
- **Material Theme**: A theme based on the Material Design guidelines, offering a modern and colorful UI.
- **Monokai**: A classic and widely appreciated dark theme known for its vivid syntax highlighting.

2.1.6 Key Takeaways

- Themes and color schemes in VS Code allow you to customize the appearance of your coding workspace.

- Themes affect the overall look and feel of VS Code, while color schemes focus on syntax highlighting.

- You can change the theme in VS Code through the settings menu.

- Additional themes can be installed from the Visual Studio Code Marketplace.

- Many themes offer customization options to fine-tune their appearance to your liking.

Customizing themes and colors in VS Code not only enhances the aesthetics of your workspace but also contributes to a more comfortable and visually pleasing coding experience. Whether you prefer a dark, vibrant theme or a light, minimalist one, VS Code provides ample options to make your workspace your own. In the next sections of this chapter, we'll explore more ways to personalize your coding environment and boost your productivity.

2.2 Managing Workspaces and Folders

In Visual Studio Code (VS Code), workspaces and folders play a crucial role in organizing your projects and customizing your development environment. Understanding how to manage workspaces and folders effectively can significantly enhance your coding workflow. In this section, we'll explore the concepts of workspaces and folders in VS Code and how to utilize them to your advantage.

2.2.1 Workspaces vs. Folders

In VS Code, both workspaces and folders are used for project management, but they serve slightly different purposes:

- **Workspace**: A workspace in VS Code is a container for one or more folders. It allows you to group related projects and define settings specific to that workspace. For example, you can have a workspace for a web application that includes folders for frontend and backend code.

- **Folder**: A folder is a directory on your filesystem. Each folder in a workspace represents a specific project or part of a project. You can open individual folders in VS Code, and they inherit the workspace's settings unless overridden.

2.2.2 Creating a Workspace

To create a new workspace in VS Code:

1. Open VS Code.

2. Click on "File" in the top menu.

3. Select "Add Folder to Workspace" or "Add File to Workspace" if you want to include a specific file.

4. Choose the folder or file you want to add to the workspace.

5. Your workspace is now created, and you can save it by clicking "File" > "Save Workspace As…" and specifying a name for the workspace file (with the .code-workspace extension).

2.2.3 Adding Folders to a Workspace

After creating a workspace, you can add folders to it:

1. In your workspace, click on the "Add Folder" icon in the Explorer panel.

2. Select the folder you want to add, and it will become part of the workspace.

3. You can repeat this process to add multiple folders to your workspace.

2.2.4 Switching Between Workspaces

To switch between different workspaces in VS Code:

1. Click on "File" > "Open Workspace..."

2. Browse to the location of your workspace file (with the .code-workspace extension).

3. Select the workspace file, and it will open with all the folders and settings you defined.

2.2.5 Workspace Settings

Each workspace in VS Code can have its own settings that override global settings. These workspace-specific settings are stored in the settings.json file within the .vscode folder in your workspace.

To configure workspace settings:

1. Open your workspace in VS Code.

2. Click on the gear icon in the lower-right corner and select "Settings."

3. You can now modify the settings in the workspace-specific settings.json file.

Workspace settings are particularly useful when you need to define project-specific configurations, such as formatter preferences or specific extensions for that project.

2.2.6 Workspaces for Multi-Project Management

Workspaces are powerful tools for managing multi-project environments. For instance, if you are developing a web application with separate frontend and backend folders, you can create a workspace that includes both folders. This allows you to open and work on both parts of the project simultaneously, with shared settings and extensions.

2.2.7 Key Takeaways
- In VS Code, workspaces and folders are used for project organization and management.

- A workspace is a container for one or more folders and allows you to define project-specific settings.

- Folders represent specific projects or parts of projects within a workspace.

- You can create and save workspaces, add folders to them, and switch between different workspaces.

- Workspace settings override global settings and can be configured in the `settings.json` file within the `.vscode` folder of the workspace.

Effectively using workspaces and folders in VS Code helps you organize your projects, streamline your workflow, and manage complex development environments with ease. Whether you're working on a single project or juggling multiple projects, leveraging workspaces and folders enhances your productivity and keeps your coding environment well-structured.

2.3 Keyboard Shortcuts and Efficiency Tips

Keyboard shortcuts are an essential aspect of improving your productivity in Visual Studio Code (VS Code). VS Code provides a plethora of keyboard shortcuts for various tasks, and mastering them can significantly speed up your coding workflow. In this section, we'll explore some essential keyboard shortcuts and efficiency tips to help you become more proficient with the editor.

2.3.1 Basic Navigation Shortcuts

- **Ctrl+P (Cmd+P on macOS)**: Opens the Quick Open dialog, allowing you to quickly search for and open files within your project.

- **Ctrl+Tab (Cmd+Tab on macOS)**: Switches between open files or tabs.

- **Ctrl+ (Cmd+ on macOS)**: Toggles the integrated terminal.

- **Ctrl+- (Cmd+- on macOS)**: Navigates backward through your code's history, similar to a web browser's back button.

- **Ctrl+Shift+- (Cmd+Shift+- on macOS)**: Navigates forward through your code's history, similar to a web browser's forward button.

2.3.2 Code Editing Shortcuts

- **Ctrl+D (Cmd+D on macOS)**: Selects the word under the cursor or the next occurrence of the selected text. You can use it to quickly select multiple occurrences for editing simultaneously.

- **Ctrl+Shift+L (Cmd+Shift+L on macOS)**: Selects all occurrences of the currently selected text.

- **Ctrl+/ (Cmd+/ on macOS)**: Comments or uncomments the selected lines or the current line if nothing is selected.

- **Ctrl+Enter (Cmd+Enter on macOS)**: Inserts a new line below the current line, even if the cursor is in the middle of a line.

- **Ctrl+Shift+Enter (Cmd+Shift+Enter on macOS)**: Inserts a new line above the current line, even if the cursor is in the middle of a line.

2.3.3 Multi-Cursor and Selection Shortcuts

- **Alt+Click (Option+Click on macOS)**: Allows you to add multiple cursors by clicking at different positions in your code.

- **Ctrl+Alt+Down (Cmd+Option+Down on macOS)**: Inserts a cursor below the current line, creating a multi-cursor selection.

- **Ctrl+Alt+Up (Cmd+Option+Up on macOS)**: Inserts a cursor above the current line, creating a multi-cursor selection.

- **Ctrl+U (Cmd+U on macOS)**: Undo the last cursor operation, useful for refining your multi-cursor selections.

2.3.4 Search and Replace Shortcuts

- **Ctrl+F (Cmd+F on macOS)**: Opens the Find dialog for searching within the current file.

- **Ctrl+H (Cmd+H on macOS)**: Opens the Replace dialog for searching and replacing text within the current file.

- **Ctrl+Shift+F (Cmd+Shift+F on macOS)**: Opens the Find in Files dialog for searching across your entire project.

- **Ctrl+F2 (Cmd+F2 on macOS)**: Selects all occurrences of the word under the cursor, allowing you to quickly rename variables or symbols.

2.3.5 Integrated Terminal Shortcuts

- **Ctrl+ (Cmd+ on macOS)**: Toggles the integrated terminal.

- **Ctrl+Shift+ (Cmd+Shift+ on macOS)**: Creates a new integrated terminal instance.

- **Ctrl+C (Cmd+C on macOS)**: Interrupts the currently running command in the terminal.

2.3.6 Customizing Keyboard Shortcuts

VS Code allows you to customize keyboard shortcuts to fit your preferences and workflow. You can modify existing shortcuts or create your own. To customize keyboard shortcuts:

1. Open the command palette with Ctrl+Shift+P (Cmd+Shift+P on macOS).

2. Search for "Preferences: Open Keyboard Shortcuts."

3. You can then search for specific commands or keybindings and customize them by clicking the pencil icon or adding your own keybindings in the keybindings.json file.

2.3.7 Key Takeaways

- Keyboard shortcuts are essential for improving productivity in VS Code.

- Basic navigation shortcuts help you quickly switch between files, tabs, and the integrated terminal.

- Code editing shortcuts simplify tasks like selecting text, commenting, and adding new lines.

- Multi-cursor and selection shortcuts enable you to work efficiently with multiple cursors.

- Search and replace shortcuts make it easy to find and modify code.

- The integrated terminal can be controlled with keyboard shortcuts for quick access and operation.

Mastering keyboard shortcuts in VS Code is a key step towards becoming a more efficient and productive developer. By incorporating these shortcuts into your daily coding routine, you'll be able to navigate, edit, and manage your code with greater ease and speed, ultimately enhancing your coding experience.

2.4 Extensions and Plugins: Enhancing Functionality

Extensions are one of the defining features of Visual Studio Code (VS Code) that make it a versatile and powerful code editor. They allow you to extend and enhance the functionality of VS Code to suit your specific development needs. In this section, we'll explore the world of extensions and how they can supercharge your coding experience.

2.4.1 What Are Extensions?

Extensions, also known as plugins, are packages of code that add new features or capabilities to VS Code. They can range from simple language support for a programming language to complex tools and integrations with other development tools and services. Extensions are created and maintained by the VS Code community, making it a rich ecosystem of tools and resources.

2.4.2 Installing Extensions

To install an extension in VS Code:

1. Click on the Extensions icon in the sidebar or use the keyboard shortcut Ctrl+Shift+X (Cmd+Shift+X on macOS) to open the Extensions view.

2. In the search bar, enter the name or keyword related to the extension you want to install.

3. Browse through the search results and click the "Install" button next to the extension you want.

4. Once installed, the extension will appear in your list of installed extensions.

2.4.3 Popular Extension Categories

Extensions in VS Code cover a wide range of categories, catering to various development needs. Here are some popular extension categories:

- **Language Support**: These extensions provide enhanced support for specific programming languages, including syntax highlighting, code completion, and debugging capabilities.

- **Version Control**: Extensions like GitLens enhance your version control experience by providing detailed information about code changes and history.

- **Code Linters and Formatters**: Extensions like ESLint and Prettier help you maintain consistent code quality by highlighting errors and formatting your code.

- **Debugging Tools**: VS Code offers extensions for debugging various programming languages, making it a powerful debugging environment.

- **Themes and Color Schemes**: Customize the look and feel of VS Code with themes and color schemes tailored to your preferences.

- **Productivity Tools**: Extensions like Live Share enable collaborative coding, while others improve code navigation and refactoring.

- **Docker and Container Tools**: If you work with containers, there are extensions that provide integration and management features for Docker.

- **Database Tools**: Extensions for database management and querying, such as SQL Server (mssql) and MySQL (msql), are available to streamline database-related tasks.

- **Serverless and Cloud Development**: Extensions for AWS, Azure, and other cloud platforms help you develop and deploy serverless and cloud-native applications.

- **Web Development**: For web developers, extensions for HTML, CSS, JavaScript, and popular frameworks like React and Angular are widely available.

2.4.4 Managing Extensions

You can manage your installed extensions in VS Code easily:

- **Disable**: If you want to temporarily disable an extension, you can do so by clicking the gear icon on the extension in the Extensions view and selecting "Disable."

- **Uninstall**: To remove an extension from your system, click the gear icon on the extension and select "Uninstall."

- **Settings**: Some extensions come with their own settings that can be customized. You can access these settings by clicking the gear icon on the extension and selecting "Extension Settings."

2.4.5 Creating Your Own Extensions

For advanced users and developers, it's possible to create your own extensions for VS Code. The official documentation and guides provide resources to get you started with extension development. Creating custom extensions can be beneficial when you have specific requirements or need to integrate with your own tools.

2.4.6 Key Takeaways

- Extensions are packages of code that extend the functionality of VS Code.

- You can easily install extensions from the VS Code Marketplace or through the Extensions view.

- VS Code's extension ecosystem covers a wide range of categories, including language support, version control, productivity tools, and more.

- Managing installed extensions allows you to enable, disable, or uninstall extensions as needed.

- Advanced users can create their own extensions to meet specific development needs.

Extensions are a fundamental part of what makes VS Code a popular choice among developers. They allow you to tailor your development environment to match your workflow, making coding more efficient and enjoyable. As you explore the VS Code Marketplace and discover extensions that suit your needs, you'll find that they significantly enhance your coding experience.

2.5 Setting Up User and Workspace Settings

In Visual Studio Code (VS Code), you have the flexibility to configure settings at both the user and workspace levels. This allows you to customize your coding environment to your preferences and adapt it to specific projects. In this section, we'll delve into the concept of user and workspace settings and how to set them up effectively.

2.5.1 User Settings vs. Workspace Settings

User Settings apply to your entire VS Code installation and are consistent across all workspaces and projects. These settings are ideal for configurations that you want to apply globally, such as your preferred code editor theme, font size, and keybindings.

Workspace Settings, on the other hand, are specific to a particular workspace or project. They allow you to define configurations that are tailored to the requirements of a particular project, including settings like linters, code formatter preferences, and specific extensions.

2.5.2 User Settings

To access and configure User Settings in VS Code:

1. Click on "File" > "Preferences" > "Settings."

2. You can also use the keyboard shortcut Ctrl+, (Cmd+, on macOS).

3. User Settings are presented as a JSON file that you can modify. You can search for specific settings and customize them according to your preferences.

4. Changes made to User Settings apply to your entire VS Code installation.

2.5.3 Workspace Settings

Workspace Settings in VS Code are stored in a settings.json file within the .vscode folder of your project's workspace. This allows you to define project-specific configurations.

To set up Workspace Settings:

1. Open your workspace in VS Code.

2. Click on "File" > "Preferences" > "Settings" or use the keyboard shortcut Ctrl+, (Cmd+, on macOS).

3. In the top-right corner, click on the {} icon to open the settings.json file specific to your workspace.

4. Customize the settings within this file according to your project's requirements.

5. Save the settings.json file.

Workspace-specific settings take precedence over User Settings, allowing you to fine-tune your development environment for each project.

2.5.4 Common Configuration Settings

Here are some common settings you may want to configure in both User and Workspace Settings:

*   **Editor Preferences**: Customize editor settings like font size, line height, tab size, and word wrap.

- **Theme**: Set your preferred color theme for the code editor.

- **Keybindings**: Define custom keyboard shortcuts or modify existing ones.

- **File Associations**: Configure file associations to open specific file types with the desired editor or extension.

- **Language and File-Specific Settings**: Customize settings for specific programming languages or file types, such as code formatting rules, linters, and code actions.

- **Extensions**: Manage and configure extensions, including their settings and keybindings.

- **Version Control**: Configure version control settings for Git, such as user name and email.

- **Workspace Folders**: Define the folders that should be included in the workspace.

2.5.5 Syncing Settings

VS Code provides extensions like "Settings Sync" that allow you to sync your settings and configurations across multiple VS Code installations. This is particularly useful if you work on different machines or want to maintain consistency in your development environment.

2.5.6 Key Takeaways

- User Settings apply globally to your entire VS Code installation, while Workspace Settings are specific to individual projects.

- User Settings can be accessed and customized through the settings UI or by editing the settings.json file.

- Workspace Settings are stored in a settings.json file within the .vscode folder of your workspace.

- Customize settings such as editor preferences, themes, keybindings, language-specific configurations, and version control settings.

- Extensions like "Settings Sync" enable you to sync your settings across multiple VS Code installations.

Customizing User and Workspace Settings in VS Code allows you to create a coding environment that suits your workflow and project-specific needs. Whether it's adjusting the editor's appearance, defining coding conventions, or setting up project-specific linters, mastering these settings helps you work more efficiently and consistently across different projects.

Chapter 3: Coding Efficiently in Visual Studio Code

3.1 Intelligent Code Completion

Intelligent code completion is a powerful feature in Visual Studio Code (VS Code) that enhances your productivity by providing context-aware code suggestions as you type. This feature, often referred to as "autocomplete" or "intellisense," helps you write code faster and with fewer errors. In this section, we'll explore how to make the most of intelligent code completion in VS Code.

3.1.1 Getting Started with Code Completion

VS Code's code completion feature is enabled by default, and it provides suggestions for:

- Keywords and symbols from the current programming language.
- Variables and functions in the current file.
- Variables and functions from imported modules or libraries.

To trigger code completion, start typing and a dropdown list of suggestions will appear. You can navigate through the suggestions using the arrow keys and select the desired completion by pressing Enter or Tab.

3.1.2 Context-Aware Suggestions

One of the strengths of VS Code's code completion is its context-awareness. It considers the current scope, the programming language you're using, and even your coding style to provide relevant suggestions. For example:

- If you're writing JavaScript, it will suggest JavaScript-specific keywords and methods.
- If you're inside a function, it will suggest variables declared in that function.
- If you've imported a library, it will suggest functions and objects from that library.

3.1.3 Triggering Code Completion Manually

In addition to automatic code completion, you can trigger it manually at any time by using keyboard shortcuts:

- Ctrl+Space (Cmd+Space on macOS): This shortcut forces code completion suggestions to appear, even if you haven't started typing.

- Ctrl+Shift+Space (Cmd+Shift+Space on macOS): This keyboard shortcut shows parameter hints for function calls, helping you remember the expected arguments.

3.1.4 Snippets and Emmet Abbreviations

VS Code also includes support for code snippets and Emmet abbreviations. Snippets are predefined code blocks that can be inserted by typing a trigger word and pressing Tab.

41

Emmet is a powerful toolkit for web developers that allows you to expand abbreviations into HTML or CSS code. For example, typing ul>li*3 and then pressing Tab will generate an unordered list with three list items.

3.1.5 Customizing Code Completion

VS Code allows you to customize code completion to better fit your needs. You can modify settings related to code suggestions, such as enabling or disabling specific sources of suggestions, changing the delay before suggestions appear, and more.

To access code completion settings:

1.   Click on "File" > "Preferences" > "Settings."

2.   Search for "Suggest" in the search bar to find relevant suggestions settings.

3.   You can modify these settings to tailor code completion to your liking.

3.1.6 Code Completion with Extensions

Extensions in VS Code can enhance code completion further by adding language-specific features or suggestions for specific frameworks or libraries. For example, an extension for a JavaScript framework might provide suggestions for framework-specific components and attributes.

3.1.7 Key Takeaways

- Intelligent code completion in VS Code provides context-aware suggestions to help you write code faster and with fewer errors.

- It suggests keywords, symbols, variables, and functions based on the current scope and language.

- You can trigger code completion manually using keyboard shortcuts.

- Snippets and Emmet abbreviations allow for quick code generation.

- Code completion settings can be customized to fit your preferences.

- Extensions can extend code completion with language-specific features and suggestions.

Intelligent code completion is a valuable tool for developers, whether you're writing code in a familiar language or exploring a new one. By taking advantage of code completion in VS Code and customizing it to match your workflow, you can write code more efficiently and with greater accuracy, ultimately boosting your productivity.

3.2 Code Navigation and Refactoring Tools

Efficient code navigation and refactoring are essential skills for any developer, and Visual Studio Code (VS Code) offers a range of tools and shortcuts to help you master these tasks. In this section, we'll explore code navigation techniques, such as finding and jumping to symbols, as well as refactoring tools to improve your code's structure and readability.

3.2.1 Go to Definition and Peek Definition

Go to Definition

VS Code allows you to quickly jump to the definition of a variable, function, class, or method by using the "Go to Definition" feature. To use it:

1. Place your cursor on the symbol you want to explore (e.g., a function name).

2. Press F12 or right-click and select "Go to Definition."

3. VS Code will navigate to the file and location where the symbol is defined, allowing you to see its implementation.

Peek Definition

Alternatively, you can use the "Peek Definition" feature to view a symbol's definition without leaving your current file:

1. Place your cursor on the symbol you want to inspect.

2. Press Alt+F12 or right-click and select "Peek Definition."

3. A peek window will open, displaying the symbol's definition inline.

"Peek Definition" is useful for quickly referencing code without switching between files.

3.2.2 Find All References

Finding all references to a symbol is a powerful way to understand how it's used throughout your codebase. In VS Code, you can achieve this by:

1. Placing your cursor on the symbol you want to find references for.

2. Pressing Shift+F12 or right-clicking and selecting "Find All References."

3. VS Code will display a list of all occurrences of the symbol, including their file locations. You can navigate through the list and jump to each reference as needed.

3.2.3 Renaming Symbols

Renaming symbols, such as variables, functions, or classes, can be done safely in VS Code with the "Rename Symbol" feature. To rename a symbol:

1. Place your cursor on the symbol you want to rename.

2. Press F2 or right-click and select "Rename Symbol."

3. Enter the new name for the symbol and press Enter.

VS Code will automatically update all references to the symbol throughout your codebase, ensuring consistency and reducing the risk of errors.

3.2.4 Code Refactoring

Refactoring is the process of restructuring code to improve its design, readability, and maintainability. VS Code supports various refactoring actions, depending on the programming language and extensions you're using. Common refactoring tasks include:

- Extracting code into functions or methods.
- Reorganizing import statements.
- Simplifying conditional statements.

Refactoring actions can typically be accessed through the context menu when you right-click on code or by using keyboard shortcuts. The availability of specific refactoring actions may vary depending on your coding context and extensions.

3.2.5 Keyboard Shortcuts for Navigation and Refactoring

Efficient code navigation and refactoring often rely on keyboard shortcuts for speed and convenience. Familiarizing yourself with the following keyboard shortcuts can significantly enhance your coding experience:

- F12: Go to Definition.
- Alt+F12: Peek Definition.
- Shift+F12: Find All References.
- F2: Rename Symbol.

Additionally, you can explore and customize keyboard shortcuts by going to "File" > "Preferences" > "Keyboard Shortcuts" in VS Code.

3.2.6 Extensions for Advanced Refactoring

For more advanced refactoring capabilities, consider installing extensions tailored to your programming language or framework. These extensions often provide additional refactorings and code analysis tools to help you maintain high-quality code.

3.2.7 Key Takeaways

- Code navigation features in VS Code, such as "Go to Definition" and "Peek Definition," help you explore and understand code quickly.

- "Find All References" allows you to locate all occurrences of a symbol throughout your codebase.

- "Rename Symbol" lets you safely rename variables, functions, or classes with automatic updates to references.

- Code refactoring is essential for improving code quality and maintainability.

- Keyboard shortcuts streamline code navigation and refactoring tasks.

- Extensions can provide advanced refactoring capabilities tailored to specific programming languages and frameworks.

By mastering code navigation and refactoring tools in Visual Studio Code, you can not only work more efficiently but also improve the overall quality and maintainability of your codebase. These features are essential for developers striving to write clean, organized, and maintainable code.

3.3 Debugging Made Simple

Debugging is a critical part of software development, and Visual Studio Code (VS Code) offers a robust set of debugging tools to make the process efficient and effective. In this section, we'll explore how to set up and use the debugging features in VS Code to identify and fix issues in your code.

3.3.1 Setting Up Debugging Environments

Before you start debugging, you need to set up your debugging environment. This typically involves configuring launch configurations that specify how your code should be executed and debugged. VS Code supports debugging for various programming languages and environments, such as Node.js, Python, and web browsers.

To set up a debugging environment:

1. Open the file you want to debug.

2. Click on the debugging icon in the left sidebar or use the keyboard shortcut F5.

3. If you don't have a launch configuration set up, VS Code will prompt you to create one. A launch configuration defines how your code is executed and debugged, including which executable to run and any necessary command-line arguments.

4. Configure your launch configuration based on your project's requirements.

5. Save the launch configuration file.

3.3.2 Debugging Features

Once your debugging environment is set up, you can take advantage of the following debugging features in VS Code:

45

Breakpoints

Breakpoints are markers you place in your code to pause its execution at specific points. To set a breakpoint, click in the gutter to the left of the code line where you want the breakpoint. When the code reaches a breakpoint, it will pause, allowing you to inspect variables, step through code, and more.

Stepping Through Code

While debugging, you can step through your code using the following actions:

- **Step Over (F10)**: Executes the current line and moves to the next line. If the current line contains a function call, it will not step into the function but will execute it and move to the next line.

- **Step Into (F11)**: If the current line contains a function call, it will step into the function, allowing you to debug the function's code.

- **Step Out (Shift+F11)**: If you've stepped into a function and want to return to the calling function, use this to step out of the current function's execution.

Variables and Watches

While debugging, you can view and inspect variables and expressions. VS Code provides a "Variables" panel that displays the current values of variables, making it easy to identify issues.

You can also add watches to monitor specific variables or expressions continuously. Watches are particularly useful for tracking the values of variables over time as you step through code.

Call Stack

The call stack panel displays the hierarchy of function calls leading to the current point in the code. It helps you understand how your program reached its current state and can be instrumental in debugging complex issues.

Debug Console

The debug console allows you to execute arbitrary code and view the output during debugging. You can use it to test small code snippets or evaluate expressions to understand their behavior.

Conditional Breakpoints

You can make breakpoints conditional by right-clicking on a breakpoint and adding a condition. The code will only break when the condition evaluates to true, which is helpful for debugging specific scenarios.

3.3.3 Remote Debugging Capabilities

VS Code supports remote debugging, allowing you to debug code running on remote servers or devices. This is particularly useful for web development, server-side debugging, or debugging applications on IoT devices.

3.3.4 Debugging Configuration Options

VS Code provides various configuration options to customize your debugging experience. You can set up multi-target debugging for multi-process applications, configure source maps for better debugging in minified or transpiled code, and specify additional environment variables.

3.3.5 Debugging Extensions

Extensions in VS Code can enhance your debugging experience by providing language-specific debugging tools, additional features, and integrations with third-party services and platforms.

3.3.6 Debugging Tips

Here are some debugging tips to help you effectively identify and resolve issues:

- Use meaningful variable names and comments to make your code more understandable during debugging.

- Test your code in small, isolated parts to pinpoint issues more easily.

- Experiment with conditional breakpoints to break execution only when certain conditions are met.

- Take advantage of watches and the debug console to inspect and evaluate expressions.

- Learn keyboard shortcuts for debugging actions to work efficiently.

- Use the call stack to trace the path of execution and identify where issues may have originated.

3.3.7 Key Takeaways

- Debugging is a crucial aspect of software development, and VS Code provides robust debugging tools.

- Setting up debugging environments involves configuring launch configurations that specify how your code should be executed and debugged.

- Debugging features in VS Code include breakpoints, stepping through code, inspecting variables, and evaluating expressions.

- Remote debugging capabilities allow you to debug code running on remote servers or devices.

- Debugging extensions can enhance your debugging experience with language-specific tools and integrations.

- Effective debugging relies on meaningful variable names, small testing units, and knowledge of debugging features and tips.

Mastering debugging in Visual Studio Code is essential for identifying and fixing issues in your code efficiently. By becoming proficient with breakpoints, stepping through code, and utilizing debugging tools, you can streamline the development process and produce high-quality software with fewer bugs.

3.4 Integrated Terminal Usage

The integrated terminal in Visual Studio Code (VS Code) is a powerful tool that allows you to interact with your development environment without leaving the code editor. In this section, we'll explore how to use the integrated terminal effectively for tasks such as running commands, managing your project, and debugging.

3.4.1 Accessing the Integrated Terminal

You can access the integrated terminal in VS Code in several ways:

1. **View > Terminal**: Clicking on this menu option opens a new integrated terminal panel at the bottom of the window.

2. **Ctrl+ (Cmd+ on macOS)**: Pressing this keyboard shortcut toggles the integrated terminal panel's visibility.

3. **Terminal Icon**: Clicking on the terminal icon in the sidebar's activity bar also opens or focuses the integrated terminal.

3.4.2 Customizing the Terminal

VS Code allows you to customize the integrated terminal to suit your preferences. You can change settings such as the default shell, terminal font, colors, and more.

To access terminal settings:

1. Click on "File" > "Preferences" > "Settings."

2. In the search bar, type "terminal" to find relevant settings.

3. You can modify these settings according to your preferences.

3.4.3 Running Commands

The integrated terminal in VS Code allows you to run various commands, including:

- **Shell Commands**: You can execute shell commands directly in the terminal. For example, you can navigate to your project directory, install dependencies, and run build scripts.

- **Programming Language Interpreters**: If you're working with a programming language like Python or Node.js, you can run scripts and interact with the language's REPL (Read-Eval-Print Loop) within the terminal.

- **Version Control**: You can use the terminal for version control operations, such as committing changes, pushing to a remote repository, or resolving merge conflicts.

- **Debugging**: When debugging, you can view debugging output and interact with debugging sessions in the terminal.

3.4.4 Multiple Terminals

VS Code supports multiple terminal instances, allowing you to work on different tasks simultaneously. You can open additional terminals by clicking the "+" button in the integrated terminal panel or using the keyboard shortcut Ctrl+Shift+ (Cmd+Shift+` on macOS).

Each terminal instance maintains its shell session, allowing you to switch between tasks without losing context.

3.4.5 Terminal Split View

You can split the integrated terminal view horizontally or vertically to have multiple terminal panes open at once. This is useful when you need to monitor multiple logs or run different commands simultaneously.

To split the terminal:

1. Click the "Split Terminal" button in the terminal panel.

2. Alternatively, you can use the keyboard shortcuts Ctrl+\ (Cmd+ on macOS) for horizontal split and Ctrl+| (Cmd+| on macOS) for vertical split.

3.4.6 Debugging in the Terminal

When debugging your code, the integrated terminal can display debugging output and allow you to interact with debugging sessions. This is particularly useful for languages like Python or Node.js, where you can see console output and input within the same window.

3.4.7 Running Tasks

VS Code allows you to define and run tasks directly from the integrated terminal using task configurations. You can create tasks for common operations like building, testing, or deploying your project and execute them with simple commands.

3.4.8 Key Takeaways

- The integrated terminal in VS Code provides a convenient way to interact with your development environment.

- You can customize the terminal's appearance and behavior to suit your preferences.

- The terminal is useful for running shell commands, working with programming language interpreters, version control, and debugging.

- Multiple terminal instances and split views help you manage multiple tasks efficiently.

- You can run tasks directly from the integrated terminal using task configurations.

The integrated terminal in Visual Studio Code is a versatile tool that streamlines your development workflow. Whether you're running commands, managing multiple tasks, or debugging your code, the integrated terminal provides a seamless way to interact with your project without leaving the code editor.

3.5 Version Control Integration

Version control is a fundamental aspect of modern software development, enabling teams to collaborate, track changes, and manage code effectively. Visual Studio Code (VS Code) offers seamless integration with popular version control systems, such as Git, making it easy to work with repositories and manage code history. In this section, we'll explore how to use version control integration in VS Code to enhance your development workflow.

3.5.1 Initializing a Repository

If you're starting a new project, you can initialize a version control repository directly from within VS Code. Here's how to do it with Git:

1. Open your project folder in VS Code.

2. Click on the Source Control icon in the left sidebar (it looks like a branch).

3. Click on the "Initialize Repository" button.

4. Select the folder where you want to initialize the Git repository and confirm.

Once your repository is initialized, you can start tracking changes and committing code.

3.5.2 Cloning a Repository

If you're joining an existing project hosted on a version control platform like GitHub, you can clone the repository to your local machine using VS Code:

1. Open VS Code.

2. Click on "File" > "Add Folder to Workspace."

3. Select the folder where you want to clone the repository.

4. Click on the Source Control icon, and then click on the "Clone Repository" button.

5. Enter the repository's URL and the destination folder on your local machine.

6. Click "Clone" to download the repository.

VS Code will clone the repository and open it in your workspace, allowing you to work on the code.

3.5.3 Git Integration

VS Code's Git integration is one of its standout features. You can perform common Git operations, such as committing changes, pushing to remote repositories, pulling updates, and resolving merge conflicts, directly from the editor.

Here are some essential Git-related tasks in VS Code:

- **Committing Changes**: After making changes to your code, you can stage and commit them using the Source Control panel. Provide a commit message to describe your changes, and then click the checkmark icon to commit.

- **Branch Management**: You can create and switch between branches, merge branches, and resolve conflicts through the Source Control panel. This allows you to work on different features or bug fixes simultaneously.

- **Push and Pull**: Pushing your local changes to a remote repository and pulling updates from a remote repository can be done with a few clicks in the Source Control panel.

- **History and Blame**: You can view the commit history of a file, compare different versions, and use the "Blame" feature to see who made each change in a file.

3.5.4 Version Control Providers

VS Code supports multiple version control providers, including Git, Azure DevOps, GitHub, and more. Depending on your project's hosting platform, you can choose the appropriate provider and seamlessly integrate it with your workflow.

3.5.5 Visual Studio Code GitLens Extension

The GitLens extension for VS Code is a popular tool that enhances Git integration further. It provides a wealth of information about your code's history, including line-by-line annotations with commit details, authorship, and commit messages. GitLens is a valuable asset for exploring code evolution and understanding who made specific changes.

3.5.6 Key Takeaways

- VS Code offers seamless integration with version control systems like Git.

- You can initialize a new Git repository or clone an existing one directly within VS Code.

- Git integration in VS Code allows you to perform common version control tasks, including committing changes, managing branches, pushing and pulling from remote repositories, and reviewing code history.

- Multiple version control providers are supported, allowing you to choose the one that matches your project's hosting platform.

- The GitLens extension provides enhanced Git functionality, such as detailed code annotations and commit history exploration.

Using version control integration in Visual Studio Code is crucial for effective collaboration and code management in software development projects. Whether you're a solo developer or part of a team, the ability to track changes, collaborate on code, and manage your project's history is essential for maintaining code quality and ensuring the integrity of your software.

Chapter 4: Extensions and the Marketplace

4.1 Navigating the Extension Marketplace

Visual Studio Code's extensibility is a key factor in its popularity among developers. Extensions enhance its functionality, enabling you to tailor the editor to your specific needs and workflows. In this section, we'll explore how to navigate the Extension Marketplace within Visual Studio Code, find the right extensions for your tasks, and install them to supercharge your coding experience.

4.1.1 Accessing the Extension Marketplace

To access the Extension Marketplace in VS Code, follow these steps:

1. Open Visual Studio Code.

2. Click on the Extensions icon in the left sidebar, which resembles a square puzzle piece.

3. You'll be taken to the Extensions view, where you can explore and search for extensions.

4.1.2 Browsing Extensions

The Extension Marketplace offers a vast collection of extensions created by the community to enhance your development environment. You can explore these extensions by browsing categories, searching for specific functionalities, or checking out the "Featured" section for popular extensions.

- **Categories**: Extensions are organized into categories like "Programming Languages," "Debuggers," "Themes," and more. Click on a category to view relevant extensions.

- **Search**: Use the search bar in the Extensions view to search for extensions by name, functionality, or author.

- **Featured**: The "Featured" section highlights popular and noteworthy extensions, making it easy to discover new tools.

4.1.3 Extension Details

When you click on an extension in the marketplace, you'll see detailed information about it, including its description, version history, installation statistics, and user reviews. Take the time to review this information to ensure the extension meets your requirements.

4.1.4 Installing Extensions

To install an extension in Visual Studio Code:

1. Navigate to the Extension Marketplace and find the extension you want to install.

2. Click the "Install" button next to the extension.

3. After installation, you may need to reload VS Code to activate the extension fully.

4.1.5 Managing Installed Extensions

Once you've installed extensions, you can manage them easily:

- **Enable/Disable**: You can enable or disable an extension by clicking the gear icon next to its name in the Extensions view. Disabled extensions won't be active but can be re-enabled when needed.

- **Uninstall**: If you no longer need an extension, click the gear icon and select "Uninstall" to remove it from your VS Code installation.

4.1.6 Extension Recommendations

Visual Studio Code may provide recommendations for extensions based on your coding habits and the programming languages you use. These recommendations can help you discover useful extensions tailored to your needs.

4.1.7 Keeping Extensions Updated

Regularly updating your extensions is important to ensure they are compatible with the latest version of VS Code and to benefit from bug fixes and new features. VS Code provides automatic updates for installed extensions by default.

4.1.8 Installing Extensions from the Command Line

You can also install extensions from the command line using the code command with the --install-extension flag. For example:

```
code --install-extension author.extension-name
```

This method can be useful for automating extension installation as part of your development environment setup.

4.1.9 Managing Extensions Remotely

If you use Visual Studio Code remotely on a different machine or server, you can manage your extensions remotely as well. Extensions installed locally will not be available in the remote environment by default, so you may need to install them separately in that environment.

4.1.10 Key Takeaways

- Visual Studio Code's extensibility is a major advantage, allowing you to enhance your coding experience with community-contributed extensions.

- The Extension Marketplace is the central hub for discovering and installing extensions.

- You can browse extensions by categories, search for specific functionality, and explore featured extensions.

- Always review extension details, version history, and user reviews before installation.

- Managing installed extensions is easy through the Extensions view, where you can enable, disable, or uninstall extensions.

- Keeping extensions updated is essential for compatibility and security.

- You can install extensions from the command line using the code command.

- When working in remote environments with VS Code, remember to manage your extensions accordingly.

Exploring and utilizing extensions from the Visual Studio Code Extension Marketplace allows you to tailor your development environment to your unique needs. Whether you're looking for language support, debugging tools, or productivity enhancements, the marketplace offers a wide range of extensions to choose from, making Visual Studio Code a versatile and customizable code editor.

4.2 Must-Have Extensions for Developers

The Visual Studio Code Extension Marketplace is a treasure trove of extensions that can significantly enhance your development workflow. In this section, we'll explore a curated list of must-have extensions for developers that cover various aspects of coding, from code editing and debugging to project management and collaboration.

4.2.1 ESLint
- **Extension Name**: ESLint
- **Description**: ESLint is a popular JavaScript and TypeScript linter that helps you maintain consistent code style and catch potential issues in your code. This extension integrates ESLint seamlessly into VS Code, providing real-time linting and auto-fixing capabilities.

4.2.2 Prettier - Code Formatter
- **Extension Name**: Prettier - Code Formatter
- **Description**: Prettier is an opinionated code formatter that automatically formats your code to adhere to a consistent style. This extension ensures that your code is always properly formatted as you write, saving you from manual formatting efforts.

4.2.3 GitLens

- **Extension Name**: GitLens
- **Description**: GitLens is a powerful extension that supercharges your Git integration in VS Code. It provides detailed information about code changes, commit history, and code authorship directly in the editor. You can explore code evolution with ease and gain insights into the history of your codebase.

4.2.4 Bracket Pair Colorizer 2

- **Extension Name**: Bracket Pair Colorizer 2
- **Description**: This extension enhances code readability by coloring matching brackets, parentheses, and braces with the same color. It's especially helpful when dealing with nested code blocks, making it easier to identify opening and closing brackets.

4.2.5 Live Server

- **Extension Name**: Live Server
- **Description**: Live Server is a handy extension for web developers. It allows you to launch a local development server with live reloading capabilities. This means that as you make changes to your HTML, CSS, or JavaScript files, the browser automatically updates to reflect those changes, streamlining your web development workflow.

4.2.6 Docker

- **Extension Name**: Docker
- **Description**: If you work with containers, the Docker extension is essential. It provides integration with Docker, allowing you to manage containers, images, and Docker Compose files directly from within VS Code. You can build, run, and debug containerized applications efficiently.

4.2.7 Visual Studio IntelliCode

- **Extension Name**: Visual Studio IntelliCode
- **Description**: IntelliCode is an AI-assisted extension that enhances your coding productivity. It offers intelligent code completions and suggestions based on patterns observed in millions of code repositories. This extension can significantly speed up your coding by suggesting relevant code snippets and methods.

4.2.8 Remote - SSH

- **Extension Name**: Remote - SSH
- **Description**: If you need to work on remote servers or virtual machines, the Remote - SSH extension simplifies the process. It allows you to connect to remote machines and code as if you were working locally. You can edit files, run commands, and utilize VS Code extensions in a remote environment seamlessly.

4.2.9 REST Client

- **Extension Name**: REST Client

- **Description**: The REST Client extension lets you interact with RESTful APIs directly from VS Code. You can write and send HTTP requests with ease, view responses, and save request collections for future use. It's a valuable tool for testing and debugging APIs.

4.2.10 Live Share

- **Extension Name**: Live Share
- **Description**: Live Share enables real-time collaboration between developers. You can share your VS Code session with others, allowing them to view and edit your code, debug together, and communicate via built-in chat and audio features. It's perfect for pair programming and remote collaboration.

4.2.11 Code Spell Checker

- **Extension Name**: Code Spell Checker
- **Description**: Code Spell Checker helps you catch spelling and grammar errors in your code and comments. It provides suggestions for correcting typos and improving code readability. This extension ensures that your code is not only functional but also well-written.

4.2.12 Jupyter

- **Extension Name**: Jupyter
- **Description**: If you work with Jupyter notebooks for data science and machine learning, this extension is a must. It provides rich support for Jupyter notebooks within VS Code, allowing you to create, edit, and run notebooks seamlessly. You can also use interactive widgets and data visualization tools.

4.2.13 Docker Compose

- **Extension Name**: Docker Compose
- **Description**: Docker Compose is an extension that complements the Docker extension. It simplifies the management of multi-container applications defined in Docker Compose files. You can start, stop, and manage Docker Compose services directly from the editor.

4.2.14 Code Runner

- **Extension Name**: Code Runner
- **Description**: Code Runner allows you to quickly run code snippets in various programming languages without needing to create a separate project or file. It's a handy tool for testing small code snippets and verifying the behavior of code segments.

4.2.15 Rainbow Brackets

- **Extension Name**: Rainbow Brackets
- **Description**: Similar to Bracket Pair Colorizer, Rainbow Brackets enhances code readability by colorizing nested brackets with distinct colors. It's particularly useful when working with deeply nested code structures.

4.2.16 CodeTime

- **Extension Name**: CodeTime
- **Description**: CodeTime is a productivity tool that helps you track and improve your coding habits. It provides insights into your coding patterns, time spent on different projects, and daily coding streaks. It can motivate you to stay focused and productive.

4.2.17 Bookmarks

- **Extension Name**: Bookmarks
- **Description**: Bookmarks allow you to add and navigate bookmarks within your code. It's a simple yet effective way to mark important lines or sections of code that you want to revisit later.

4.2.18 Git History

- **Extension Name**: Git History
- **Description**: Git History is another Git-related extension that provides an interactive Git history viewer within VS Code. You can view commit details, changes, and diffs directly in the editor, making it easier to understand code history.

4.2.19 Quokka.js

- **Extension Name**: Quokka.js
- **Description**: Quokka.js is a JavaScript and TypeScript live scratchpad for VS Code. It allows you to evaluate code snippets as you type, providing instant feedback on variables, expressions, and function results. It's a valuable tool for experimenting with code.

4.2.20 CodeTour

- **Extension Name**: CodeTour
- **Description**: CodeTour is a collaborative guide and walkthrough extension for your codebase. It enables you to create guided tours that walk through your code, explaining its structure and functionality. It's useful for onboarding new team members or documenting complex codebases.

These must-have extensions cover a wide range of development tasks and can significantly boost your productivity when working with Visual Studio Code. Whether you're a web developer, data scientist, or working in any other coding domain, these extensions can help streamline your workflow, improve code quality, and enhance your overall coding experience.

4.3 Creating Your Own Extensions

Visual Studio Code (VS Code) is known for its extensibility, and one of the exciting aspects of this extensibility is the ability for developers to create their own extensions. Whether you want to customize your coding environment, automate repetitive tasks, or share useful tools with the community, creating VS Code extensions allows you to tailor the editor to your specific needs. In this section, we'll explore the basics of creating your own VS Code extensions.

4.3.1 Why Create Your Own Extension?

There are several reasons why you might want to create your own VS Code extension:

- **Customization**: You can create extensions to customize your coding environment, such as adding new themes, snippets, or keybindings.

- **Automation**: Extensions can automate repetitive tasks, making your development workflow more efficient. For example, you can create an extension that formats code automatically upon saving a file.

- **Integration**: If you use other development tools or services, you can create extensions to integrate them seamlessly with VS Code.

- **Community Contribution**: Creating an extension that solves a common problem or provides a useful feature can benefit the VS Code community. You can share your extension on the VS Code Marketplace for others to use.

4.3.2 Extension Components

A VS Code extension typically consists of the following components:

- **Package.json**: This file contains metadata about your extension, such as its name, version, description, and dependencies. It also specifies the extension's activation events.

- **Extension Scripts**: You can write extension scripts using JavaScript or TypeScript. These scripts define the functionality of your extension, such as commands, keybindings, and language support.

- **Extension Manifest**: The manifest file, usually named `extension.js` or `extension.ts`, serves as the entry point for your extension. It defines the extension's behavior and registers commands, keybindings, and other features.

- **Language Support**: If your extension provides language support, it includes language grammar definitions, snippets, and IntelliSense configurations.

- **UI Components**: If your extension has a user interface, you'll define UI components using HTML, CSS, and possibly JavaScript.

4.3.3 Getting Started

To create your own VS Code extension, follow these general steps:

1. **Set Up Your Development Environment**: Ensure you have Node.js and npm (Node Package Manager) installed. You'll also need to install Yeoman and the VS Code Extension Generator.

2. **Generate a New Extension**: Use the Yeoman generator to create a new extension project. This will scaffold the necessary files and structure for your extension.

3. **Code Your Extension**: Write the code for your extension, including defining commands, keybindings, and other features. You can use the VS Code Extension API to access various functionalities of the editor.

4. **Test Your Extension**: Test your extension in a development instance of VS Code to ensure it behaves as expected. Debugging tools are available to help you identify and fix issues.

5. **Package Your Extension**: Once your extension is ready, package it into a `.vsix` file. This file can be published to the VS Code Marketplace or shared with others.

6. **Publish Your Extension**: If you want to share your extension with the community, you can publish it to the VS Code Marketplace. This allows other VS Code users to discover and install your extension.

4.3.4 Extension API

The VS Code Extension API provides a wide range of features and capabilities that you can leverage when creating extensions. Some of the key areas of the API include:

- **Commands**: You can register custom commands that perform specific actions within VS Code. For example, you can create a command that formats the current code file.

- **Keybindings**: Define custom keybindings that trigger your extension's commands.

- **Language Support**: Extend VS Code's language support by providing syntax highlighting, code snippets, and IntelliSense for a specific programming language.

- **Debugging**: Create debugging extensions to support debugging in specific languages or platforms.

- **UI Components**: Design and display user interface components within VS Code, such as panels, status bars, and tree views.

- **Extension Settings**: Define settings for your extension that users can customize in their VS Code settings.

- **Workspace Configuration**: Configure your extension to work differently based on the current workspace or folder.

- **Publishing and Licensing**: Learn how to publish your extension to the VS Code Marketplace and choose the appropriate licensing.

4.3.5 Extension Development Resources

Developing VS Code extensions can be a rewarding experience, but it may require some learning if you're new to extension development. Fortunately, there are plenty of resources available:

- **VS Code Extension API Documentation**: The official documentation provides detailed information on the available API and how to use it.

- **Extension Samples**: The VS Code team maintains a repository of extension samples that you can use as a reference.

- **Community and Forums**: You can engage with the VS Code community on forums and discussion boards to seek help, share your experiences, and collaborate on extension development.

- **Extensions Marketplace**: Study existing extensions to see how they are structured and learn from their code.

- **Extensions Generator**: Use the Yeoman generator for VS Code extensions

---

4.4 Community Contributions and Support

The Visual Studio Code (VS Code) ecosystem thrives on community contributions and support. As an open-source code editor, VS Code benefits from the active involvement of developers worldwide who create extensions, provide feedback, contribute to the core codebase, and help others in the community. In this section, we'll explore the importance of community contributions and how you can engage with and support the VS Code community.

4.4.1 The Power of Community

The success of VS Code can be attributed in large part to its vibrant and supportive community. This community contributes to the editor's growth and evolution by:

- **Creating Extensions**: Developers from around the world create and share extensions that enhance VS Code's functionality. These extensions cater to various programming languages, frameworks, and tools.

- **Reporting Issues**: Users and developers actively report bugs and issues they encounter while using VS Code. This feedback is invaluable in improving the editor's stability and performance.

- **Contributing Code**: The VS Code repository on GitHub welcomes contributions from the community. Developers can submit pull requests to fix bugs, add features, or improve documentation.

- **Answering Questions**: The VS Code community actively participates in online forums and platforms to help answer questions and solve problems for fellow users.

- **Providing Feedback**: Users share their experiences and suggestions, helping the VS Code team prioritize features and improvements.

4.4.2 Engaging with the VS Code Community

Here are some ways you can engage with and contribute to the VS Code community:

1. *Use and Share VS Code*: Begin by using VS Code for your development tasks. If you find it beneficial, share your experiences with others. Word-of-mouth recommendations are powerful.

2. *Contribute to Extensions*: If you have the skills, consider creating your own VS Code extensions to address specific needs. You can then share these extensions with the community on the VS Code Marketplace.

3. *Report Bugs and Issues*: When you encounter bugs or issues while using VS Code, don't hesitate to report them on GitHub. Providing clear and detailed information about the problem helps the development team address it more effectively.

4. *Contribute Code*: If you're comfortable with coding, you can contribute to the core codebase of VS Code. Check out the GitHub repository, explore the issues marked as "help wanted," and consider submitting pull requests.

5. *Participate in Forums*: Join online forums and discussion boards related to VS Code, such as the VS Code GitHub Discussions, Reddit, or Stack Overflow. Engaging in these communities allows you to learn from others and share your knowledge.

6. *Share Your Setup*: Share your VS Code setup, including your favorite extensions, keybindings, and tips, on social media or developer platforms. This can help others discover useful tools and configurations.

7. *Teach and Mentor*: If you're experienced with VS Code, consider mentoring newer users. You can create tutorials, walkthroughs, or video content to help newcomers get started.

8. *Translate Documentation*: Help translate VS Code's documentation into different languages to make it more accessible to a global audience.

9. *Advocate for Accessibility*: Advocate for and contribute to accessibility improvements in VS Code to ensure it can be used by individuals with disabilities.

4.4.3 Supporting the VS Code Project

Supporting the VS Code project goes beyond code contributions. Financial support can also help ensure the sustainability of the project. Here are a few ways to support VS Code:

1. *Donate*: *Consider making a financial donation to support the ongoing development of VS Code. Donations can help cover infrastructure costs and fund development efforts.*

2. *Corporate Sponsorship*: *If you work for a company that relies on VS Code, encourage your organization to consider corporate sponsorship or providing paid development time for VS Code contributions.*

3. *Promote VS Code*: *Help promote VS Code within your organization or community. Encourage its adoption and use among colleagues or fellow developers.*

4. *Participate in Hackathons*: *Join hackathons or coding events related to VS Code. These events often focus on improving the editor or creating innovative extensions.*

5. *Advocate for Open Source*: *Advocate for the principles of open source software and the importance of community-driven development.*

4.4.4 Recognizing Contributors

The VS Code team recognizes the efforts of community contributors in various ways:

- **Maintainer Interaction**: Maintainers actively engage with contributors on GitHub, reviewing and merging pull requests, and providing feedback and guidance.

- **Acknowledgment**: Contributors who submit code or help with documentation are acknowledged in the project's release notes and changelogs.

- **Extensions Showcase**: Outstanding extensions created by community members may be featured in the VS Code Marketplace or other promotional materials.

- **Events and Conferences**: The VS Code team often participates in and sponsors events, conferences, and meetups where contributors and users can connect and collaborate.

By actively participating in the VS Code community and contributing your skills and knowledge, you can play a role in shaping the future of this popular code editor and help ensure its continued success. Whether you're a developer, user, or supporter, your involvement is valuable to the community and the growth of Visual Studio Code.

4.5 Keeping Extensions Updated

One of the key aspects of maintaining a smooth and productive development environment with Visual Studio Code (VS Code) is keeping your extensions up to date. Extensions are integral to the functionality and versatility of VS Code, and their regular updates ensure that you have access to the latest features, bug fixes, and improvements. In this section, we'll explore why it's essential to keep your extensions updated and how to manage extension updates effectively.

4.5.1 The Importance of Extension Updates

Keeping your extensions updated offers several advantages:

*1. **Bug Fixes**: Extension updates often include bug fixes that address issues reported by users. By updating, you can resolve problems and ensure a more stable development experience.*

*2. **Performance Improvements**: Extensions are continuously optimized for better performance. Updating them can lead to improved responsiveness and reduced resource usage.*

*3. **New Features**: Extensions are regularly enhanced with new features and capabilities. Updating ensures that you have access to the latest functionality that can boost your productivity.*

*4. **Compatibility**: VS Code itself receives updates, and extension developers work to ensure compatibility with the latest VS Code versions. Updating extensions helps prevent compatibility issues and ensures a seamless experience.*

*5. **Security**: Extension updates may include security fixes to address vulnerabilities. Staying up to date is crucial for keeping your development environment secure.*

*6. **Extension Dependencies**: Some extensions depend on specific versions of other extensions or libraries. Updating ensures that all dependencies are in sync.*

4.5.2 Managing Extension Updates

Managing extension updates in VS Code is straightforward:

*1. **Automatic Updates**: By default, VS Code automatically checks for and installs extension updates in the background. When updates are available, you'll see a notification in the bottom-right corner of the window.*

*2. **Manual Updates**: If you prefer more control over updates, you can disable automatic updates in the settings and choose to update extensions manually. To manually update an extension, follow these steps:*

- Open the Extensions view by clicking the square icon on the left sidebar or using the shortcut `Ctrl+Shift+X` (Windows/Linux) or `Cmd+Shift+X` (macOS).
- In the Extensions view, you'll see a list of installed extensions. If updates are available, an "Update" button will appear next to each extension.
- Click the "Update" button for the extensions you want to update.

3. **Extension Settings**: *You can configure extension-specific settings to control their update behavior. Extension settings may include options for enabling or disabling automatic updates, specifying update intervals, or customizing update notifications.*

4. **Workspace Recommendations**: *VS Code can provide recommendations for extensions that are helpful in a specific workspace or project. These recommendations often point to well-maintained and popular extensions that can enhance your workflow.*

4.5.3 Best Practices for Extension Updates

To ensure a smooth extension update process and maintain a well-maintained VS Code environment, consider the following best practices:

1. **Regularly Check for Updates**: *Even if you have automatic updates enabled, it's a good practice to periodically check for updates manually. This ensures that you're aware of any changes or new features in your extensions.*

2. **Review Release Notes**: *Before updating an extension, review its release notes. Release notes provide information about what's new, bug fixes, and any breaking changes. This helps you understand what to expect after the update.*

3. **Backup Settings**: *Before updating extensions, consider backing up your VS Code settings. Extensions may introduce changes that affect your workspace configuration, and having a backup ensures you can revert if necessary.*

4. **Keep a Lean Extension List**: *While it's tempting to install numerous extensions, try to keep your list lean by regularly evaluating which extensions you truly need. Uninstall extensions that you no longer use or that have overlapping functionality.*

5. **Update VS Code**: *Keep the VS Code editor itself up to date. New versions of VS Code often come with performance improvements and compatibility enhancements that can benefit your extensions.*

6. **Report Issues**: *If you encounter issues with an extension after updating, don't hesitate to report them to the extension's developer. Constructive feedback can help improve the extension for all users.*

7. **Stay Informed**: *Stay informed about updates and changes in the VS Code ecosystem. Follow official VS Code channels, extension developers, and relevant communities to receive notifications and announcements.*

By following these best practices, you can ensure that your extensions are up to date, your development environment is stable and secure, and you're making the most of the latest features and improvements offered by Visual Studio Code and its extensions. Keeping your extensions updated is a small but essential part of maintaining an efficient and productive coding environment.

66

Chapter 5: Languages and Frameworks

5.1 Support for Major Programming Languages

Visual Studio Code (VS Code) is a versatile code editor that provides support for a wide range of programming languages and frameworks. Whether you are a web developer, data scientist, game developer, or working in any other domain, chances are that you will find support for your preferred language in VS Code. In this section, we'll explore the extensive language support that makes VS Code a popular choice among developers.

5.1.1 Language Server Protocol

One of the key reasons behind the broad language support in VS Code is the Language Server Protocol (LSP). LSP is an open standard that allows language servers to communicate with code editors, including VS Code. A language server is a separate program that provides language-specific intelligence, such as syntax checking, code completion, and error checking.

LSP separates the language-specific functionality from the code editor, enabling better integration of multiple languages. It ensures a consistent and efficient experience for developers, regardless of the programming language they are using.

5.1.2 Built-in Language Features

VS Code includes built-in language features that provide a solid foundation for various programming languages. These features include:

- **Syntax Highlighting**: VS Code can highlight the syntax of your code, making it easier to read and understand. It uses color-coded text to distinguish between keywords, variables, strings, and other elements.

- **Auto-indentation**: The editor can automatically indent your code according to the language's conventions, ensuring consistent formatting.

- **Bracket Matching**: VS Code helps you match brackets, parentheses, and other delimiters, reducing the chances of syntax errors.

- **Code Folding**: You can collapse sections of code to focus on specific parts of your codebase, which is especially useful in large projects.

- **Comments and Documentation**: VS Code supports writing comments and documentation in various formats, making it easier to create well-documented code.

5.1.3 IntelliSense and Autocompletion

One of the standout features of VS Code is its IntelliSense capability, which provides intelligent code completion suggestions as you type. IntelliSense is language-aware and context-aware, offering suggestions for variables, functions, classes, and even method signatures.

The availability and accuracy of IntelliSense depend on the language support provided by extensions. Many popular programming languages have dedicated extensions that enhance the IntelliSense experience in VS Code. These extensions often include type inference, parameter hints, and documentation pop-ups.

5.1.4 Debugging Support

VS Code offers debugging support for a wide variety of programming languages. Debuggers are available as extensions and can be configured to work with your specific language and environment. You can set breakpoints, inspect variables, and step through your code to identify and fix issues.

5.1.5 Language Extensions

For languages that are not natively supported by VS Code, you can rely on language-specific extensions provided by the community. These extensions often include features like syntax highlighting, code formatting, and IntelliSense for the respective language.

Popular languages like Python, JavaScript, Java, C++, and many others have well-maintained extensions that bring rich language support to VS Code.

5.1.6 Polyglot Development

VS Code's support for multiple languages makes it an ideal choice for polyglot development, where you work with multiple programming languages within a single project. The editor can seamlessly switch between language configurations, allowing you to develop full-stack applications or complex systems with ease.

5.1.7 Custom Language Support

If you have specific language requirements that are not covered by existing extensions, you can create your own language support extension for VS Code. The extension can define syntax highlighting rules, code snippets, and IntelliSense features tailored to your language.

In summary, VS Code's support for major programming languages is a testament to its flexibility and extensibility. Whether you are a seasoned developer or just starting, you can find a rich ecosystem of extensions and tools that enhance your coding experience in your preferred programming language. The combination of built-in features, extensions, and the Language Server Protocol makes VS Code a versatile and powerful code editor for a wide range of development tasks.

5.2 Tailoring Visual Studio Code for JavaScript

JavaScript is one of the most widely used programming languages for web development, and Visual Studio Code (VS Code) provides excellent support for JavaScript development. In this section, we'll explore how you can tailor VS Code to make it a powerful JavaScript development environment.

5.2.1 JavaScript Language Features

VS Code includes a rich set of features for JavaScript developers:

- **Syntax Highlighting**: JavaScript code is highlighted for easy readability. This helps you distinguish between keywords, variables, and strings.

- **IntelliSense**: VS Code provides intelligent code completion and suggestions for JavaScript. It understands the structure of your code and offers context-aware recommendations.

- **ESLint Integration**: You can integrate ESLint, a popular JavaScript linter, into VS Code. ESLint helps you maintain code quality by catching errors and enforcing coding standards.

- **Debugging**: VS Code offers a powerful JavaScript debugger that allows you to set breakpoints, inspect variables, and step through your code for debugging purposes.

- **Code Formatting**: Use the built-in code formatter (Prettier) or customize your formatting rules to ensure consistent code style.

5.2.2 JavaScript Extensions

While VS Code provides excellent JavaScript support out of the box, you can enhance your development experience further by installing JavaScript-specific extensions. Some popular JavaScript extensions include:

- **ESLint**: The ESLint extension provides real-time linting and code analysis for JavaScript. It highlights errors and coding style violations as you type.

- **npm Intellisense**: This extension offers auto-completion for npm modules in your JavaScript code, making it easy to import and use external libraries.

- **Debugger for Chrome**: If you're working on web applications, this extension allows you to debug JavaScript code running in the Chrome browser directly from VS Code.

- **JSDoc Comments**: Simplify documenting your JavaScript code with JSDoc comment support. This extension helps you generate JSDoc comments for your functions and classes.

5.2.3 Customization for JavaScript

To tailor VS Code specifically for JavaScript development, consider the following customization options:

- **Keybindings**: Customize keyboard shortcuts to streamline your workflow. Create keybindings for common tasks or extensions you frequently use.

- **Snippets**: VS Code supports code snippets. You can create your own JavaScript code snippets for frequently used patterns or boilerplate code.

- **Themes**: Choose a theme that suits your coding preferences. There are numerous themes available, including those optimized for JavaScript development.

- **Extensions**: Explore the VS Code Marketplace for JavaScript-related extensions. You'll find extensions for popular frameworks like React, Angular, and Vue.js, as well as libraries like Redux and Axios.

- **Workspace Settings**: Configure workspace-specific settings in your project's .vscode folder. This allows you to define preferences, linters, and formatting rules that apply only to your JavaScript project.

- **Integrated Terminal**: Use the integrated terminal in VS Code for running JavaScript scripts, npm commands, or managing your project without leaving the editor.

5.2.4 Node.js Development

If you're working with server-side JavaScript using Node.js, VS Code provides excellent support. You can create Node.js projects, debug Node.js applications, and use the integrated terminal for running Node.js scripts.

Extensions like "Node.js" and "npm" provide enhanced Node.js development features and integration.

5.2.5 JavaScript Frameworks

VS Code's versatility extends to popular JavaScript frameworks like React, Angular, and Vue.js. There are dedicated extensions and tools tailored for each of these frameworks. These extensions offer features like component templates, syntax highlighting, IntelliSense, and project scaffolding.

Whether you're building a single-page application with React, a dynamic web app with Angular, or a progressive web app with Vue.js, you'll find tools and extensions in VS Code that cater to your needs.

5.2.6 Debugging in the Browser

For web development, debugging JavaScript in the browser is essential. VS Code provides extensions like "Debugger for Chrome" and "Debugger for Firefox" that allow you to connect the editor to your browser's developer tools. This enables you to debug client-side JavaScript code directly from VS Code.

5.2.7 Collaboration and Version Control

VS Code also supports collaboration and version control for JavaScript projects. You can integrate Git for version control and use extensions like "Live Share" for real-time collaborative coding sessions with teammates.

In conclusion, Visual Studio Code offers a feature-rich and customizable environment for JavaScript development. Its support for syntax highlighting, IntelliSense, debugging, and a vast extension ecosystem make it a top choice for JavaScript developers working on web and Node.js projects. By customizing your VS Code setup with the right extensions and settings, you can optimize your JavaScript development workflow and boost productivity.

5.3 Python Development in Visual Studio Code

Visual Studio Code (VS Code) is a popular choice for Python development due to its versatility, robust extension ecosystem, and excellent support for the Python programming language. In this section, we'll delve into the features and tools that make Python development in VS Code a seamless and efficient experience.

5.3.1 Python Language Features

VS Code provides a set of built-in features tailored for Python development:

- **Syntax Highlighting**: Python code is highlighted for improved readability, with different colors for keywords, variables, and strings.

- **IntelliSense**: VS Code offers intelligent code completion, suggestions, and auto-imports for Python. It understands your code's structure and context, making coding faster and less error-prone.

- **Code Formatting**: VS Code can automatically format your Python code using popular formatters like Black or autopep8. Consistent code style is easily achieved.

- **Linter Integration**: You can integrate Python linters like pylint or flake8 to catch and fix code quality issues, enforce coding standards, and identify errors as you write code.

- **Debugging**: VS Code includes a powerful Python debugger that allows you to set breakpoints, inspect variables, and step through your code to troubleshoot issues effectively.

5.3.2 Python Extensions

While VS Code offers great Python support out of the box, you can further enhance your Python development environment by installing Python-specific extensions:

- **Python**: The official Python extension for VS Code provides features like IntelliSense, debugging, code formatting, and more. It's essential for a smooth Python development experience.

- **Python Docstring Generator**: Simplify documentation by generating docstrings for your Python functions and classes using this extension. Proper documentation is crucial for code readability and maintainability.

- **Jupyter**: If you work with Jupyter notebooks, the Jupyter extension for VS Code allows you to create, edit, and run notebooks seamlessly within the editor.

- **Python Test Explorer**: This extension integrates test frameworks like pytest and unittest into VS Code, making it easier to run and manage your Python tests.

5.3.3 Customization for Python

To tailor VS Code specifically for Python development, consider the following customization options:

- **Virtual Environments**: Create and manage virtual environments for your Python projects. VS Code can detect and use the correct environment for your workspace.

- **Python Interpreters**: Configure the Python interpreter used for your projects. This is especially important if you work with multiple Python versions or virtual environments.

- **Code Snippets**: Use and create Python code snippets for frequently used patterns or boilerplate code. VS Code supports custom snippets to boost productivity.

- **Themes**: Choose a theme that suits your coding preferences. VS Code offers a wide range of themes, including those optimized for Python development.

- **Linting and Formatting**: Customize linting and formatting rules to align with your project's coding standards. You can adjust settings for linters like pylint or flake8.

- **Keybindings**: Create custom keyboard shortcuts to streamline your Python development workflow.

5.3.4 Python Web Development

If you're working on web development projects with Python, VS Code has you covered. You can use extensions like "Django" for Django framework support or "Flask" for Flask framework support. These extensions offer features like code snippets, project templates, and debugging for web applications.

5.3.5 Data Science and Machine Learning

For data science and machine learning projects in Python, VS Code provides excellent support. You can install extensions like "Python Data Science" to access Jupyter notebooks, data visualization tools, and libraries such as Pandas and Matplotlib. Additionally, you can integrate with popular machine learning frameworks like TensorFlow and PyTorch.

5.3.6 Python Version Control

Integrate Git or other version control systems into your Python projects within VS Code. You can commit changes, view commit history, and manage branches without leaving the editor. This ensures that your Python code is well-tracked and maintained.

5.3.7 Collaboration and Remote Development

VS Code's "Live Share" extension enables real-time collaborative coding sessions, making it easy to work on Python projects with teammates regardless of their physical location. Remote development extensions also allow you to develop, run, and debug Python code on remote servers or containers.

In summary, Visual Studio Code offers a feature-rich and customizable environment for Python development. Its support for syntax highlighting, IntelliSense, debugging, and a vast extension ecosystem makes it a top choice for Python developers working on a wide range of projects, from web development to data science and machine learning. By customizing your VS Code setup with the right extensions and settings, you can optimize your Python development workflow and boost productivity.

5.4 Exploring C# and .NET Capabilities

Visual Studio Code (VS Code) is not limited to specific programming languages, and it offers robust support for C# and the .NET ecosystem. In this section, we will explore the capabilities and tools available for C# developers using VS Code.

5.4.1 C# Language Features

VS Code provides a set of features tailored for C# development:

- **Syntax Highlighting**: C# code is syntax-highlighted to improve readability, helping you distinguish between keywords, variables, and strings.

- **IntelliSense**: VS Code offers intelligent code completion, suggestions, and auto-imports for C#. It understands the structure of your code and context, making coding more efficient and reducing errors.

- **Code Formatting**: You can automatically format your C# code using built-in formatters like OmniSharp, ensuring consistent code style.

- **Debugging**: VS Code includes a powerful debugger for C# that allows you to set breakpoints, inspect variables, and step through your code to identify and fix issues.

- **Unit Testing**: C# developers can utilize extensions like "NUnit Test Adapter" or "xUnit Test Explorer" to perform unit testing within the editor.

5.4.2 .NET Core and .NET 5+ Development

VS Code is an excellent choice for developing applications using .NET Core and the latest .NET 5+ versions. It supports a wide range of project types, including console applications, web applications, and more. You can create, build, and run .NET projects directly within the editor.

5.4.3 C# Extensions

Enhance your C# development experience in VS Code by installing C#-specific extensions:

- **C# for Visual Studio Code (powered by OmniSharp)**: This official C# extension provides essential features like IntelliSense, code formatting, and debugging support.

- **C# XML Documentation Comments**: Simplify documenting your C# code by generating XML documentation comments for methods, classes, and properties.

- **C# Extensions**: Explore a variety of extensions for specific C# frameworks and libraries. For example, you can find extensions for ASP.NET, Entity Framework, and popular libraries like Newtonsoft.Json.

5.4.4 Customization for C

To tailor VS Code specifically for C# development, consider these customization options:

- **.editorconfig**: Define coding conventions and formatting rules for your C# projects by using the `.editorconfig` file. VS Code will enforce these rules for consistent code style.

- **Keybindings**: Customize keyboard shortcuts to streamline your C# development workflow. Create keybindings for common tasks or extensions you frequently use.

- **Themes**: Choose a theme that suits your coding preferences. VS Code offers numerous themes, including those optimized for C# development.

- **Linters and Code Analyzers**: Integrate code analyzers like Roslyn Analyzers into your projects to enforce coding standards and identify potential issues.

- **Project and Solution Management**: Use extensions like "C# Project Manager" to manage your C# projects and solutions effectively within VS Code.

5.4.5 .NET Core and ASP.NET Core Development

If you're working with .NET Core or ASP.NET Core, VS Code offers a smooth development experience. You can create and manage .NET Core projects, build web applications, and leverage extensions tailored for ASP.NET Core development.

5.4.6 Entity Framework Core

For database access and ORM (Object-Relational Mapping) in C#, Entity Framework Core is a popular choice. VS Code supports Entity Framework Core development, allowing you to create models, generate migrations, and interact with databases using extensions like "EF Core Power Tools."

5.4.7 Collaboration and Version Control

VS Code supports collaboration and version control for C# projects. You can integrate Git or other version control systems, commit changes, view commit history, and manage branches without leaving the editor. Extensions like "Live Share" facilitate real-time collaborative coding sessions with teammates.

5.4.8 Unity Game Development

C# is commonly used for game development with the Unity game engine. VS Code is a suitable choice for Unity development, with extensions that provide Unity-specific features, code completion, and debugging support.

In conclusion, Visual Studio Code is a versatile code editor that offers robust capabilities for C# and .NET development. Whether you are building web applications, console applications, games with Unity, or working on other C# projects, VS Code provides a feature-rich environment with extensive support for C# language features, debugging, and a wide range of extensions. By customizing your VS Code setup and installing relevant extensions, you can optimize your C# development workflow and enhance productivity.

5.5 Other Languages: From PHP to Go

Visual Studio Code (VS Code) isn't limited to a specific set of programming languages. It offers extensive support for various programming languages, making it a versatile code editor for a wide range of developers. In this section, we'll explore how you can use VS Code for languages beyond JavaScript, Python, and C#.

5.5.1 PHP Development

If you're a PHP developer, you can take advantage of VS Code's features for PHP development. VS Code provides syntax highlighting, IntelliSense, debugging support, and extensions for PHP development. You can also integrate tools like Composer for dependency management and PHPUnit for unit testing.

5.5.2 Ruby and Ruby on Rails

Ruby developers can utilize VS Code for Ruby and Ruby on Rails projects. The editor offers syntax highlighting, code navigation, and debugging support for Ruby. Extensions like "Ruby" and "Ruby on Rails" provide additional features and project templates for Rails applications.

5.5.3 Java Development

While VS Code is known for its lightweight nature, it also supports Java development. You can use extensions like "Java Extension Pack" to add Java language support, debugging capabilities, and integration with popular build tools like Maven and Gradle.

5.5.4 Rust Programming

Rust is gaining popularity for systems programming, and VS Code offers extensions like "Rust (rls)" for Rust language support. You can write, build, and debug Rust code directly within the editor, making it a viable choice for Rust developers.

5.5.5 Go Programming

Go (Golang) developers can benefit from VS Code's support for the Go programming language. The "Go" extension provides features like IntelliSense, code formatting, and debugging support for Go projects. You can also set up Go workspaces and efficiently navigate Go code.

5.5.6 TypeScript and Front-End Development

If you work with TypeScript for front-end development, VS Code is an excellent choice. TypeScript is a superset of JavaScript, and VS Code provides robust support for TypeScript features like type checking and code navigation. You can also use extensions for popular front-end frameworks like React, Angular, and Vue.js.

5.5.7 Swift and iOS Development

While Xcode is the primary development environment for Swift and iOS, VS Code can be used for Swift development with extensions like "Swift Language" and "Swifty." You can write Swift code, but for full iOS app development, Xcode is still necessary.

5.5.8 Dart and Flutter

Dart is the programming language used for building Flutter apps, and VS Code provides excellent support for Dart and Flutter development. With the "Flutter" extension, you can create, debug, and test Flutter applications efficiently.

5.5.9 Web Development with HTML and CSS

For web development, VS Code offers robust support for HTML and CSS. You can benefit from features like syntax highlighting, code completion, and live previews. Extensions like "Live Server" provide a local development server for testing your web applications.

5.5.10 Shell Scripting and DevOps

If you're involved in shell scripting or DevOps tasks, VS Code can be a valuable tool. It supports various shell scripting languages like Bash and PowerShell. You can also use extensions to integrate with version control systems, cloud services, and containerization tools.

5.5.11 LaTeX and Technical Writing

For LaTeX and technical writing, VS Code provides extensions like "LaTeX Workshop" that simplify the creation of documents, including research papers, articles, and reports. You can benefit from real-time previews and LaTeX-specific tools.

In conclusion, Visual Studio Code is a versatile code editor that caters to a wide spectrum of programming languages and development scenarios. Whether you're a PHP developer, a Ruby enthusiast, a Java programmer, or working with languages like Rust, Go, or Swift, VS Code offers a feature-rich environment with language-specific support, debugging capabilities, and a vast extension ecosystem. By customizing your VS Code setup and installing relevant extensions, you can adapt the editor to suit your preferred programming language and streamline your development workflow.

Chapter 1: Introduction to Visual Studio Code

- 1.1. The Evolution of Code Editors: A Brief History
- 1.2. Visual Studio Code: An Overview
- 1.3. Key Features That Set Visual Studio Code Apart
- 1.4. The User Interface: A Tour
- 1.5. Installing and Setting Up Visual Studio Code

Chapter 2: Customizing Your Workspace

- 2.1. Personalizing Themes and Colors
- 2.2. Managing Workspaces and Folders
- 2.3. Keyboard Shortcuts and Efficiency Tips
- 2.4. Extensions and Plugins: Enhancing Functionality
- 2.5. Setting Up User and Workspace Settings

Chapter 3: Coding Efficiently in Visual Studio Code

- 3.1. Intelligent Code Completion
- 3.2. Code Navigation and Refactoring Tools
- 3.3. Debugging Made Simple
- 3.4. Integrated Terminal Usage
- 3.5. Version Control Integration

Chapter 4: Extensions and the Marketplace

- 4.1. Navigating the Extension Marketplace
- 4.2. Must-Have Extensions for Developers
- 4.3. Creating Your Own Extensions
- 4.4. Community Contributions and Support
- 4.5. Keeping Extensions Updated

Chapter 5: Languages and Frameworks

- 5.1. Support for Major Programming Languages
- 5.2. Tailoring Visual Studio Code for JavaScript
- 5.3. Python Development in Visual Studio Code
- 5.4. Exploring C# and .NET Capabilities
- 5.5. Other Languages: From PHP to Go

Chapter 6: Source Control Integration

- 6.1. Understanding Git Integration
- 6.2. Committing and Pushing Changes
- 6.3. Branch Management and Merging
- 6.4. Resolving Merge Conflicts
- 6.5. Advanced Git Features and Extensions

Chapter 7: Debugging and Problem Solving

- 7.1. Setting Up Debugging Environment
- 7.2. Breakpoints and Watchers
- 7.3. Inspecting Variables and Stack Traces
- 7.4. Remote Debugging Capabilities
- 7.5. Solving Common Debugging Issues

Chapter 8: Testing Your Code

- 8.1. Introduction to Testing in Visual Studio Code
- 8.2. Setting Up Testing Frameworks
- 8.3. Writing and Running Tests
- 8.4. Test Coverage and Reporting
- 8.5. Automated Testing and Continuous Integration

Chapter 9: Advanced Editing Features

- 9.1. Multi-Cursor and Snippets
- 9.2. Code Folding and Regions
- 9.3. Regular Expression in Search and Replace
- 9.4. File Comparisons and Merging

- 9.5. Advanced Formatting and Beautification Tools

Chapter 10: Optimizing Performance

- 10.1. Improving Startup Time and Efficiency
- 10.2. Managing Memory and CPU Usage
- 10.3. Troubleshooting Performance Issues
- 10.4. Best Practices for High-Performance Coding
- 10.5. Leveraging Hardware Resources

Chapter 11: Customizing the Look and Feel

- 11.1. Themes and Icon Packs
- 11.2. Customizing Font and Display Settings
- 11.3. Accessibility Features
- 11.4. Personalizing the Sidebar and Panels
- 11.5. Creating a Comfortable Coding Environment

Chapter 12: Collaboration and Remote Development

- 12.1. Pair Programming with Live Share
- 12.2. Remote Development Extensions
- 12.3. Collaborating Across Different Platforms
- 12.4. Code Reviews and Pull Requests
- 12.5. Managing Projects and Teams

Chapter 13: The Command Palette and Shortcuts

- 13.1. Mastering the Command Palette
- 13.2. Essential Keyboard Shortcuts
- 13.3. Customizing Shortcuts
- 13.4. Command Line Integration
- 13.5. Efficiency Tips and Tricks

Chapter 14: Integrating with Other Tools and Services

- 14.1. Connecting with Cloud Services
- 14.2. Using Docker in Visual Studio Code
- 14.3. Integration with Database Tools
- 14.4. Working with REST APIs and Postman
- 14.5. Combining with Other Development Tools

Chapter 15: Mobile and Web Development

- 15.1. Setting Up for Web Development
- 15.2. Mobile Development with React Native and Flutter
- 15.3. Responsive Design and Cross-Browser Testing

- 15.4. JavaScript Frameworks: Angular, Vue.js, and More
- 15.5. Building Progressive Web Apps

Chapter 16: Scripting and Automation

- 16.1. Automating Repetitive Tasks
- 16.2. Building and Running Scripts
- 16.3. Task Runners and Build Tools
- 16.4. Custom Automation Workflows
- 16.5. Using Visual Studio Code for DevOps

Chapter 17: Data Science and Machine Learning

- 17.1. Setting Up for Data Science Workflows
- 17.2. Python and R Integration
- 17.3. Working with Jupyter Notebooks
- 17.4. Visualization Tools and Libraries
- 17.5. Machine Learning Model Development

Chapter 18: Security and Version Control

- 18.1. Ensuring Code Security
- 18.2. Managing Dependencies and Security Updates
- 18.3. Working with Version Control Systems
- 18.4. Best Practices for Secure Coding
- 18.5. Handling Sensitive Data and Credentials

Chapter 19: Tailoring Visual Studio Code for Enterprise Use

- 19.1. Large-Scale Deployment Strategies
- 19.2. Managing Licenses and Compliance
- 19.3. Enterprise-Level Customizations
- 19.4. Security in an Enterprise Environment
- 19.5. Training and Support for Teams

Chapter 20: The Future of Visual Studio Code

- 20.1. Emerging Trends in Development
- 20.2. Visual Studio Code in the Next Decade
- 20.3. Community and Open Source Contributions
- 20.4. Integrating AI and Machine Learning Tools
- 20.5. Staying Ahead with Visual Studio Code

Chapter 6: Source Control Integration

6.1. Understanding Git Integration

Source control, also known as version control, is a crucial aspect of modern software development. It allows developers to track changes, collaborate effectively, and maintain a history of code revisions. In Visual Studio Code (VS Code), Git integration is a fundamental feature that streamlines source control tasks. In this section, we will explore how to understand and use Git integration within VS Code.

What is Git?

Git is a distributed version control system (DVCS) designed to handle projects of all sizes efficiently. It was created by Linus Torvalds in 2005 and has since become the standard for version control in the software development industry. Git enables multiple developers to work on a project simultaneously while keeping track of changes and managing code collaboration seamlessly.

Why Use Git Integration in VS Code?

Visual Studio Code offers built-in Git support to simplify source control tasks directly from your code editor. Using Git within VS Code provides several benefits:

1. **Seamless Integration:** Git is seamlessly integrated into VS Code, allowing you to perform Git operations without leaving the editor.

2. **Visual Representation:** VS Code provides a visual representation of your Git repository's status, making it easier to understand and manage changes.

3. **Efficient Workflow:** You can stage, commit, and push changes with a few clicks, streamlining your workflow.

4. **Branch Management:** Easily create, switch, and merge branches within VS Code.

5. **Conflict Resolution:** Resolve merge conflicts directly within the editor, with helpful tools to guide you through the process.

Getting Started with Git in VS Code

To start using Git in VS Code, follow these steps:

1. **Install Git:** If you haven't already, install Git on your system. You can download it from the official Git website (https://git-scm.com/).

2. **Open a Project:** Open your project folder in VS Code.

3. **Initialize a Repository:** If your project isn't already a Git repository, you can initialize one using the "Initialize Repository" option in the source control view.

4. **Staging Changes:** Use the source control view to stage your changes. You can do this by clicking the "+" icon next to the files you want to stage.

5. **Commit Changes:** After staging your changes, provide a commit message and commit them. This creates a new commit in your Git history.

6. **Push to Remote:** If you're collaborating with others, you can push your commits to a remote repository, such as GitHub or GitLab.

Key Git Concepts

To effectively use Git in VS Code, it's essential to understand some key Git concepts:

- **Repository:** A Git repository is a folder or directory that contains your project's files and their history.

- **Commit:** A commit is a snapshot of your project's state at a specific point in time. It records changes to your files along with a commit message describing the changes.

- **Branch:** A branch is a parallel line of development. You can create branches to work on new features or fixes independently.

- **Merge:** Merging combines changes from one branch into another. It's often used to integrate feature branches into the main branch.

- **Pull:** Pulling retrieves changes from a remote repository and integrates them into your local branch.

- **Conflict:** A conflict occurs when Git can't automatically merge changes from different branches. Manual intervention is needed to resolve conflicts.

Conclusion

Understanding Git integration in Visual Studio Code is essential for efficient source control management. Git's powerful features combined with VS Code's user-friendly interface make it easy to track changes, collaborate with others, and maintain a well-organized codebase. In the following sections, we will delve deeper into various Git operations and best practices for effective version control within VS Code.

6.2. Committing and Pushing Changes

Once you have a Git repository set up in Visual Studio Code (VS Code), the next steps involve committing and pushing changes to your version control system. This section will guide you through the process of committing your code changes and pushing them to a remote repository, such as GitHub or GitLab.

Committing Changes

Committing changes in Git means creating a snapshot of the current state of your project. Each commit represents a logical unit of work and includes a message explaining the changes made. Commits help you keep track of the project's history and facilitate collaboration with other developers.

To commit changes in VS Code:

1. **Stage Your Changes:** Before committing, you need to stage the changes you want to include in the commit. You can do this from the Source Control panel by clicking the "+" icon next to the files you want to stage. Alternatively, you can stage all changes by clicking the "+" icon at the top of the panel.

2. **Provide a Commit Message:** After staging your changes, you must provide a meaningful commit message that describes what the commit accomplishes. A good commit message is concise and informative.

3. **Commit the Changes:** Click the checkmark icon (✓) in the Source Control panel to commit your changes. Alternatively, you can use the keyboard shortcut Ctrl+Enter (Windows/Linux) or Cmd+Enter (macOS).

4. **View Commit History:** You can view your commit history in the Source Control panel to see a list of all your commits.

Pushing changes in Git means uploading your committed changes from your local repository to a remote repository, like GitHub or GitLab. This allows you to share your work with others and collaborate on the project.

To push changes in VS Code:

1. **Ensure You're Connected:** Make sure you are connected to the remote repository where you want to push your changes. You may need to set up a remote repository and configure your Git credentials if you haven't already.

2. **Push Commits:** Click the circular arrow icon (↻) in the Source Control panel to push your commits to the remote repository. Alternatively, you can use the keyboard shortcut Ctrl+Shift+P (Windows/Linux) or Cmd+Shift+P (macOS) and type "Git: Push."

3. **Enter Credentials (If Necessary):** If you haven't previously configured your Git credentials for the remote repository, VS Code may prompt you to enter your username and password or a personal access token.

4. **View Remote Changes:** After a successful push, you can view your changes on the remote repository's web interface. This is where other collaborators can access your code.

Here are some best practices for committing and pushing changes in Git:

- **Commit Frequently:** Make small, frequent commits rather than large, infrequent ones. This makes it easier to track changes and collaborate with others.

- **Write Meaningful Commit Messages:** Write clear and descriptive commit messages that explain what the commit accomplishes. Follow a consistent format and keep messages concise.

- **Review Changes Before Committing:** Review your changes in VS Code's built-in diff viewer before committing to ensure you are committing the intended changes.

- **Pull Before Push:** Always pull changes from the remote repository before pushing your own changes to avoid conflicts.

- **Use Branches:** Create branches for new features or bug fixes to isolate your changes from the main development branch.

- **Push Regularly:** Don't forget to push your commits regularly to the remote repository to keep it up-to-date.

By following these best practices, you can effectively manage your code changes, collaborate with your team, and maintain a well-organized Git workflow in Visual Studio Code.

6.3. Branch Management and Merging

In the context of source control and version management, branches play a crucial role in keeping your development process organized and efficient. In Visual Studio Code (VS Code), you can manage branches seamlessly, enabling you to work on different features or bug fixes simultaneously without interfering with each other's work. This section will explore branch management and merging within VS Code.

What Are Branches?

In Git, a branch is a parallel line of development that represents a distinct line of code changes. Branches allow you to work on different features, bug fixes, or experiments without affecting the main codebase. Each branch has its own set of commits, which provides isolation and flexibility in the development process.

Branches in VS Code can be created and managed easily, making it a powerful tool for collaborative development.

Creating a Branch

To create a new branch in VS Code:

1. Open the Source Control panel by clicking on the Source Control icon in the left sidebar or by using the keyboard shortcut Ctrl+Shift+G (Windows/Linux) or Cmd+Shift+G (macOS).

2. Click on the branch name at the bottom left corner of the panel. This will open the branch switcher.

3. Click on the "Create new branch" button (the plus icon) and enter a name for your new branch. Make sure the name is descriptive and related to the task or feature you're working on.

4. Press Enter, and the new branch will be created. VS Code will automatically switch to the newly created branch, so you're ready to start working on it.

Switching Between Branches

Switching between branches in VS Code is straightforward:

1. Open the Source Control panel if it's not already open.

2. Click on the branch name at the bottom left corner to open the branch switcher.

3. Select the branch you want to switch to from the list of available branches.

VS Code will update your workspace to the selected branch, allowing you to work on the code specific to that branch.

Merging Branches

Merging is the process of integrating changes from one branch into another, typically from a feature branch into the main development branch. To merge branches in VS Code:

1. Ensure you are on the branch where you want to merge changes. This is usually the branch you want to update with changes from another branch.

2. Open the Source Control panel.

3. Click on the three dots icon (ellipsis) to access the menu.

4. Choose "Pull, Push, and Sync" from the menu.

5. Select the branch you want to merge changes from in the dialog box.

6. Click the "Pull" button. VS Code will fetch the changes from the selected branch and merge them into your current branch.

Handling Merge Conflicts

Sometimes, when you merge branches, Git may encounter conflicts—situations where the same lines of code have been modified in both branches. VS Code provides a helpful interface to resolve merge conflicts:

1. After attempting a merge, if conflicts arise, VS Code will display them in the file with conflict markers (<<<<<<<, =======, and >>>>>>>).

2. Click on a conflict marker to choose the version of the code you want to keep, or manually edit the code to resolve the conflict.

3. After resolving conflicts, save the file.

4. Open the Source Control panel, and you will see the conflicted file listed with a "Resolve" button. Click it to mark the conflict as resolved.

5. Commit the changes to finalize the merge.

Branch Management Best Practices

Here are some best practices for effective branch management in VS Code:

- Use descriptive branch names that convey the purpose of the branch.

- Create separate branches for new features, bug fixes, and experiments to keep your codebase organized.

- Regularly pull changes from the main development branch to stay up-to-date and minimize conflicts.

- Review and test your code changes on your branch before merging them into the main branch.

- Delete branches that are no longer needed to keep your repository clean.

By following these practices and mastering branch management in VS Code, you can maintain a smooth and efficient development workflow, collaborate effectively with your team, and keep your codebase in good shape. Branches are a powerful tool in Git, and using them wisely can greatly enhance your development experience.

6.4. Resolving Merge Conflicts

Merge conflicts are a common occurrence in collaborative development when multiple contributors work on the same codebase. When two or more branches have made conflicting changes to the same part of a file, Git cannot automatically determine which changes to accept. In such cases, you'll need to manually resolve the conflicts. This section will guide you through the process of resolving merge conflicts in Visual Studio Code (VS Code).

When a merge conflict occurs, Git will mark the conflicted areas in the affected files. These marks look like this:

```
<<<<<<< HEAD
// Your changes
=======
// Incoming changes
>>>>>>> branch-name
```

- `<<<<<<< HEAD` indicates the start of your changes.
- `=======` separates your changes from incoming changes.
- `>>>>>>> branch-name` indicates the end of incoming changes.

You'll need to decide which changes to keep and which to discard, and then remove the conflict markers.

Steps to Resolve Merge Conflicts

To resolve merge conflicts in VS Code:

1. **Open the Affected File:** First, open the file with the merge conflict in VS Code. The file will display the conflict markers as described above.

2. **Review and Edit:** Carefully review the conflicting sections and decide which changes to keep. You can edit the code directly in the file to resolve the conflicts. Remove the conflict markers (`<<<<<<< HEAD`, `=======`, and `>>>>>>> branch-name`) once you've made your decisions.

3. **Save the File:** After resolving conflicts, save the file.

4. **Mark as Resolved:** In the Source Control panel, you'll see a list of files with merge conflicts. Right-click on the conflicted file and select "Mark as Resolved." This action informs Git that you have resolved the conflicts.

5. **Commit Changes:** Finally, commit the changes. You can do this by opening the Source Control panel, adding a commit message describing the resolution, and clicking the commit button.

Using VS Code's Built-in Merge Conflict Resolution

VS Code provides a helpful built-in merge conflict resolution tool that makes the process more user-friendly. Here's how to use it:

1. Open the file with a merge conflict in VS Code.

2. In the Source Control panel, click on the file with conflicts. VS Code will display a side-by-side view with your changes on the left and incoming changes on the right.

3. You can click the buttons in the gutter (the vertical bar on the left) to accept your changes, incoming changes, or both for each conflicting section.

4. Use the "Accept All Current" or "Accept All Incoming" buttons at the top to quickly accept all changes from one side.

5. Once you've resolved all conflicts, save the file.

6. In the Source Control panel, right-click on the conflicted file and select "Mark as Resolved."

7. Commit your changes as usual.

Additional Tips for Conflict Resolution

- Communicate with your team: If you're resolving conflicts in a collaborative project, it's essential to communicate with other contributors to ensure everyone is on the same page regarding conflict resolution.

- Test thoroughly: After resolving conflicts, thoroughly test your code to ensure that the changes work as expected and haven't introduced new issues.

- Keep commits clean: When committing resolved conflicts, use clear and concise commit messages that describe the conflict resolution.

By following these steps and best practices, you can effectively manage and resolve merge conflicts in Visual Studio Code, ensuring that your collaborative development efforts proceed smoothly and without code conflicts hampering progress.

6.5. Advanced Git Features and Extensions

In addition to basic Git functionalities, Visual Studio Code (VS Code) offers a range of advanced features and extensions that can enhance your Git workflow. These tools can help streamline your development process, improve code quality, and facilitate collaboration. This section will explore some of the advanced Git features and extensions available in VS Code.

1. GitLens Extension

GitLens is a popular extension for VS Code that provides an array of advanced Git features right within your code editor. Some of its key features include:

- **Blame Annotations:** GitLens shows blame annotations in your code, allowing you to see who last modified each line and when.

- **Code Lens:** It adds code lens indicators above your code, displaying information about changes and authors. You can click these indicators to access additional details.

- **File History:** View detailed file history, including commit messages, authors, and changes over time.

- **Compare and Diff:** Compare changes between commits, branches, or tags right within VS Code.

2. Git Graph Extension

The **Git Graph** extension provides an interactive and visually appealing way to visualize your Git repository's history. With Git Graph, you can:

- View and interact with your commit history as a graph.

- See branches, commits, and tags in a clear and intuitive manner.

- Create and manage branches directly from the graph.

- Merge branches easily by dragging and dropping.

- Rebase, cherry-pick, and perform other Git operations effortlessly.

3. Git History Extension

The **Git History** extension offers a detailed and interactive view of your Git repository's history. It provides features like:

- Detailed commit history with commit messages, authors, and timestamps.

- Searching for commits by keywords or authors.

- Viewing and comparing changes between commits.

- Cherry-picking and reverting commits.

4. Gitignore Support

VS Code includes built-in support for `.gitignore` files. These files specify which files and directories should be ignored by Git when tracking changes. VS Code can automatically generate `.gitignore` files based on your project's programming language and environment.

To create a `.gitignore` file in VS Code:

1. Right-click on the root folder of your project in the Explorer sidebar.

2. Select "New File."

3. Name the file `.gitignore`.

4. Open the .gitignore file and add the patterns for files and directories you want to exclude from version control.

5. Git Stash

Git stash is a powerful feature for temporarily saving changes that you're not ready to commit. It allows you to switch branches or perform other Git operations without committing incomplete work.

To stash changes in VS Code:

1. Open the Source Control panel.

2. Click the three dots (ellipsis) icon to access the menu.

3. Choose "Stash Changes."

4. Provide a name for the stash, and VS Code will save your changes.

You can later apply or delete stashed changes as needed.

6. Git Workspaces

VS Code supports the concept of Git workspaces, which allows you to have multiple projects open in the same window, each with its own Git repository. You can switch between workspaces easily, making it convenient to work on multiple projects simultaneously.

To create a new workspace in VS Code:

1. Open your first project in VS Code.

2. Click on "File" in the top menu.

3. Select "Add Folder to Workspace" and choose the second project folder.

4. Save the workspace by selecting "File" > "Save Workspace As."

These advanced Git features and extensions can significantly improve your Git workflow within Visual Studio Code. Depending on your project's complexity and your specific needs, you can choose the extensions and tools that enhance your productivity and code quality.

7.1. Setting Up Debugging Environment

Setting up a debugging environment is a crucial aspect of software development. Debugging helps identify and fix issues in your code, making it more reliable and efficient. Visual Studio Code (VS Code) offers a robust debugging environment that supports multiple programming languages and frameworks. In this section, we will explore how to set up and configure a debugging environment in VS Code.

1. Installing the Necessary Extensions

Before you can start debugging in VS Code, you need to install the relevant extensions for your programming language or framework. VS Code has a vast marketplace of extensions, many of which provide debugging support for specific languages or platforms.

To install an extension for debugging:

1. Open VS Code.

2. Go to the Extensions view by clicking on the square icon in the sidebar or pressing Ctrl+Shift+X (or Cmd+Shift+X on macOS).

3. Search for the extension related to your programming language or framework (e.g., "Python" or "Node.js").

4. Click the "Install" button next to the extension you want to use.

5. Once the extension is installed, you may need to configure it by specifying the path to your runtime or interpreter. Refer to the extension's documentation for guidance.

2. Creating a Launch Configuration

A launch configuration in VS Code defines how your application should be launched and debugged. It specifies details such as the entry file, command-line arguments, environment variables, and more.

To create a launch configuration:

1. Open your project in VS Code.

2. Click on the Debugging view by clicking on the bug icon in the sidebar or pressing Ctrl+Shift+D (or Cmd+Shift+D on macOS).

3. Click the gear icon to create a new launch configuration.

4. Select the type of application you are debugging (e.g., Node.js, Python, Java).

5. VS Code will generate a basic launch configuration. Customize it according to your project's requirements. You may need to specify the program entry point, arguments, environment variables, and more.

6. Save the launch configuration by clicking the diskette icon or pressing Ctrl+S (or Cmd+S on macOS).

3. Setting Breakpoints

Breakpoints are markers in your code where the debugger should pause execution so you can inspect variables and step through your code. To set a breakpoint:

1. Open the file where you want to set a breakpoint.

2. Click in the gutter (the vertical bar on the left) next to the line where you want the breakpoint to be.

3. A red dot will appear, indicating the breakpoint.

4. Starting the Debugger

To start debugging your application:

1. Ensure you have a valid launch configuration selected in the Debugging view.

2. Click the green play button (or press F5) to start debugging.

3. Your application will run, and execution will pause at the first breakpoint.

5. Debugging Actions

Once your application is paused at a breakpoint, you can perform various debugging actions:

- Step Over (F10): Execute the current line and move to the next one.
- Step Into (F11): If the current line calls a function, step into that function.
- Step Out (Shift+F11): Finish executing the current function and return to its caller.
- Continue (F5): Resume normal execution until the next breakpoint is encountered.
- Restart (Ctrl+Shift+F5 or Cmd+Shift+F5 on macOS): Restart the debugging session.
- Stop (Shift+F5): Stop the debugging session and terminate the application.

6. Inspecting Variables

You can inspect the values of variables while debugging. In the Debugging view, you will find a Variables section that displays the variables in the current scope. You can also hover over variables in your code to see their values.

7. Debugging Console

The Debugging Console allows you to execute code and evaluate expressions during debugging. You can open the console by clicking the "Debug Console" tab in the Debugging view. This can be helpful for testing code snippets or investigating issues interactively.

Setting up a debugging environment in Visual Studio Code is essential for efficient and effective software development. Whether you are working on web applications, server-side code, or other types of software, VS Code's debugging features can help you identify and resolve issues quickly, leading to more reliable and stable applications.

7.2. Breakpoints and Watchers

Breakpoints and watchers are powerful debugging tools that help developers identify and resolve issues in their code effectively. Visual Studio Code (VS Code) provides a user-friendly interface for setting breakpoints and adding watchers to variables, making the debugging process more efficient and intuitive.

Setting Breakpoints

Breakpoints are markers placed in your code that pause program execution when reached, allowing you to inspect variables and step through code to identify issues. Here's how to set breakpoints in VS Code:

1. Open the source file you want to debug in the editor.

2. Click in the gutter (the vertical bar to the left of the code) next to the line where you want to set a breakpoint. A red dot will appear, indicating the breakpoint.

3. You can set multiple breakpoints throughout your code to pause execution at different points.

4. When your code runs in debugging mode, it will halt at breakpoints, allowing you to examine the program's state and variables.

Working with Breakpoints

Once breakpoints are set, you can perform various actions to control program execution:

- **Continue Execution (F5):** Resumes program execution until the next breakpoint is reached or until the program finishes running.

- **Step Over (F10):** Executes the current line and moves to the next one. If the current line contains a function call, it will execute the entire function and stop at the next line in the current scope.

- **Step Into (F11):** If the current line contains a function call, it steps into that function, allowing you to debug the function's code. If there is no function call, it behaves like "Step Over."

- **Step Out (Shift+F11):** Finishes executing the current function and returns to the caller. Useful when you want to exit a function and return to the higher-level code.

- **Restart (Ctrl+Shift+F5 or Cmd+Shift+F5 on macOS):** Restarts the debugging session, allowing you to run your code from the beginning.

- **Stop (Shift+F5):** Stops the debugging session and terminates the program.

Adding Watchers

Watchers are expressions that you can add to your debugging session to monitor the values of variables or expressions continuously. Here's how to add watchers in VS Code:

1. While debugging, open the Debugging view by clicking on the bug icon in the sidebar or pressing Ctrl+Shift+D (or Cmd+Shift+D on macOS).

2. In the Debugging view, locate the "Watch" section.

3. Click the "Add Watch Expression" button (a plus icon) to create a new watcher.

4. Enter the variable name or expression you want to watch. For example, you can enter myVariable to monitor the value of a variable named myVariable.

5. Press Enter to add the watcher.

6. The value of the watcher will be displayed in the "Watch" section, and it will be continuously updated as the program executes.

Conditional Breakpoints

In addition to regular breakpoints, you can set conditional breakpoints that pause execution only when a specified condition is met. To set a conditional breakpoint:

1. Right-click on an existing breakpoint in the gutter.

2. Select "Edit Breakpoint."

3. In the dialog that appears, enter the condition. For example, you can use i == 10 to break when the variable i equals 10.

4. Click "Save."

Conditional breakpoints are handy for debugging specific scenarios or when you want to avoid stopping at a breakpoint during routine executions.

Data Tips

While debugging, you can hover over variables in your code to see their current values without adding them as watchers explicitly. VS Code displays a tooltip-like data tip with the variable's value, type, and other relevant information.

Breakpoints and watchers are indispensable tools for debugging and diagnosing issues in your code. By strategically placing breakpoints and monitoring variables with watchers, you can gain valuable insights into your program's behavior and streamline the debugging process in Visual Studio Code.

7.3. Inspecting Variables and Stack Traces

When debugging code in Visual Studio Code (VS Code), inspecting variables and stack traces is crucial for understanding the state of your program and identifying issues. VS Code provides powerful tools for inspecting variables and navigating stack traces during debugging sessions.

Inspecting Variables

While debugging, you can easily inspect the values of variables, objects, and expressions to gain insights into your program's behavior. Here's how to inspect variables in VS Code:

1. Set breakpoints at the desired locations in your code.

2. Start a debugging session by clicking the "Run and Debug" button or pressing F5.

3. When the program pauses at a breakpoint, you can view variable values in several ways:

   - **Hover over variables:** Hover your mouse pointer over a variable in your code, and a tooltip-like data tip will appear, displaying the variable's current value.

   - **Watchers:** Add variables or expressions as watchers in the Debugging view. The values of these watchers will be continuously updated as the program runs.

   - **Debug Console:** Open the Debug Console panel at the bottom of the VS Code window. You can use it as an interactive REPL (Read-Eval-Print Loop) to evaluate expressions and display variable values.

   - **Variables panel:** In the Debugging view, there is a "Variables" panel that displays all variables in the current scope. You can expand objects and drill down into their properties.

4. You can also modify variables' values during debugging, which can be helpful for testing different scenarios.

Navigating Stack Traces

Understanding the call stack is essential for debugging, especially when dealing with exceptions or errors. VS Code provides tools for navigating and exploring the call stack, which shows the sequence of function calls leading to the current point in your code. Here's how to navigate stack traces:

1. When your program pauses at a breakpoint or encounters an exception, open the "Call Stack" panel in the Debugging view.

2. The "Call Stack" panel displays the function calls in reverse order, with the current function at the top. You can see the function names and the files where they are defined.

3. Clicking on a stack frame in the "Call Stack" panel takes you to that function's source code, allowing you to inspect variables and step through the code.

4. Use the "Step Into" (F11) and "Step Out" (Shift+F11) commands to move up and down the call stack, navigating between function calls.

5. By understanding the call stack, you can trace the execution path and pinpoint the source of errors or unexpected behavior.

Exception Handling

When an unhandled exception occurs during debugging, VS Code provides valuable information to help you diagnose the issue. You can inspect the exception object, view its properties, and navigate the call stack to identify where the exception originated.

To catch and handle exceptions during debugging, you can set up exception breakpoints. Exception breakpoints pause the program when a specific type of exception is thrown, allowing you to investigate the problem.

In summary, inspecting variables and navigating stack traces are essential skills for effective debugging in Visual Studio Code. By using these features, you can gain a deep understanding of your code's behavior, identify issues, and diagnose and fix errors efficiently during debugging sessions.

7.4. Remote Debugging Capabilities

Visual Studio Code (VS Code) offers robust support for remote debugging, allowing developers to debug code running on remote machines, containers, or even in the cloud. Remote debugging capabilities are invaluable when working on distributed systems, microservices, or remote development environments.

Setting Up Remote Debugging

To start remote debugging in VS Code, follow these general steps:

1. **Install VS Code on Your Local Machine:** Ensure that you have VS Code installed on your local development machine, where you will run VS Code as your primary code editor.

2. **Install VS Code on the Remote Machine:** Install a compatible version of VS Code on the remote machine where your code is running or hosted. You can also use VS

Code's Remote Development extensions for specific scenarios, such as SSH, WSL (Windows Subsystem for Linux), or Docker containers.

3. **Open Your Project Locally:** Open your project's source code on your local machine using VS Code.

4. **Configure Launch Settings:** Create a launch configuration in VS Code that specifies the remote debugging settings, including the remote host and port, authentication method (if required), and the application's entry point.

5. **Start the Remote Debugging Session:** Use VS Code's debugging features to start a remote debugging session. This typically involves selecting the appropriate launch configuration and triggering the debugger to attach to the remote code.

6. **Debug Remotely:** Once the debugging session is established, you can set breakpoints, inspect variables, and use all debugging features as if you were debugging code locally.

Remote Development Scenarios

VS Code's remote debugging capabilities support various development scenarios:

- **SSH:** You can use VS Code to remotely debug code running on a remote server or virtual machine via SSH. This is useful for Linux-based development environments.

- **WSL (Windows Subsystem for Linux):** If you are using WSL on Windows, you can debug code running within the WSL environment, even if your code editor is on the Windows side.

- **Docker Containers:** VS Code can attach to code running inside Docker containers, allowing you to debug applications within isolated containers.

- **Remote Development Containers:** You can create and develop within development containers, which encapsulate your entire development environment. VS Code's Remote - Containers extension simplifies this workflow.

- **Cloud-Based Development:** VS Code can connect to cloud-based development environments, including cloud IDEs or remote servers provided by cloud providers. This is particularly useful for collaborative or distributed teams.

Troubleshooting Remote Debugging

Remote debugging may involve additional challenges compared to local debugging, such as network connectivity issues, authentication, or environment-specific configurations. Here are some tips for troubleshooting remote debugging:

- **Network Connectivity:** Ensure that your local machine can connect to the remote host. Verify that firewalls, network security rules, and SSH configurations are correctly set up.

- **Authentication:** If authentication is required to access the remote machine, make sure you provide the necessary credentials in your launch configuration.

- **SSH Keys:** When using SSH for remote debugging, ensure that your SSH keys are correctly configured and accessible from your local machine.

- **Port Forwarding:** Check that the remote debugging port (usually specified in your launch configuration) is open and properly forwarded to the remote machine.

- **Remote Environment Consistency:** Ensure that the remote environment matches your development setup, including dependencies and runtime configurations.

- **VS Code Extensions:** Install the necessary VS Code extensions for remote development, such as the Remote - SSH or Remote - Containers extensions, depending on your scenario.

Remote debugging in VS Code empowers developers to work effectively in various development scenarios and across different environments. Whether you're debugging code on remote servers, within containers, or in the cloud, VS Code's remote debugging capabilities streamline the development and debugging process.

7.5. Solving Common Debugging Issues

Debugging is an integral part of software development, but it can sometimes be challenging and frustrating. In this section, we'll explore common debugging issues you might encounter and strategies to resolve them effectively.

1. Debugging Information Not Visible:
- **Issue:** Sometimes, debugging information is not visible or obscured due to UI elements or the layout of your code editor.

- **Solution:** Adjust the layout of your code editor to make more room for debugging information. You can also dock the Debug Console or Variables panel to keep them visible.

2. Breakpoints Not Hitting:
- **Issue:** Breakpoints you've set are not being hit during debugging sessions.

- **Solution:** Verify that your breakpoints are set in executable code and not in comments or empty lines. Ensure that your code is being executed and that there are no conditional statements preventing breakpoints from being hit.

3. Code Not Pausing at Breakpoints:
- **Issue:** Your code runs continuously without pausing at breakpoints.

- **Solution:** Check if you are running your code in "Release" mode instead of "Debug" mode. Ensure that the breakpoints are correctly set and that you are debugging the right process or script.

4. Debugging Slow or Unresponsive:
- **Issue:** Debugging is slow or becomes unresponsive, making it difficult to interact with debugging features.

- **Solution:** Close unnecessary applications or processes consuming system resources. Reduce the number of open files in your code editor, and consider optimizing your code to improve performance.

5. Exception Handling:
- **Issue:** Unhandled exceptions or errors are causing your debugging sessions to terminate abruptly.

- **Solution:** Set exception breakpoints to catch specific types of exceptions. Ensure that your code includes proper error handling to prevent crashes during debugging.

6. Misconfigured Debugging Environment:
- **Issue:** Debugging environments, such as launch configurations or paths, are not set up correctly.

- **Solution:** Double-check your launch configurations, paths, and debugging settings. Ensure that your project structure matches the configuration.

7. Dependencies and Environment:
- **Issue:** Debugging issues arise due to differences in dependencies or environmental configurations between your development and production environments.

- **Solution:** Use package managers like npm or pip to manage dependencies consistently. Consider using virtual environments or containerization to ensure reproducible environments.

8. Outdated Debugging Extensions:
- **Issue:** Debugging extensions in your code editor are outdated or incompatible with your project.

- **Solution:** Keep your debugging extensions up to date, and check for compatibility with your code editor and project. Remove or replace extensions causing conflicts.

9. Network-Related Issues:
- **Issue:** Debugging network-related code can be challenging, and issues may not be related to your code.

- **Solution:** Use debugging tools like Wireshark or browser developer tools to inspect network traffic. Ensure that your network settings, ports, and security groups are correctly configured.

10. Inconsistent Debugging Environment:
- **Issue:** Debugging works inconsistently across different machines or environments.

- **Solution:** Use version control to track and share your project's configuration. Document environment setup steps to ensure consistency.

11. Memory and Resource Issues:
- **Issue:** Debugging can be affected by high memory usage or resource constraints.

- **Solution:** Monitor system resources during debugging sessions. Optimize your code for memory efficiency, and consider using profiling tools to identify resource bottlenecks.

12. IDE-Specific Issues:
- **Issue:** Debugging issues may be specific to your integrated development environment (IDE).

- **Solution:** Check for IDE-specific updates or patches. Consider switching to a different IDE or code editor if issues persist.

Debugging can be challenging, but with patience and the right strategies, you can overcome common debugging issues effectively. By understanding these challenges and their solutions, you can become a more efficient and effective debugger, ultimately improving your software development process.

Chapter 8: Testing Your Code

8.1. Introduction to Testing in Visual Studio Code

Testing is an essential aspect of software development, ensuring that your code functions correctly, reliably, and consistently. In this section, we'll introduce you to testing in Visual Studio Code and explore its significance in the development process.

Why Testing Matters

Testing plays a crucial role in software development for several reasons:

1. **Bug Detection:** Testing helps identify and rectify bugs, errors, and unexpected behavior in your code. By systematically testing your code, you can catch issues early in the development process, making them easier and less costly to fix.

2. **Quality Assurance:** Testing ensures the quality and reliability of your software. It helps guarantee that your application works as expected under various conditions, reducing the risk of critical failures in production.

3. **Code Maintenance:** Writing tests alongside your code (test-driven development or TDD) facilitates code maintenance. Tests act as documentation, providing insights into how different parts of your code should behave.

4. **Regression Prevention:** Regression testing verifies that new code changes do not introduce new issues or break existing functionality. This prevents previously working features from breaking due to code updates.

5. **Confidence in Code Changes:** Comprehensive test suites give developers confidence when making code changes. Knowing that tests will catch regressions allows for more frequent and safer updates.

Types of Testing

Visual Studio Code supports various types of testing, including:

1. **Unit Testing:** Unit tests focus on individual components or functions, verifying that they behave correctly in isolation. Unit tests are typically written by developers for specific code units.

2. **Integration Testing:** Integration tests examine how different components or modules work together. They verify that the interactions between various parts of your code function as intended.

3. **Functional Testing:** Functional tests assess whether the entire application or specific features behave correctly from a user's perspective. These tests mimic user interactions and validate the expected outcomes.

4. **Performance Testing:** Performance tests evaluate the speed, responsiveness, and resource usage of your application. They help identify bottlenecks and optimize code for better performance.

5. **Security Testing:** Security tests aim to identify vulnerabilities and weaknesses in your application's security mechanisms. They help ensure that your software is resistant to attacks and data breaches.

6. **Regression Testing:** Regression tests confirm that code changes do not introduce new issues or regressions. These tests are crucial when updating and maintaining software.

Testing Frameworks and Libraries

Visual Studio Code offers a range of extensions and integrations with popular testing frameworks and libraries for different programming languages. Some widely used testing frameworks include:

- **JUnit:** A popular framework for Java unit testing.
- **JUnit 5:** The latest version of JUnit, offering improved features and flexibility.
- **pytest:** A testing framework for Python, known for its simplicity and extensibility.
- **Mocha:** A JavaScript testing framework that works well with Node.js.
- **Jest:** A JavaScript testing framework developed by Facebook for React and JavaScript applications.
- **RSpec:** A testing framework for Ruby, known for its expressive syntax.

In addition to these frameworks, you can find extensions and plugins for other languages and testing tools in the Visual Studio Code Marketplace. These tools simplify test setup, execution, and reporting, making it easier to adopt testing practices in your development workflow.

Writing Your First Test

To get started with testing in Visual Studio Code, you'll typically follow these steps:

1. **Install a Testing Framework:** If your project doesn't already use a testing framework, choose one that suits your programming language and install it. You can usually do this using a package manager like npm, pip, or gem.

2. **Write a Test:** Create a test file or directory in your project and write your first test. Tests are typically written using a framework-specific syntax. For example, in JUnit for Java, you might use @Test annotations to define test methods.

3. **Run Tests:** Use the testing framework's command or extension in Visual Studio Code to run your tests. This typically generates a report indicating which tests passed and which failed.

4. **Debugging Tests:** If a test fails, use Visual Studio Code's debugging features to pinpoint the issue in your code. You can set breakpoints, inspect variables, and step through the code to identify the problem.

5. **Refine and Iterate:** After identifying issues, make code changes and rerun the tests. Continue refining your code until all tests pass, ensuring that your software meets the desired quality standards.

By adopting testing practices in your development workflow, you can produce more reliable and maintainable software while reducing the likelihood of critical issues in production. In the following sections, we will delve deeper into different aspects of testing in Visual Studio Code, including setting up testing frameworks, writing tests, and automating test runs.

8.2. Setting Up Testing Frameworks

Setting up a testing framework in Visual Studio Code is a crucial step in ensuring the quality and reliability of your code. In this section, we'll guide you through the process of setting up common testing frameworks for different programming languages.

JavaScript and Node.js

Mocha and Chai

Mocha is a widely used JavaScript testing framework that works well with Node.js. It provides a versatile and extensible testing environment. To set up Mocha and Chai, a popular assertion library, follow these steps:

1. **Initialize Your Project**: If you haven't already, create a Node.js project and navigate to the project directory in your terminal.

2. **Install Mocha and Chai**: Use npm (Node Package Manager) to install Mocha and Chai as development dependencies:

```
npm install --save-dev mocha chai
```

3. **Create a Test Directory**: It's a good practice to organize your tests in a separate directory. Create a directory named test in your project root:

```
mkdir test
```

4. **Write Your First Test**: Inside the test directory, create a JavaScript file for your tests, e.g., test.js. Write your first test using Mocha and Chai. Here's a simple example:

```
const chai = require('chai');
const expect = chai.expect;

describe('Example Test Suite', () => {
  it('should pass this test', () => {
    expect(true).to.be.true;
  });
});
```

5. **Run Tests**: In Visual Studio Code, open the integrated terminal and run your tests using the mocha command:

```
npx mocha test/test.js
```

Replace test/test.js with the path to your test file. You should see the test results in the terminal.

Jest (For React and JavaScript)

Jest is a popular testing framework developed by Facebook, primarily used for testing React applications and JavaScript code. Setting up Jest in Visual Studio Code is straightforward:

1. **Initialize Your Project**: If you haven't already, create a JavaScript or React project and navigate to the project directory in your terminal.

2. **Install Jest**: Use npm to install Jest as a development dependency:

```
npm install --save-dev jest
```

3. **Create a Test Directory**: Just like with Mocha, create a test directory in your project root:

```
mkdir test
```

4. **Write Your First Test**: Inside the test directory, create a JavaScript file for your tests, e.g., test.js. Write your first Jest test:

```
test('adds 1 + 2 to equal 3', () => {
  expect(1 + 2).toBe(3);
});
```

5. **Run Tests**: Use the following command to run Jest tests:

```
npx jest
```

Jest will automatically discover and run your test files, displaying the results in the terminal.

pytest

pytest is a popular testing framework for Python. It simplifies the process of writing and running tests. To set up pytest in Visual Studio Code for a Python project, follow these steps:

1. **Initialize Your Project**: Create a Python project if you haven't already and navigate to the project directory in your terminal.

2. **Install pytest**: Use pip (Python package manager) to install pytest:

   ```
   pip install pytest
   ```

3. **Write Your First Test**: Create a Python file for your tests, e.g., `test_myapp.py`. Write your first pytest test:

   ```python
   def test_addition():
       assert 1 + 1 == 2
   ```

4. **Run Tests**: In Visual Studio Code, open the integrated terminal and run your tests using the `pytest` command:

   ```
   pytest test_myapp.py
   ```

   Replace `test_myapp.py` with the path to your test file.

Setting up testing frameworks in Visual Studio Code is an essential part of the development process, ensuring that your code functions correctly and reliably. By following the steps mentioned above for your programming language of choice, you can start writing and running tests effectively to maintain code quality.

8.3. Writing and Running Tests

Writing and running tests is an integral part of software development, as it helps ensure the correctness and reliability of your code. Visual Studio Code provides support for various testing frameworks and tools, making it convenient to write, manage, and execute tests within your development workflow.

Choosing a Testing Framework

Before you start writing tests in Visual Studio Code, you'll need to choose a testing framework that's appropriate for your programming language and project requirements. Here are some commonly used testing frameworks for different languages:

- **Mocha and Chai**: Mocha is a versatile JavaScript testing framework that works well with Node.js. Chai is a popular assertion library often used alongside Mocha.

- **Jest**: Jest is a widely used testing framework, especially for React applications and JavaScript code.

Python

- **pytest**: pytest is a popular testing framework for Python that simplifies test writing and execution.

Java

- **JUnit**: JUnit is a widely used testing framework for Java applications.

Ruby

- **RSpec**: RSpec is a behavior-driven development (BDD) framework for Ruby.

C

- **NUnit**: NUnit is a popular testing framework for C#.

Go

- **testing**: Go has a built-in testing package that's simple to use.

Setting Up Your Testing Environment

Once you've chosen a testing framework, you'll need to set up your testing environment. This typically involves the following steps:

1. **Install the Testing Framework**: Use your programming language's package manager (e.g., npm, pip, gem) to install the testing framework and any necessary dependencies.

2. **Create a Test Directory**: It's a good practice to organize your tests in a separate directory. Create a directory (e.g., `tests` or `test`) in your project's root directory.

3. **Write Your Tests**: Create test files within the test directory. Depending on the testing framework, tests are typically written as functions or methods that assert expected outcomes.

4. **Configure Test Runner**: Configure your testing framework or test runner to discover and run your tests. This configuration may involve specifying the test directory, patterns for test file discovery, and any additional options.

Running Tests in Visual Studio Code

Visual Studio Code provides built-in support for running tests using various extensions and plugins specific to your programming language. Here's a general overview of how to run tests within Visual Studio Code:

1. **Select a Test**: Open the file containing the test you want to run. In the test file, you can often find options to run individual tests, test suites, or the entire test file.

2. **Run Tests**: Use the appropriate command or shortcut to run the selected tests. This might involve right-clicking on the test, using a keyboard shortcut, or accessing a context menu.

3. **View Test Output**: Visual Studio Code will display the test output in the integrated terminal or a dedicated test runner panel. You can view the results, including passed and failed tests, any error messages, and test execution times.

4. **Debug Tests**: If a test fails or behaves unexpectedly, you can use the integrated debugger to set breakpoints and step through your code to identify and fix issues.

5. **Configure Test Settings**: Depending on your testing framework, you may have options to configure test settings, such as specifying a different test runner, test output format, or test coverage analysis.

Remember that the exact steps and commands for running tests may vary depending on your chosen testing framework and Visual Studio Code extensions. It's essential to refer to the documentation for your specific framework and any relevant extensions for detailed instructions on configuring and running tests effectively.

In conclusion, Visual Studio Code provides a versatile environment for writing and running tests across different programming languages. By choosing the right testing framework, setting up your testing environment, and using the available extensions and tools, you can ensure the quality and reliability of your code through comprehensive testing practices.

8.4. Test Coverage and Reporting

Test coverage is a critical aspect of ensuring the quality and reliability of your software. It measures how much of your codebase is exercised by your tests. Higher test coverage indicates that more parts of your code have been tested, reducing the likelihood of undetected bugs and issues. Visual Studio Code provides tools and extensions that help you measure test coverage and generate detailed reports.

Understanding Test Coverage

Test coverage is typically expressed as a percentage, representing the proportion of code lines, functions, or statements that have been executed during testing. The main types of code coverage include:

*   **Statement Coverage**: Measures the percentage of executable statements in your code that have been executed during testing.

- **Branch Coverage**: Measures the percentage of decision points (branches) in your code that have been exercised.

- **Function Coverage**: Measures the percentage of functions or methods that have been called during testing.

- **Line Coverage**: Measures the percentage of lines of code that have been executed.

- **Path Coverage**: Measures the percentage of possible code execution paths that have been tested.

Setting Up Test Coverage

To get started with test coverage in Visual Studio Code, you'll need to follow these general steps:

1. **Choose a Test Coverage Tool**: Depending on your programming language and project, you'll need to select a test coverage tool or library that integrates with Visual Studio Code. Some common test coverage tools include Istanbul for JavaScript, coverage.py for Python, and JaCoCo for Java.

2. **Install and Configure the Tool**: Install the chosen test coverage tool as a project dependency or globally, depending on your preference. Configure the tool to work with your testing framework, specifying the test command and output paths.

3. **Run Tests with Coverage**: Use your testing framework to run your tests with coverage analysis enabled. This may involve specific command-line options or configurations.

4. **View Coverage Reports**: Once tests have been executed with coverage analysis, the tool will generate coverage reports. Visual Studio Code can display these reports in various formats, including HTML, XML, or JSON.

Visualizing Coverage Reports

Visual Studio Code offers extensions that can help you visualize coverage reports directly within the editor. These extensions provide interactive visual representations of your code, highlighting covered and uncovered portions. You can often see coverage information alongside your code, making it easier to identify areas that need additional testing.

Interpreting Coverage Reports

While high test coverage is desirable, it's essential to understand that achieving 100% coverage may not always be practical or necessary. Some code paths may be challenging to test, such as error handling or rare edge cases. Therefore, it's crucial to use your judgment and domain knowledge to prioritize testing efforts.

Here are some key points to consider when interpreting coverage reports:

- Focus on critical and complex code: Prioritize testing for code that has a significant impact on the application's functionality and where bugs could lead to severe issues.

- Use coverage as a guideline: Test coverage is a valuable metric, but it should not be the sole measure of code quality. Effective testing involves a combination of unit, integration, and functional tests.

- Consider edge cases: Ensure that your tests cover edge cases, boundary conditions, and unexpected scenarios that can reveal hidden issues.

- Regularly review and update tests: As your codebase evolves, update your tests to reflect changes in functionality, and review coverage reports to identify areas that may need additional testing.

In conclusion, test coverage and reporting are essential practices for maintaining code quality and reliability. Visual Studio Code, in combination with the right test coverage tools and extensions, provides a powerful platform for measuring, visualizing, and improving your test coverage. By leveraging these tools, you can identify areas of your codebase that require attention and reduce the risk of undiscovered bugs in your software.

8.5. Automated Testing and Continuous Integration

Automated testing and continuous integration (CI) are integral parts of modern software development workflows. They help ensure code quality, catch bugs early, and streamline the development and deployment processes. In this section, we'll explore how Visual Studio Code can be used in conjunction with automated testing and CI tools to enhance your development workflow.

Automated Testing

Automated testing involves writing scripts or test cases that can be executed automatically to verify the correctness of your code. Visual Studio Code provides excellent support for various programming languages and testing frameworks, making it easy to write and run automated tests.

Writing Automated Tests

1. **Test Framework Integration**: Depending on your programming language and project, you can choose from a variety of testing frameworks (e.g., JUnit for Java, pytest for Python, Mocha for JavaScript). Visual Studio Code offers extensions that provide code snippets and IntelliSense for these frameworks, making it easier to write tests.

2. **Test Creation**: Create test files or test suites that mirror the structure of your application code. Write test cases to cover various scenarios, including normal functionality, edge cases, and error conditions.

3. **Assertions**: Use assertion libraries or built-in assertion functions to verify that the expected outcomes match the actual results of your code.

Running Automated Tests

1. **Test Explorer**: Visual Studio Code has extensions like "Test Explorer" that integrate with popular test runners. They allow you to discover and run your tests directly from the editor. Test results are displayed in a user-friendly format, highlighting passing and failing tests.

2. **Code Lens**: In-code indicators (Code Lens) can show you how many tests cover a specific function or method, making it easier to see which parts of your codebase are well-tested.

3. **Debugging Tests**: You can also debug your tests within Visual Studio Code, setting breakpoints and inspecting variables to diagnose issues.

Continuous Integration (CI)

Continuous Integration is a practice where code changes are automatically built, tested, and deployed to a shared environment, typically multiple times a day. CI ensures that code changes do not introduce regressions and can be integrated seamlessly into the existing codebase.

Setting Up CI with Visual Studio Code

1. **Select a CI Service**: Choose a CI service such as GitHub Actions, Travis CI, CircleCI, Jenkins, or Azure DevOps, depending on your project's hosting platform and requirements.

2. **Configuration Files**: Create configuration files (e.g., `.github/workflows/main.yml` for GitHub Actions) in your project repository to define the CI workflow. These files specify the steps to build, test, and deploy your application.

3. **Automated Builds**: CI services can automatically trigger builds and tests whenever code changes are pushed to the repository. They provide a dedicated environment for testing and reporting results.

4. **Integration with Version Control**: CI services are tightly integrated with version control systems like Git. They can automatically detect changes, clone your repository, and execute the CI workflow.

5. **Test Reporting**: CI services generate detailed test reports, including information about failing tests and code coverage. These reports help you identify and fix issues quickly.

Benefits of Automated Testing and CI

- **Early Bug Detection**: Automated tests catch bugs and regressions early in the development process, reducing the effort required to fix them.

- **Code Quality**: CI ensures that code is built and tested consistently. This promotes code quality and reliability.

- **Fast Feedback**: Developers receive quick feedback on the impact of their code changes through automated test results and CI pipelines.

- **Streamlined Workflow**: CI automates repetitive tasks such as building and testing, freeing developers to focus on writing code.

- **Confidence in Deployment**: CI pipelines provide confidence that code changes are safe to deploy to production.

In summary, Visual Studio Code's support for automated testing and its integration with CI services empower developers to maintain code quality, catch issues early, and streamline the development process. By incorporating these practices into your workflow, you can ensure that your software is robust, reliable, and ready for deployment.

9.1. Multi-Cursor and Snippets

Efficiency in coding is essential, and Visual Studio Code offers powerful features to speed up your development workflow. In this section, we'll explore multi-cursor editing and code snippets, two features that can significantly boost your productivity.

Multi-Cursor Editing

Multi-cursor editing is a feature that allows you to place multiple cursors in your code, enabling simultaneous editing of multiple locations. This can be a huge time-saver when you need to make similar changes in various parts of your codebase.

How to Use Multi-Cursor Editing
1. **Basic Multi-Cursor**: To add additional cursors, you can hold down the Alt (or Option on macOS) key and click in multiple locations in your code. Alternatively, you can use Ctrl + Alt + Down Arrow to add cursors below the current line.

2. **Column Selection**: You can also create a rectangular selection by holding Shift + Alt and dragging your mouse or using Ctrl + Shift + Alt + Arrow Keys.

3. **Multi-Cursor Selection with Keyboard Shortcuts**: Use Ctrl + D to select the next instance of the word under the cursor or Ctrl + U to unselect the last instance.

4. **Multi-Cursor with Find and Replace**: Press Ctrl + F to open the Find widget, then Alt + Enter to select all instances. Now, you can edit them simultaneously.

5. **Column (Box) Selection**: Press Alt while selecting text with the mouse to create a column (box) selection. This is handy for editing columns of text.

6. **Multi-Cursor in a Specific Selection**: You can also use `Ctrl + Shift + L` to select all instances of the word under the cursor, or `Ctrl + Shift + P` to open the command palette and search for "Add Cursors to Line Ends."

Code Snippets

Code snippets are predefined code templates that can be quickly inserted into your code. They are useful for inserting boilerplate code, repetitive structures, or commonly used patterns.

Using Code Snippets

1. **Built-In Snippets**: Visual Studio Code comes with a variety of built-in code snippets. For example, type `for` and press `Tab` to insert a `for` loop snippet.

2. **User-Defined Snippets**: You can create your custom code snippets to suit your development needs. To create a user-defined snippet, go to "File" > "Preferences" > "User Snippets" and select the language for which you want to add snippets. Then, define your snippet with a trigger word and the code template.

3. **Tab Stops and Variables**: Snippets can include placeholders known as "tab stops" and "variables." These allow you to quickly navigate through and customize the inserted code. Use `${1}` for the first tab stop, `${2}` for the second, and so on. Variables like `${TM_FILENAME}` can automatically insert values like the current file's name.

4. **Expansion**: After triggering a snippet, you can use the `Tab` key to move between tab stops and replace their contents with your code.

5. **Snippet Suggestions**: Visual Studio Code suggests snippets as you type, making it easy to discover and use them.

Benefits of Multi-Cursor Editing and Snippets

- **Increased Productivity**: These features speed up coding tasks and reduce repetitive typing, leading to faster development.

- **Consistency**: Snippets help maintain code consistency by enforcing standardized patterns and structures.

- **Fewer Errors**: With multi-cursor editing, you can make changes in multiple places simultaneously, reducing the chances of introducing errors.

- **Customization**: You can create custom snippets tailored to your project's specific requirements.

Incorporating multi-cursor editing and code snippets into your Visual Studio Code workflow can significantly enhance your coding efficiency, making you a more productive and effective developer.

9.2. Code Folding and Regions

Efficiently managing large code files is crucial for maintaining code readability and navigation. Visual Studio Code provides features like code folding and regions to help you organize and simplify complex codebases.

Code Folding

Code folding allows you to collapse sections of your code, hiding details that you don't need to see at the moment. This feature is particularly useful when working with long functions, classes, or sections of code that you want to hide temporarily.

How to Use Code Folding

1. **Fold All**: You can fold all code sections by clicking the small minus sign (-) in the gutter area (the vertical strip on the left side of the editor) or by using the keyboard shortcut Ctrl + K, Ctrl + 0 (zero).

2. **Unfold All**: To expand all folded code sections, click the small plus sign (+) in the gutter area or use the shortcut Ctrl + K, Ctrl + J.

3. **Fold/Unfold Specific Sections**: Hover over the line of code you want to fold or unfold, and click the small fold/unfold icon that appears.

4. **Fold by Indentation**: Visual Studio Code can automatically fold code blocks based on their indentation level. To enable this feature, go to "File" > "Preferences" > "Settings," search for "folding" and set "Folding Strategy" to "indentation."

Code Regions

Code regions are a way to group and organize sections of your code, making it easier to navigate and collapse related parts. While code regions are not a native feature of all programming languages, they are supported in languages like C# and C++.

How to Use Code Regions

1. **Creating a Region**: To create a code region, you need to use a specific comment format recognized by your programming language. For example, in C#:

```
#region MyRegion
// Your code here
#endregion
```

    This will create a collapsible region named "MyRegion."

2. **Folding Regions**: You can fold or unfold regions by clicking the small triangle next to the region's name or by using the keyboard shortcuts provided by your language extension. In C#, it's typically Ctrl + M, Ctrl + M.

3. **Naming Regions**: It's a good practice to provide descriptive names for your regions to indicate their purpose.

4. **Nested Regions**: Some languages allow you to nest regions inside each other, providing a more granular organization of your code.

Benefits of Code Folding and Regions

- **Improved Readability**: Code folding helps reduce clutter, making it easier to focus on the relevant parts of your code.

- **Quick Navigation**: Regions provide a way to quickly jump to specific sections of your code, enhancing your navigation speed.

- **Organized Code**: Regions allow you to logically group related code, improving code organization and maintainability.

- **Customization**: You can customize code folding behavior and region naming to suit your preferences and project requirements.

By utilizing code folding and regions, you can effectively manage and navigate through even the most extensive codebases, resulting in a more efficient and organized development experience.

9.3. Regular Expression in Search and Replace

Regular expressions, often abbreviated as regex or regexp, are powerful tools for pattern matching and manipulation of text. Visual Studio Code supports regular expressions in its search and replace functionality, allowing you to perform complex text operations with ease.

Using Regular Expressions in Search

When searching for text in Visual Studio Code, you can enable regular expression mode by clicking the . * icon in the search bar or by using the keyboard shortcut Ctrl + F7. Once in regex mode, you can use regular expressions to find patterns in your code. Here are some common regex patterns and their meanings:

- .: Matches any single character except a newline character.
- *: Matches zero or more occurrences of the preceding character or group.
- +: Matches one or more occurrences of the preceding character or group.
- ?: Matches zero or one occurrence of the preceding character or group.
- []: Defines a character class, matching any single character inside the brackets.
- [^]: Defines a negated character class, matching any character not inside the brackets.

- ( ): Groups characters together for more complex patterns.
- | : Acts as an OR operator, matching either the pattern on its left or right.

For example, if you want to find all occurrences of the word "color" spelled either as "color" or "colour," you can use the regex pattern `colou?r` in the search bar.

Regular expressions can also be used in the replace functionality of Visual Studio Code. After performing a search in regex mode, you can enable regex mode in the replace input field by clicking the `.*` icon or by using the keyboard shortcut `Ctrl + Alt + R`.

In the replace field, you can use matched groups from your search pattern by referencing them as $1, $2, etc. For example, if you want to swap the order of the first and last name in a list of names, you can use the following regex pattern in the search bar:

Search: `(\w+)\s+(\w+)`

Replace: `$2 $1`

This will swap the first and last names for all matching patterns.

Here are some tips for effectively using regular expressions in Visual Studio Code:

1. **Practice**: Regular expressions can be complex, so it's essential to practice and experiment with them. You can use online regex testers to validate your patterns before applying them in your code.

2. **Use Capturing Groups**: Capturing groups (...) allow you to extract specific parts of a matched pattern and use them in replacement strings.

3. **Escape Special Characters**: Special characters like ., *, +, ?, (), [], and {} have special meanings in regex. If you want to match them literally, you need to escape them with a backslash \.

4. **Check the Documentation**: Each programming language may have slight variations in regular expression syntax. Consult the documentation or resources specific to your language for detailed information.

5. **Test and Validate**: Regular expressions can sometimes behave unexpectedly. Always test and validate your regex patterns on sample data to ensure they work as intended.

6. **Be Mindful of Efficiency**: Complex regex patterns can be computationally expensive, especially on large files. Use regex judiciously and consider their impact on performance.

With regular expressions, you can perform advanced search and replace operations, making it easier to manipulate and transform text in your code files. It's a valuable skill for any developer working with text-based data.

9.4. File Comparisons and Merging

Visual Studio Code provides functionality for comparing and merging files, which is particularly useful when collaborating on projects with multiple contributors or when managing code versions. In this section, we'll explore how to perform file comparisons and merging within the code editor.

Comparing Files

File comparison allows you to view the differences between two versions of a file. To compare two files in Visual Studio Code, follow these steps:

1. Open the first file you want to compare.

2. Open the second file in a new tab or navigate to it within the same workspace.

3. Right-click on the second file's tab and select "Compare Active File with…" from the context menu.

4. In the file picker, select the file you want to compare with the active file.

Visual Studio Code will open a new tab displaying the compared content with added lines highlighted in green, removed lines in red, and modified lines with both colors.

You can also use the keyboard shortcut Ctrl + K, Ctrl + D to compare the active file with the last file you compared.

Merging Changes

When working on a collaborative project, merging changes from different contributors is a common task. Visual Studio Code provides a built-in merge conflict resolution tool to help you manage conflicts efficiently.

To resolve a merge conflict:

1. Open the file with the merge conflict.

2. You will see the conflicting sections marked with <<<<<<<, =======, and >>>>>>> markers. These indicate the conflicting changes from different contributors.

3. Manually edit the conflicting sections to resolve the conflict. You can choose to keep one version, combine both versions, or write a completely new solution.

116

4. Save the file once you've resolved the conflict.

5. Use the source control features (e.g., Git) to commit the resolved file with the conflict resolved.

Extensions for Enhanced Merge Conflict Resolution

While Visual Studio Code offers basic merge conflict resolution capabilities, you can enhance this functionality by installing extensions like "GitLens" or "Merge Conflict."

These extensions provide visual aids and additional features for managing merge conflicts, such as side-by-side comparison, inline conflict markers, and easier navigation through conflict resolutions.

Visual Studio Code as a Git Merge Tool

You can also configure Visual Studio Code as your default merge and diff tool for Git. To set it up, use the following Git commands:

```
git config --global merge.tool vscode
git config --global mergetool.vscode.cmd "code --wait $MERGED"
git config --global diff.tool vscode
git config --global difftool.vscode.cmd "code --wait --diff $LOCAL $REMOTE"
```

With this configuration, you can use Git commands like `git mergetool` and `git difftool` to launch Visual Studio Code for merging and diffing files.

Conclusion

File comparisons and merging are essential tools for managing code changes and collaborating effectively with others. Visual Studio Code provides built-in functionality for comparing files and resolving merge conflicts, making it a versatile code editor for team projects. Additionally, extensions and Git integration can enhance your ability to handle complex merge scenarios.

9.5. Advanced Formatting and Beautification Tools

Formatting and code styling are crucial aspects of writing clean and maintainable code. Visual Studio Code offers various advanced formatting and beautification tools that help developers adhere to coding standards and keep their code organized. In this section, we'll explore these tools and how to use them effectively.

1. Auto-Formatting on Save

Visual Studio Code allows you to automatically format your code every time you save a file. This feature ensures that your code consistently follows the specified coding style. To enable auto-formatting on save, follow these steps:

- Open Visual Studio Code settings (`File > Preferences > Settings` or `Ctrl + ,`).

- Search for "format on save" in the settings search bar.

- Check the "Editor: Format On Save" option to enable it.

- You can also configure the default formatter and specific languages' formatters in the settings.

2. Built-in Formatters

Visual Studio Code includes built-in formatters for various programming languages. These formatters automatically adjust your code's indentation, spacing, and style to match the language's conventions. To use them, simply open a file and press `Shift + Alt + F` (or `Shift + Option + F` on macOS). The editor will apply the appropriate formatter for the active language.

3. EditorConfig Support

EditorConfig is a popular tool for defining and maintaining consistent coding styles across different editors and IDEs. Visual Studio Code provides built-in support for EditorConfig files. To utilize this feature:

- Create an `.editorconfig` file in your project's root directory or the directory containing your source code.

- Define coding style rules for various file types, specifying indentation, line endings, and more.

- Visual Studio Code will automatically detect and apply the rules from the `.editorconfig` file.

4. Custom Code Styling with Settings

You can customize your code styling preferences in Visual Studio Code using workspace or user settings. This allows you to specify rules such as indentation size, tab or space usage, and maximum line length. To access settings:

- Go to `File > Preferences > Settings` or use the shortcut `Ctrl + ,`.

- Search for the language-specific settings by typing the language name (e.g., "javascript") in the search bar.

- Modify the settings as per your coding style preferences.

5. Using ESLint and Prettier

For JavaScript and TypeScript development, ESLint and Prettier are widely used tools for code formatting and linting. Visual Studio Code seamlessly integrates with both, providing real-time feedback and auto-fix suggestions. To set up ESLint and Prettier:

- Install the ESLint and Prettier extensions from the Visual Studio Code Marketplace.

- Configure ESLint and Prettier in your project by creating `.eslintrc` and `.prettierrc` files.

- Customize ESLint rules and Prettier options to match your code style.

- Enjoy automatic code formatting and linting as you type.

6. Custom Code Snippets

Visual Studio Code allows you to create custom code snippets that speed up your coding workflow. You can define your snippets for frequently used code patterns. To create custom snippets:

- Open the command palette (`Ctrl + Shift + P`) and search for "Preferences: Configure User Snippets."

- Choose the language for which you want to create a snippet or select "New Global Snippets file."

- Define your custom code snippets using JSON format.

- Use your custom snippets by typing their trigger keyword and pressing `Tab` to expand.

7. Extensions for Code Formatting

Visual Studio Code has a rich extension ecosystem, and many extensions are dedicated to code formatting and styling. Some popular extensions include "Beautify," "Format HTML," and "Sort lines." These extensions provide additional formatting options and support for various file types.

Conclusion

Advanced formatting and beautification tools in Visual Studio Code empower developers to maintain clean and consistent code. Whether it's automatic formatting, EditorConfig support, custom code styling, or extensions, Visual Studio Code offers a versatile set of features to enhance your coding experience and make your code more readable and maintainable. By adopting these tools and best practices, you can write code that is not only functional but also aesthetically pleasing and easy to collaborate on with other developers.

10.1. Improving Startup Time and Efficiency

The startup time and overall efficiency of Visual Studio Code are critical factors in providing a smooth development experience. As developers, we often switch between projects and tasks, and any delays or sluggishness in the editor can hinder our productivity. In this section, we will explore strategies to improve the startup time and efficiency of Visual Studio Code.

1. Update to the Latest Version

Keeping Visual Studio Code up to date is essential for performance improvements and bug fixes. The VS Code team regularly releases updates with optimizations, so make sure you are using the latest version. You can check for updates in the "Help" menu or configure automatic updates in the settings.

2. Optimize Extensions

Extensions can enhance your development workflow, but having too many or poorly optimized extensions can slow down VS Code. Here are some tips:

- Review your installed extensions and disable or remove any that you no longer use.

- Check if there are alternative, more lightweight extensions that provide similar functionality.

- Periodically review the performance impact of extensions using the "Extensions" view's built-in profiler.

- Disable extensions that you don't need for the current project to reduce their impact on startup time.

3. Custom Workspace Configuration

Consider creating a custom workspace configuration for each project. This allows you to specify which extensions are enabled and which settings are applied for that particular project. By minimizing the enabled extensions and tailored settings, you can improve the startup time and efficiency for that project.

4. Use Workspaces and Folders

Visual Studio Code allows you to open multiple folders and workspaces simultaneously. However, opening too many folders can consume resources and affect performance. Try to keep your workspace focused on the task at hand, and close unrelated folders when not needed.

5. Limit Large Files and Folders

Working with large files or folders with many files can slow down VS Code. Consider excluding large files or folders from your project's settings using the "files.exclude" and "search.exclude" settings. This prevents them from being indexed by the editor.

6. Adjust Git History

If your project has a long Git history with many branches and commits, VS Code might spend more time indexing it. Consider using shallow clones when setting up your repository or using Git tools to maintain a cleaner history.

7. Clear Workspace State

VS Code stores workspace-specific state information to improve startup performance. However, over time, this data can become outdated and affect startup times. You can clear the workspace state by deleting the .vscode folder in your workspace directory, but be cautious as this will reset workspace-specific settings and configurations.

8. Reduce Telemetry and Error Reporting

Visual Studio Code collects telemetry data by default to help improve the product. If you are concerned about privacy or want to reduce telemetry data sent to Microsoft, you can adjust telemetry settings in the editor's settings.

9. Optimize Hardware

Sometimes, improving startup time requires hardware upgrades. Consider upgrading your computer's CPU, RAM, or switching to a faster SSD drive. These improvements can have a significant impact on VS Code's performance, especially when working on large projects.

10. Troubleshooting and Profiling

If you are still facing performance issues after applying the above strategies, consider using built-in tools like the VS Code profiler to identify the cause of slowdowns. Profiling can help pinpoint specific extensions or operations causing performance problems.

In conclusion, optimizing the startup time and efficiency of Visual Studio Code is essential for a productive development workflow. By following these strategies and regularly reviewing your development environment, you can ensure that VS Code remains a fast and responsive editor, enabling you to focus on writing code without interruptions.

10.2. Managing Memory and CPU Usage

Efficiently managing memory and CPU usage is crucial for maintaining the performance of Visual Studio Code, especially when working on larger projects or using extensions that consume significant resources. In this section, we will explore strategies and settings to help you keep memory and CPU usage in check.

1. Limiting Concurrent Processes

Visual Studio Code can open multiple files and run various tasks simultaneously. However, this concurrency can strain your computer's resources. To limit concurrent processes, you can adjust the following settings:

- **"files.autoSave"**: Set this to **"off"** if you don't need autosaving on file changes. Autosaving too frequently can increase CPU usage.

- **"editor.maxTokenizationLineLength"**: Increase this value if you're working with very long lines of code. Lower values may lead to higher CPU usage during tokenization.

- **"files.autoGuessEncoding"**: Disabling this setting prevents VS Code from guessing file encodings, which can be resource-intensive.

2. Extension Profiling

If you suspect that an extension is causing excessive CPU or memory usage, you can use the built-in extension profiler to identify the culprit. Follow these steps:

1. Open the command palette with Ctrl+Shift+P (Windows/Linux) or Cmd+Shift+P (macOS).

2. Type "Developer: Show Running Extensions" and select it. This displays a list of currently running extensions and their CPU and memory usage.

3. Identify the extension(s) with high resource consumption and consider disabling or replacing them with more efficient alternatives.

3. Customize Search Behavior

Visual Studio Code's search feature can be resource-intensive when searching through large codebases. You can optimize the search behavior by adjusting the following settings:

- **"search.exclude"**: Exclude folders and file types from search indexing to reduce memory and CPU usage.

- **"search.useRipgrep"**: Enable Ripgrep for faster and more efficient searching. Ripgrep is an external tool that can significantly reduce CPU usage during searches.

4. Extension Recommendations

Consider using extensions that help manage memory and CPU usage:

- **"Settings Sync"**: This extension allows you to sync your settings across devices, making it easier to manage resource-efficient configurations.

- **"Peacock"**: Peacock allows you to colorize the title bar of your VS Code instance based on the workspace you are in. It can help visually distinguish different instances, reducing the likelihood of accidentally running multiple instances and increasing resource usage.

- **"VS Code Intellicode"**: This extension provides intelligent code completion suggestions, which can improve code writing efficiency and reduce the need for resource-intensive manual searches.

5. Increase Heap Memory

You can allocate more heap memory to Visual Studio Code if you frequently work with large projects. To do this, follow these steps:

1. Open the user or workspace settings by going to "File" > "Preferences" > "Settings" (or use the shortcut Ctrl+,).

2. Search for "heap" in the search bar.

3. Under "Edit in settings.json," add the following line to increase the heap memory (adjust the value as needed):

```
"javascript.updateImportsOnFileMove.enabled": "always"
```

4. Save the settings file.

6. Manage Large Workspace Folders

If you are working with large workspace folders, consider dividing them into smaller, more manageable sections. This can reduce the overall memory and CPU usage when loading a specific workspace.

7. Monitor Task Manager

Regularly monitor your computer's task manager or system monitor while using Visual Studio Code. This allows you to identify any resource-hungry processes and take appropriate action.

8. Close Unused Tabs and Editors

Closing tabs and editors that you no longer need can free up memory and reduce CPU usage. VS Code allows you to reopen closed tabs, so you can easily switch between files when necessary.

By implementing these strategies and customizing your settings, you can effectively manage memory and CPU usage in Visual Studio Code, ensuring a smoother and more efficient development experience.

10.3. Troubleshooting Performance Issues

While Visual Studio Code is known for its speed and efficiency, there may be situations where you encounter performance issues. These issues can manifest as slow startup times, unresponsive behavior, or high CPU and memory usage. In this section, we will explore common performance problems and how to troubleshoot them.

1. Slow Startup

Potential Causes:

- **Extensions**: Too many or poorly designed extensions can slow down startup. Some extensions may run resource-intensive tasks during startup.

- **Workspace Size**: A large workspace with numerous files and folders can increase startup time.

- **Disk Health**: Slow disk drives or insufficient free space can impact startup speed.

Troubleshooting Steps:

- **Disable Extensions**: Temporarily disable extensions to identify if any specific one is causing the slowdown. Re-enable them one by one to pinpoint the culprit.

- **Workspaces**: If possible, split large workspaces into smaller ones or open only the necessary folders to reduce startup time.

- **Upgrade Hardware**: Consider upgrading to a faster disk drive (e.g., SSD) or adding more RAM if hardware limitations are the issue.

2. High CPU and Memory Usage

Potential Causes:

- **Extensions**: Certain extensions may consume excessive CPU or memory resources, especially when working with large files.

- **Background Processes**: Some extensions or tasks might run continuously in the background, causing high resource usage.

Troubleshooting Steps:

- **Extension Profiler**: Use the extension profiler mentioned in section 10.2 to identify resource-hungry extensions.

- **Disable or Replace Extensions**: Disable or replace extensions that are causing high resource usage. Look for lightweight alternatives.

- **Workspace Management**: Split large workspaces, close unused tabs, and limit the number of concurrently opened files to reduce memory usage.

3. Unresponsive Behavior

Potential Causes:

- **Extensions**: Unoptimized or outdated extensions can lead to unresponsive behavior.

- **Complex Code**: Extremely complex or deeply nested code can strain the editor's responsiveness.

Troubleshooting Steps:

- **Update Extensions**: Ensure all your extensions are up to date, as newer versions may include performance improvements.

- **Extension Profiler**: Use the extension profiler to identify extensions causing unresponsiveness.

- **Code Complexity**: Simplify and refactor complex code when possible to improve responsiveness.

4. Inefficient Search and Indexing

Potential Causes:

- **Search Settings**: Incorrect search settings, such as searching in folders with a large number of files, can result in slow searches.

- **Outdated Index**: An outdated search index can lead to inefficient searches.

Troubleshooting Steps:

- **Search Settings**: Adjust search settings, exclude unnecessary folders, and use more specific search patterns to speed up searches.

- **Rebuild Index**: If you suspect an outdated search index, use the "Rebuild IntelliSense Index" command to rebuild it.

5. Visual Studio Code Updates

Potential Causes:

- **Outdated Version**: Using an outdated version of Visual Studio Code may result in performance issues.

Troubleshooting Steps:

- **Update Visual Studio Code**: Ensure you are using the latest version of Visual Studio Code, as updates often include performance enhancements and bug fixes.

6. Editor and Workspace Settings

Potential Causes:

- **Inefficient Settings**: Poorly configured editor settings or workspace settings can affect performance.

- **Review Settings**: Review and optimize your editor and workspace settings, especially those related to files, search, and extensions.

7. External Factors

Potential Causes:
- **Background Applications**: Other applications running in the background may consume system resources.

Troubleshooting Steps:
- **Close Unnecessary Applications**: Close any background applications or processes that may be competing for system resources while using Visual Studio Code.

8. Feedback and Reporting

If you encounter persistent performance issues that cannot be resolved through the steps mentioned above, consider providing feedback to the Visual Studio Code development team. They rely on user feedback to identify and address performance-related issues. You can report problems and share performance data through the official Visual Studio Code channels.

By following these troubleshooting steps and optimizing your setup, you can resolve many performance issues and ensure a smoother experience while using Visual Studio Code for your development tasks.

10.4. Best Practices for High-Performance Coding

Achieving high performance in coding goes beyond optimizing your development environment; it also involves writing efficient and clean code. In this section, we'll explore best practices and coding techniques that can help you write code that not only works well but also performs efficiently.

1. Use Proper Data Structures and Algorithms

Choosing the right data structures and algorithms is crucial for efficient code. Be mindful of the time complexity of operations and select appropriate structures like arrays, lists, or maps. Additionally, understand the performance characteristics of algorithms to make informed choices.

```python
# Using a dictionary for efficient lookup
employee_data = {
    "John": 35,
    "Alice": 28,
    "Bob": 42,
```

```
}
print(employee_data["Alice"])
```

2. Avoid Nested Loops

Nested loops can lead to high time complexity, especially if the inner loop iterates over a large dataset. Whenever possible, refactor code to reduce nesting or consider alternative approaches like memoization.

```
// Avoiding nested loops
for (let i = 0; i < array.length; i++) {
    for (let j = 0; j < array[i].length; j++) {
        // Code logic here
    }
}
```

3. Optimize Database Queries

When working with databases, optimize your queries to fetch only the necessary data. Use indexing, caching, and database-specific optimizations to reduce query times.

```
-- Using indexes for faster database queries
CREATE INDEX idx_users_username ON users(username);
SELECT * FROM users WHERE username = 'alice';
```

4. Minimize I/O Operations

File and network I/O can be slow, so minimize unnecessary read and write operations. Buffer data when reading or writing files, and batch network requests where possible.

```
// Using buffered I/O for better performance
try (BufferedReader br = new BufferedReader(new FileReader("data.txt"))) {
    String line;
    while ((line = br.readLine()) != null) {
        // Process each line
    }
} catch (IOException e) {
    // Handle exceptions
}
```

5. Avoid Global Variables

Global variables can lead to code that is hard to reason about and debug. Instead, encapsulate data within functions or classes to improve code maintainability and performance.

```
# Avoiding global variables
def calculate_total(items):
    total = 0
    for item in items:
        total += item
    return total
```

6. Use Lazy Loading

Load data or resources only when needed. Lazy loading can significantly reduce startup times and memory usage in applications.

```
// Lazy loading images
const image = new Image();
image.src = "image.jpg";
```

7. Profile and Benchmark Your Code

Regularly profile and benchmark your code to identify bottlenecks and areas for improvement. Use profiling tools and analyze performance data to make informed optimizations.

```
# Profiling Python code
import cProfile

def my_function():
    # Code logic here

cProfile.run("my_function()")
```

8. Optimize Memory Usage

Avoid memory leaks and excessive memory usage by managing resources carefully. Release resources explicitly when they are no longer needed, especially in languages without automatic memory management.

```
// Explicitly freeing memory in C++
int* data = new int[1000];
// Code logic here
delete[] data;
```

9. Keep Code Modular and DRY

Modular code that follows the "Don't Repeat Yourself" (DRY) principle is easier to maintain and can be more performant. Reuse functions and components to minimize redundancy and improve code quality.

```
// Reusable function to calculate the square of a number
function square(x) {
    return x * x;
}
```

10. Regularly Update Dependencies

Outdated libraries and dependencies may contain security vulnerabilities or performance issues. Keep your dependencies up to date to benefit from bug fixes and optimizations.

```
# Updating Node.js packages
npm update
```

By following these best practices and optimizing your code for performance, you can write software that not only functions correctly but also runs efficiently, ensuring a smoother user experience and reduced resource consumption.

10.5. Leveraging Hardware Resources

Leveraging hardware resources effectively is crucial for optimizing the performance of your applications. In this section, we'll explore various techniques and best practices for making the most out of your hardware, whether you're developing software for desktop computers, servers, or embedded systems.

1. Parallelism and Concurrency

Modern hardware often consists of multi-core processors, which can execute multiple tasks simultaneously. To take advantage of this, use parallelism and concurrency in your code. For instance, in languages like Python, you can use the `multiprocessing` module to run tasks in parallel.

```python
import multiprocessing

def process_data(data):
    # Process data here

if __name__ == "__main__":
    data_to_process = [...]
    with multiprocessing.Pool() as pool:
        results = pool.map(process_data, data_to_process)
```

2. GPU Acceleration

Graphics Processing Units (GPUs) are powerful hardware components that can accelerate certain computations. Consider using libraries like CUDA or OpenCL to offload computationally intensive tasks to the GPU, such as deep learning and scientific simulations.

```cpp
// Using CUDA for GPU acceleration in C++
#include <iostream>
#include <cuda_runtime.h>

__global__ void addKernel(int* a, int* b, int* c, int size) {
    int i = blockIdx.x * blockDim.x + threadIdx.x;
    if (i < size) {
        c[i] = a[i] + b[i];
    }
}
```

```c
int main() {
    // CUDA code here
    return 0;
}
```

3. Memory Management

Efficient memory usage is critical for performance. Use data structures that minimize memory overhead and avoid memory leaks. In languages like C and C++, be mindful of dynamic memory allocation and deallocation.

```c
// Dynamic memory allocation in C
int* numbers = (int*)malloc(10 * sizeof(int));
if (numbers) {
    // Use the allocated memory
    free(numbers); // Don't forget to free the memory
}
```

4. Caching and Prefetching

Modern CPUs have caching mechanisms that can significantly speed up memory access. Optimize your code to make effective use of the CPU cache. Additionally, consider prefetching data to minimize wait times for memory access.

```csharp
// Caching example in C#
class Program {
    static void Main() {
        int[] data = new int[1000000];
        long sum = 0;
        for (int i = 0; i < data.Length; i++) {
            sum += data[i];
        }
    }
}
```

5. Load Balancing

In distributed systems and server applications, load balancing ensures that hardware resources are utilized evenly. Implement load balancers to distribute incoming requests or tasks among available resources, preventing overloads and optimizing performance.

```python
# Load balancing using Python's multiprocessing
from multiprocessing import Process, Queue

def worker(task_queue, result_queue):
    while True:
        task = task_queue.get()
        if task is None:
            break
        # Process the task and put the result in the result_queue
```

```python
if __name__ == "__main__":
    tasks = [...]
    num_workers = multiprocessing.cpu_count()
    task_queue = multiprocessing.Queue()
    result_queue = multiprocessing.Queue()
    workers = [Process(target=worker, args=(task_queue, result_queue)) for _
in range(num_workers)]

    for w in workers:
        w.start()

    for task in tasks:
        task_queue.put(task)

    for _ in range(num_workers):
        task_queue.put(None)

    for w in workers:
        w.join()

    # Collect and process results from result_queue
```

6. Energy Efficiency

Consider the energy consumption of your software, especially for mobile devices and data centers. Writing energy-efficient code not only reduces costs but also has a positive environmental impact. Optimize algorithms, reduce unnecessary computation, and use sleep modes where applicable.

```java
// Reducing energy consumption in Java
while (true) {
    // Perform work
    try {
        Thread.sleep(1000); // Sleep to reduce CPU usage
    } catch (InterruptedException e) {
        Thread.currentThread().interrupt();
    }
}
```

7. Profiling and Monitoring

Regularly profile your software to identify performance bottlenecks. Use monitoring tools to gather data on hardware resource usage, such as CPU and memory. Analyze this data to make informed optimizations.

By leveraging hardware resources effectively, you can ensure that your software runs efficiently and takes full advantage of the available computing power. Whether you're developing for high-performance computing clusters or resource-constrained embedded systems, optimizing for hardware is essential for delivering responsive and capable applications.

133

Chapter 11: Customizing the Look and Feel

Section 11.1: Themes and Icon Packs

Customizing the look and feel of your coding environment in Visual Studio Code is essential for creating a workspace that suits your preferences and needs. One of the fundamental aspects of customization is choosing the right theme and icon pack to define the visual style of your editor.

Visual Studio Code offers a variety of themes and icon packs that you can easily install and apply. Themes control the color scheme and overall appearance of the editor, while icon packs replace the default icons in the sidebar and other UI elements. Let's explore how to make your coding experience more visually appealing and functional by selecting and managing themes and icon packs.

Themes

Themes in Visual Studio Code are responsible for defining the color scheme used throughout the editor. They play a significant role in making your code visually distinguishable and comfortable to read. To customize your theme, follow these steps:

1. **Open the Command Palette:** Use the shortcut Ctrl+Shift+P (Windows/Linux) or Cmd+Shift+P (macOS) to open the command palette.

2. **Search for "Color Theme":** In the command palette, start typing "Color Theme." You'll see a list of available commands related to themes.

3. **Select a Theme:** Browse the list of themes, and select the one you like by clicking on it. Visual Studio Code will apply the theme instantly.

4. **Preview Themes:** You can preview a theme before applying it. Click on a theme, and it will show you a preview in the editor. Press Esc to exit the preview mode.

5. **Customize Themes:** Some themes offer customization options. After selecting a theme, you might be prompted to customize it further. Follow the on-screen instructions to make adjustments.

6. **Install Additional Themes:** If you want to explore more themes, you can click on "Install Additional Color Themes" at the bottom of the theme list. This will take you to the Visual Studio Code Marketplace, where you can discover and install new themes.

Icon Packs

Icon packs in Visual Studio Code replace the default icons used for files, folders, and other elements in the sidebar and explorer. They can help you quickly identify different file types and improve the overall visual experience of your workspace. Here's how to manage icon packs:

1. **Open the Command Palette:** Use the shortcut Ctrl+Shift+P (Windows/Linux) or Cmd+Shift+P (macOS) to open the command palette.

2. **Search for "File Icon Theme":** In the command palette, start typing "File Icon Theme." You'll see a list of available icon packs.

3. **Select an Icon Pack:** Browse the list of icon packs, and select the one you want to use by clicking on it. Visual Studio Code will apply the icon pack immediately.

4. **Preview Icon Packs:** You can preview an icon pack before applying it. Click on an icon pack to see how it changes the icons in the explorer. Press Esc to exit the preview mode.

5. **Install Additional Icon Packs:** To explore more icon packs, click on "Install Additional File Icon Themes" at the bottom of the icon pack list. This will take you to the Visual Studio Code Marketplace, where you can discover and install new icon packs.

Customizing themes and icon packs allows you to create a coding environment that aligns with your personal style and preferences. Visual Studio Code's extensive theme and icon pack ecosystem ensures that you can find the perfect combination to make your coding experience both visually pleasing and efficient.

In the next sections, we'll delve deeper into customizing other aspects of the Visual Studio Code interface to create a comfortable coding environment tailored to your needs.

Section 11.2: Customizing Font and Display Settings

In Visual Studio Code, customizing font and display settings is an important part of creating a comfortable and efficient coding environment. Whether you prefer a specific font, font size, or line spacing, Visual Studio Code provides you with the flexibility to adjust these settings to suit your needs. Let's explore how to customize font and display settings in Visual Studio Code.

Changing the Font

Changing the font in Visual Studio Code is a straightforward process. Follow these steps:

1. **Open the Settings:** You can open the settings in Visual Studio Code by clicking on the gear icon in the lower-left corner of the window and selecting "Settings" or by using the keyboard shortcut Ctrl+, (Windows/Linux) or Cmd+, (macOS).

2. **Search for "Font Family":** In the settings search bar, type "Font Family." This will filter the settings to show font-related options.

3. **Select a Font:** In the "Font Family" setting, you can specify the font you want to use. You can either type the name of the font or select it from the dropdown list if it's installed on your system.

4. **Set the Font Size:** Below the "Font Family" setting, you'll find the "Font Size" setting. Adjust the font size to your preference by typing a numerical value or using the up and down arrows.

5. **Apply the Changes:** Once you've selected a font and adjusted the font size, Visual Studio Code will immediately apply the changes. You can see the updated font in the editor.

Line Spacing and More

Besides changing the font, Visual Studio Code allows you to customize additional display settings such as line spacing and character spacing. Here's how:

1. **Open the Settings:** Access the settings as mentioned earlier.

2. **Search for "Line Height":** In the settings search bar, type "Line Height" to find the line spacing setting.

3. **Adjust Line Height:** You can adjust the line height to increase or decrease the spacing between lines of text in the editor. Use a numerical value to set the desired line height.

4. **Search for "Letter Spacing":** To adjust character spacing, type "Letter Spacing" in the settings search bar.

5. **Modify Letter Spacing:** You can specify a value for letter spacing to control the space between characters in the editor.

6. **Apply Changes:** As you make adjustments to line height and letter spacing, Visual Studio Code will immediately reflect the changes in the editor.

Customizing font and display settings allows you to fine-tune the appearance of your code editor to match your visual preferences and readability requirements. Whether you prefer a clean and minimalistic look or a more stylized coding environment, Visual Studio Code provides the flexibility to achieve the desired display settings.

In the next sections, we'll explore accessibility features and how to personalize the sidebar and panels, further enhancing your coding experience in Visual Studio Code.

Section 11.3: Accessibility Features

Accessibility is an important aspect of software development, ensuring that software is usable by individuals with disabilities. Visual Studio Code is committed to providing a coding environment that is accessible to everyone. In this section, we'll explore the accessibility features available in Visual Studio Code.

1. Screen Reader Support

Visual Studio Code is designed to work seamlessly with screen readers such as JAWS, NVDA, and VoiceOver. It provides detailed descriptions of UI elements, making it possible for visually impaired users to navigate and interact with the editor effectively.

To enable screen reader support, follow these steps:

1. Open Visual Studio Code.

2. Go to the "File" menu and select "Preferences," then choose "Settings."

3. In the search bar, type "Accessibility Support."

4. Enable the "Accessibility Support" option by checking the box.

Once enabled, Visual Studio Code will provide improved accessibility support, making it easier for users who rely on screen readers to work with the editor.

2. High Contrast Themes

Visual Studio Code offers high contrast themes that are specifically designed for users with low vision or other visual impairments. These themes provide a high level of contrast between text and background elements, enhancing readability.

To enable a high contrast theme:

1. Open Visual Studio Code.

2. Go to the "File" menu and select "Preferences," then choose "Color Theme."

3. In the color theme selection, look for themes with "High Contrast" in their names, such as "High Contrast Dark" or "High Contrast Light."

4. Select the high contrast theme that suits your preference.

Once you've applied a high contrast theme, the editor's colors will be adjusted to provide maximum contrast, making it easier for users with visual impairments to read and work with code.

3. Keyboard Navigation

Visual Studio Code provides extensive keyboard navigation options, allowing users to navigate the editor, open files, and execute commands without relying on a mouse.

Keyboard shortcuts are an essential part of accessibility, as they provide an efficient way to interact with the software.

To explore available keyboard shortcuts and customize them to your liking:

1. Open Visual Studio Code.

2. Go to the "File" menu and select "Preferences," then choose "Keyboard Shortcuts."

3. In the keyboard shortcuts editor, you can search for specific commands and assign custom keyboard shortcuts by clicking on the pencil icon next to a command.

By making use of keyboard navigation and customized shortcuts, you can tailor Visual Studio Code's interface to match your workflow and accessibility requirements.

4. Other Accessibility Settings

Visual Studio Code offers various accessibility settings that can be customized to meet your needs. These settings include:

- **Cursor Blinking:** Adjust the cursor blinking rate to make it more visible.
- **Editor Line Numbers:** Toggle the display of line numbers in the editor.
- **Editor Word Wrap:** Enable word wrapping to prevent horizontal scrolling.
- **Editor Font Ligatures:** Control whether font ligatures are used in the editor.

To explore and modify these settings, open the "Settings" by clicking on the gear icon in the lower-left corner of the window and selecting "Settings."

Incorporating accessibility features into your coding environment not only benefits individuals with disabilities but also contributes to a more inclusive and user-friendly development experience for all users. Visual Studio Code's commitment to accessibility ensures that developers can create accessible software with ease.

Section 11.4: Personalizing the Sidebar and Panels

Visual Studio Code allows you to customize not only your code editor but also the sidebar and panels, offering a tailored development environment. In this section, we'll explore how you can personalize the sidebar and panels to optimize your workflow.

1. Sidebar Customization

1.1. Show or Hide Sidebar Sections

Visual Studio Code's sidebar, also known as the Activity Bar, provides various sections such as "Explorer," "Source Control," "Extensions," and more. You can easily show or hide these sections based on your preferences.

To show or hide sidebar sections:

1. Click on the icons in the Activity Bar to toggle sections on and off.

2. Right-click on the Activity Bar and select "View" to choose which sections to display.

1.2. Rearrange Sidebar Sections

You can also rearrange the order of sidebar sections to prioritize the ones you use most frequently. To rearrange sidebar sections:

1. Click and drag a section's icon to move it to your desired position.

2. Customize the sidebar layout to match your workflow.

2. Panel Customization

Visual Studio Code includes various panels like the "Output" panel and "Terminal" panel, which you can tailor to your needs.

2.1. Pinning Panels

You can pin panels to keep them open even when switching between files or tabs. To pin a panel:

1. Open the panel you want to pin, such as the "Output" panel.

2. Click the pin icon located at the top-right corner of the panel.

The pinned panel will remain visible and accessible, providing constant access to important information.

2.2. Panel Positioning

Visual Studio Code allows you to position panels either at the bottom or on the right side of the editor. You can choose the position that best suits your workflow.

To change the position of panels:

1. Click on the gear icon located at the top-right corner of a panel.

2. Select "Move Panel Right" or "Move Panel to Bottom" as desired.

This flexibility in panel positioning enables you to optimize screen space for coding while keeping essential panels within reach.

3. Customizing Appearance

Visual Studio Code offers several appearance customizations for the sidebar and panels:

3.1. Panel Size

You can adjust the size of panels to allocate more or less screen space to them. Hover your cursor over the panel's border until it changes to a double-headed arrow, then drag to resize the panel.

3.2. Panel Fonts and Colors

Customize the fonts, colors, and themes used within panels to match your preferred coding environment. You can modify these settings in the "Settings" by searching for "Color Theme" and "Editor: Font Family."

3.3. Panel Extensions

Extensions in the Visual Studio Code marketplace can enhance the functionality and appearance of panels. Explore extensions like "Custom CSS and JS Loader" to inject custom styles into your editor, including panels.

By personalizing the sidebar and panels, you can create a development environment that caters to your specific workflow and preferences. Whether you're streamlining your sidebar layout or customizing panel appearance, Visual Studio Code provides the tools you need to optimize your coding experience.

Section 11.5: Creating a Comfortable Coding Environment

Creating a comfortable coding environment in Visual Studio Code is crucial for productivity and enjoyment. In this section, we'll explore various tips and tricks to help you tailor your coding workspace to your liking.

1. Workspace Layout

1.1. Split View

Visual Studio Code allows you to split your workspace into multiple columns and rows, creating a flexible layout. To split your view:

1. Right-click on a file tab.

2. Select "Split Up," "Split Down," "Split Left," or "Split Right" as desired.

This feature is handy for comparing code, working on different parts of a project simultaneously, or keeping documentation open while coding.

1.2. Zen Mode

Zen Mode provides a distraction-free, full-screen writing experience. Activate it by pressing Ctrl+K Z (Windows/Linux) or Cmd+K Z (macOS). To exit Zen Mode, press Escape.

2. Customizing Themes

2.1. Install Themes

Visual Studio Code offers a variety of themes in its marketplace. Install themes that resonate with your style and preferences. To install a theme:

1. Click on the gear icon in the bottom-right corner of the window.

2. Select "Color Theme."

3. Browse and install your preferred theme.

2.2. Custom Themes

You can create custom themes or customize existing ones to match your ideal color scheme. Use the "Workbench › Color Customizations" setting in your settings.json file to make adjustments.

3. Font and Typography

3.1. Font Selection

Choose a font that is easy on the eyes and suits your taste. To change the font:

1. Open the command palette with Ctrl+Shift+P (Windows/Linux) or Cmd+Shift+P (macOS).

2. Type "Preferences: Open Settings (JSON)" and select it.

3. Add or modify the "editor.fontFamily" setting with your preferred font.

3.2. Font Size

Adjust the font size for code and UI elements to enhance readability. Use the "editor.fontSize" and "window.zoomLevel" settings to control font size and scaling.

4. Comfortable Shortcuts

Customize keyboard shortcuts to streamline your coding tasks. Use the "keybindings.json" file to define your keybindings or explore extensions that offer keybinding customization.

5. Accessibility Features

Visual Studio Code provides accessibility features to accommodate different needs. You can enable screen readers and customize accessibility settings through the settings panel.

6. Version Control Integration

If you work with version control systems like Git, customize your source control panel to fit your workflow. Pin repositories, change views, and personalize the commit message input area.

7. Extending Functionality

Explore the marketplace for extensions that enhance your coding environment. Whether it's additional language support, productivity tools, or specific integrations, extensions can make your workspace even more comfortable.

8. Personalization is Key

Remember that creating a comfortable coding environment is highly personal. Experiment with different settings, themes, and extensions to find the configuration that suits you best. Your comfort and efficiency in Visual Studio Code are essential for productive and enjoyable coding experiences.

Chapter 12: Collaboration and Remote Development

Section 12.1: Pair Programming with Live Share

Collaborative coding has become increasingly popular in the software development world, allowing developers from different locations to work together efficiently. Visual Studio Code provides a powerful feature called "Live Share" that enables real-time, remote collaboration on code projects.

What is Live Share?

Live Share is an extension in Visual Studio Code that allows developers to collaborate on a project in real-time. It provides a shared coding environment where multiple users can edit and debug code simultaneously, making it an excellent tool for pair programming, code reviews, and remote collaboration.

Setting Up Live Share

To get started with Live Share:

1. Install the "Live Share" extension from the Visual Studio Code marketplace.

2. Open the project you want to collaborate on.

3. Click the "Live Share" button in the status bar on the bottom of the window.

4. Share the generated link with your collaborators.

Features of Live Share

1. Real-Time Editing

Live Share allows multiple users to edit the same code file simultaneously. Each participant can see the changes made by others in real-time, making collaborative coding seamless.

2. Debugging Together

With Live Share, developers can debug code together. This means you can set breakpoints, step through code, and inspect variables collaboratively, even if you are working on different machines.

3. Guest and Host Roles

In a Live Share session, there are typically two roles: the host and the guest. The host is the owner of the code session, while guests join to collaborate. Roles can be switched during the session as needed.

Live Share includes shared integrated terminals, which allow participants to run commands and scripts together. It eliminates the need to switch between different terminal sessions.

5. Read-Only Mode

Participants can be granted read-only access to code or specific files, which is useful for sharing code with someone who should not make edits.

Tips for Effective Live Share Sessions

1. **Communicate**: Clear communication is essential during collaborative sessions. Use voice or text chat alongside Live Share to discuss changes and decisions.

2. **Follow the Cursor**: The "Follow Participant" feature helps you keep track of what your collaborators are doing. It's especially useful when multiple participants are working on different parts of the code.

3. **Roles and Permissions**: Be aware of the roles and permissions of participants. Hosts can control access and permissions for guests.

4. **End Sessions**: Remember to end Live Share sessions when you're done to secure your code.

Live Share is a powerful tool for collaborative coding and can greatly enhance the productivity of remote development teams or pair programming sessions. Whether you're working on a complex project, conducting code reviews, or providing remote support, Live Share makes it easy to collaborate effectively in real-time.

Section 12.2: Remote Development Extensions

Remote development has become increasingly relevant in today's globalized software development landscape. Visual Studio Code offers a range of extensions that facilitate remote development, allowing developers to work on projects hosted on remote servers or in containerized environments. These extensions make it possible to edit, debug, and run code remotely, providing a seamless development experience.

Remote - SSH

The "Remote - SSH" extension is a powerful tool for connecting to remote servers and editing code as if you were working locally. It enables developers to access their remote development environments directly from Visual Studio Code. To use this extension:

1. Install the "Remote - SSH" extension from the Visual Studio Code marketplace.

2. Use the `Remote-SSH: Connect to Host` command to establish an SSH connection to your remote server.

3. Once connected, you can open folders, edit files, and run commands as if you were on the remote machine.

This extension is particularly useful when working on projects hosted on remote servers, cloud-based virtual machines, or development environments provided by your organization.

Remote - Containers

The "Remote - Containers" extension simplifies remote development using containers, such as Docker containers. It allows you to develop within a consistent, containerized environment to ensure that your code runs consistently across different setups. Here's how to use it:

1. Install the "Remote - Containers" extension from the Visual Studio Code marketplace.

2. Open your project folder in Visual Studio Code.

3. Click the green "Remote Development" icon in the bottom left corner and select "Reopen in Container."

4. Visual Studio Code will create a development container using the configuration defined in your project's `.devcontainer` folder.

This extension is beneficial for ensuring consistent development environments and simplifying the setup of complex development stacks.

Remote - WSL (Windows Subsystem for Linux)

For Windows users, the "Remote - WSL" extension allows seamless integration with the Windows Subsystem for Linux (WSL). It enables developers to develop using the WSL environment within Visual Studio Code. To use this extension:

1. Install the "Remote - WSL" extension from the Visual Studio Code marketplace.

2. Open your project folder in Visual Studio Code.

3. Click the green "Remote Development" icon in the bottom left corner and select "Remote - WSL: New Window."

This extension is beneficial for Windows users who want to leverage the advantages of WSL for their development tasks.

Remote Development Tips

When working with remote development extensions:

- Ensure you have the necessary permissions and access credentials for remote servers or containers.

- Be mindful of network connectivity and potential latency when working remotely.

- Make use of version control systems like Git to track changes, even in remote development environments.

- Keep your extensions, tools, and development environments up-to-date to ensure a smooth remote development experience.

Remote development extensions in Visual Studio Code empower developers to work effectively on projects hosted on remote servers, within containers, or even in WSL environments. These extensions are valuable tools for distributed teams and individuals who need to maintain a consistent development experience, regardless of where their code is hosted.

Section 12.3: Collaborating Across Different Platforms

Collaboration is a fundamental aspect of modern software development. Visual Studio Code supports collaboration across different platforms through a combination of built-in features and extensions. This section explores various ways to collaborate effectively using Visual Studio Code.

Multi-Platform Collaboration

Visual Studio Code is available on Windows, macOS, and Linux, making it an excellent choice for cross-platform development. Whether your team consists of developers using different operating systems, or you need to collaborate with external contributors, Visual Studio Code ensures a consistent development environment.

Live Share

Visual Studio Code's "Live Share" extension takes collaboration to the next level. It allows developers to share their development environment with others in real-time, regardless of their physical location or the operating system they use. Key features of Live Share include:

- Real-time code editing and debugging collaboration.

- Support for multiple participants.

- Secure and granular access control.

- Integration with other extensions and services.

To use Live Share:

1. Install the "Live Share" extension from the Visual Studio Code marketplace.

2. Open your project in Visual Studio Code.

3. Click the "Live Share" button in the status bar, sign in with your Microsoft account, and start a new session.

4. Share the session link with collaborators, and they can join and start collaborating instantly.

This extension is particularly valuable for pair programming, code reviews, and troubleshooting code together with team members or external partners.

GitHub Integration

If your development workflow involves GitHub, Visual Studio Code provides a seamless integration. You can easily clone, fork, push, and pull repositories using the built-in Git support. Additionally, you can:

- Create and manage GitHub Gists directly from Visual Studio Code.

- Review and comment on pull requests.

- Browse and navigate code hosted on GitHub repositories without leaving the editor.

To set up GitHub integration:

1. Sign in to your GitHub account within Visual Studio Code.

2. Install the "GitHub Pull Requests" and "GitHub Repositories" extensions to access more GitHub-specific features.

This integration streamlines the collaboration process when your project relies on GitHub for version control and issue tracking.

Collaborative Development Workflows

To collaborate effectively across different platforms:

- Ensure that everyone in your team uses a consistent set of extensions and tools to maintain a unified development experience.

- Use version control systems like Git for code management, and establish clear branching and merging strategies.

- Leverage code review tools and practices to maintain code quality and consistency.

- Communicate clearly with team members, and document your development processes and guidelines.

Collaboration across different platforms is essential for distributed teams and open-source projects. Visual Studio Code's multi-platform support, Live Share extension, and GitHub integration offer powerful tools to facilitate seamless collaboration, regardless of the geographical location or operating system of team members.

Section 12.4: Code Reviews and Pull Requests

Code reviews are a critical part of maintaining code quality and ensuring that the software development process runs smoothly. Visual Studio Code provides several features and extensions to facilitate code reviews and manage pull requests effectively.

Setting Up Code Review Environments

Before diving into code reviews, ensure that you have a version control system like Git set up for your project. Visual Studio Code seamlessly integrates with Git, making it easier to manage changes and collaborate with your team.

Installing Git

If you don't already have Git installed, you can download it from the official website (https://git-scm.com/). After installation, make sure to configure Git with your name and email address using the following commands in your terminal:

```
git config --global user.name "Your Name"
git config --global user.email "youremail@example.com"
```

Initializing a Git Repository

To initialize a new Git repository in your project folder, open a terminal and navigate to the project directory. Run the following commands:

```
git init
```

Managing Pull Requests

Pull requests (PRs) are a standard way to propose changes and collaborate on code within a Git repository. Visual Studio Code streamlines the process of creating, reviewing, and merging pull requests, particularly if your project is hosted on GitHub.

Creating a Pull Request

To create a pull request in Visual Studio Code:

1. Ensure you are on a branch that contains your changes.

2. Open the source control view by clicking the source control icon in the sidebar.

3. Click the three dots icon (ellipsis) to open the context menu, and select "Create Pull Request."

4. Follow the prompts to set up the title, description, and reviewer(s) for your pull request.

5. Click "Create Pull Request," and your changes will be submitted for review.

Reviewing Code

As a reviewer, you can easily review code changes within Visual Studio Code. Open the pull request from the "Pull Requests" section in the source control view, or by clicking a link to the pull request on your project's hosting platform (e.g., GitHub).

Within the pull request view, you can:

- Review changes in files and provide comments.

- Use the built-in diff viewer to see what was added, modified, or deleted.

- Approve or request changes to the code.

- Start discussions with other reviewers and the author.

Code Review Extensions

Visual Studio Code offers extensions that enhance the code review process further. The "GitHub Pull Requests" extension, for instance, provides a richer interface for managing pull requests on GitHub-hosted repositories, including the ability to assign reviewers, view checks, and more.

To install this extension:

1. Open the Extensions view by clicking the square icon in the sidebar.

2. Search for "GitHub Pull Requests" and install it.

Best Practices for Code Reviews

To make the most out of your code reviews:

- Keep reviews focused and concise, focusing on the code's functionality, readability, and maintainability.

- Follow coding style guidelines and adhere to best practices agreed upon by your team.

- Be respectful and constructive in your feedback, promoting a positive and collaborative atmosphere.

- Ensure timely reviews to prevent bottlenecks in the development process.

Code reviews are an integral part of modern software development. Visual Studio Code, combined with Git and code review extensions, provides a powerful environment for conducting efficient and effective code reviews and managing pull requests. By following best practices and maintaining a collaborative spirit, teams can ensure high-quality code and a smoother development workflow.

Section 12.5: Managing Projects and Teams

Visual Studio Code is not just an individual code editor; it also provides tools and extensions for managing projects and collaborating with teams. Whether you are working on a small project or contributing to a large-scale application, Visual Studio Code has features to streamline project management and foster team collaboration.

Project Management Extensions

Visual Studio Code offers various extensions for project management, helping you keep track of tasks, milestones, and project progress. These extensions integrate with popular project management platforms and provide a unified view of your project within the editor.

Popular Project Management Extensions

1. **Todo Tree**: The Todo Tree extension allows you to track TODO comments and other annotations within your codebase. It supports various formats like TODO, FIXME, and custom keywords, helping you manage tasks and code improvements.

2. **GitHub Projects**: If your project is hosted on GitHub, the GitHub Projects extension lets you view, create, and manage project boards and issues directly from Visual Studio Code. It provides a seamless way to keep your project organized.

3. **Asana**: The Asana extension integrates with the Asana project management platform. You can create, view, and manage tasks, projects, and conversations within Visual Studio Code while collaborating with your team on Asana.

4. **Trello**: If you use Trello for project management, the Trello extension allows you to access and manage your Trello boards and cards without leaving the editor. It's a convenient way to stay on top of your project's tasks.

Team Collaboration and Communication

Effective team collaboration is crucial for the success of any project. Visual Studio Code offers features and extensions that facilitate communication and collaboration among team members.

Live Share

Visual Studio Code's Live Share extension enables real-time collaborative coding sessions. With Live Share, you can share your coding environment with team members, allowing them to edit, debug, and review code together. It's especially useful for pair programming and solving coding challenges as a team.

Several extensions integrate with popular chat and communication tools like Slack, Microsoft Teams, and Discord. These extensions enable you to receive notifications, join discussions, and stay connected with your team without leaving Visual Studio Code.

Version Control and Teamwork

Version control is essential for managing code changes and collaborating effectively with your team. Visual Studio Code's built-in Git integration provides robust version control capabilities, making it easy to work on projects with multiple contributors.

When working with a team, consider the following best practices:

- Use a branching strategy like GitFlow to manage feature development and releases.

- Regularly commit and push your changes to the repository to ensure visibility and collaboration.

- Resolve merge conflicts promptly to maintain a clean and functional codebase.

- Leverage code reviews and pull requests to ensure code quality and alignment with project goals.

- Document your code, processes, and decisions to facilitate knowledge sharing within the team.

Visual Studio Code, combined with project management extensions and team collaboration tools, empowers developers to work efficiently on projects of all sizes. By adopting best practices and maintaining open communication within your team, you can maximize the benefits of Visual Studio Code for project management and collaboration.

Chapter 13: The Command Palette and Shortcuts

Section 13.1: Mastering the Command Palette

The Command Palette is a powerful feature in Visual Studio Code that allows you to access various commands and features quickly. It's an essential tool for improving your productivity and efficiency when working with the editor. In this section, we will explore the Command Palette, how to open it, and some of its most useful commands.

What is the Command Palette?

The Command Palette is a text-based interface that lets you search for and execute various commands in Visual Studio Code. You can think of it as a command center for the editor, where you can access features, settings, extensions, and more, all from a single input field.

Opening the Command Palette

To open the Command Palette, you can use the following methods:

1. **Keyboard Shortcut**: The quickest way to open the Command Palette is by using the keyboard shortcut Ctrl + Shift + P (Windows/Linux) or Cmd + Shift + P (macOS). This will bring up the input field at the top of the editor.

2. **View Menu**: You can also open it from the "View" menu by selecting "Command Palette" or by clicking on the icon that looks like a magnifying glass and a pencil in the top-right corner of the editor.

3. **Quick Open**: While using the Quick Open feature (accessible via Ctrl + P or Cmd + P), you can press Ctrl + Shift + P or Cmd + Shift + P to switch to the Command Palette directly.

Using the Command Palette

Once you've opened the Command Palette, you can start typing to search for a specific command or feature. As you type, the Command Palette will provide suggestions based on your input. You can use the arrow keys to navigate through the suggestions or continue typing to narrow down the list.

Here are some common use cases for the Command Palette:

1. Running Commands

You can use the Command Palette to run various commands in Visual Studio Code. For example, you can type "Open File" to quickly open a file or "Toggle Line Comment" to comment or uncomment lines of code.

2. Accessing Settings

To access settings quickly, you can type "Preferences: Open Settings" in the Command Palette. This will open the settings.json file where you can configure your editor's settings.

3. Installing Extensions

Installing extensions is also easy with the Command Palette. Typing "Extensions: Install Extensions" will allow you to search for and install extensions directly from within Visual Studio Code.

4. Searching for Files

If you want to find a specific file in your project, you can use the "Files: Open File" command. Just start typing the file name, and the Command Palette will display matching files.

5. Running Tasks

If you have defined tasks in your project's tasks.json file, you can execute them using the Command Palette. Type "Run Task" and select the task you want to run.

Customizing the Command Palette

Visual Studio Code allows you to customize the Command Palette to suit your workflow. You can create your own keybindings for frequently used commands or even add custom user-defined tasks. This level of customization can significantly boost your productivity by giving you quick access to the actions that matter most to you.

In conclusion, mastering the Command Palette is a fundamental skill for becoming proficient with Visual Studio Code. It provides a fast and efficient way to access features and commands, making your development workflow smoother and more productive. Whether you're a beginner or an experienced user, the Command Palette is a tool you'll find indispensable for working effectively in Visual Studio Code.

Section 13.2: Essential Keyboard Shortcuts

In addition to the Command Palette, Visual Studio Code offers a wide range of keyboard shortcuts that can significantly speed up your coding and navigation tasks. Learning and using these shortcuts efficiently can make you a more productive developer. In this section, we will explore some essential keyboard shortcuts that every Visual Studio Code user should be familiar with.

Keyboard Shortcut Basics

Before diving into specific keyboard shortcuts, let's cover some basics:

- **Key Combinations**: Keyboard shortcuts typically involve a combination of keys. For instance, Ctrl + S means holding the "Ctrl" key and pressing "S" simultaneously.

- **Platform Differences**: Some shortcuts may vary slightly depending on your operating system. We will provide both Windows/Linux and macOS shortcuts where applicable.

- **Customization**: Visual Studio Code allows you to customize keyboard shortcuts to suit your preferences. You can access these settings by opening the Command Palette (Ctrl + Shift + P or Cmd + Shift + P) and typing "Preferences: Open Keyboard Shortcuts."

Essential Keyboard Shortcuts

1. **Save File**: Probably the most commonly used shortcut. To save your current file, use Ctrl + S (Windows/Linux) or Cmd + S (macOS).

2. **Undo and Redo**: You can undo your last action with Ctrl + Z (Windows/Linux) or Cmd + Z (macOS). To redo, use Ctrl + Shift + Z (Windows/Linux) or Cmd + Shift + Z (macOS).

3. **Cut, Copy, and Paste**: These standard editing shortcuts work as expected: Ctrl + X (cut), Ctrl + C (copy), and Ctrl + V (paste) on Windows/Linux, or Cmd + X, Cmd + C, and Cmd + V on macOS.

4. **Find and Replace**: Open the find dialog with Ctrl + F (Windows/Linux) or Cmd + F (macOS). To replace, use Ctrl + H (Windows/Linux) or Cmd + Option + F (macOS).

5. **Toggle Sidebar**: Hide or show the sidebar with Ctrl + B (Windows/Linux) or Cmd + B (macOS).

6. **Navigate Files**: Quickly switch between open files with Ctrl + Tab (Windows/Linux) or Cmd + Tab (macOS).

7. **Open Integrated Terminal**: Access the integrated terminal with Ctrl + (backtick) (Windows/Linux) or Cmd + (backtick) (macOS).

8. **Go to Definition**: Jump to the definition of a variable or function with F12 (Windows/Linux/macOS).

9. **Find All References**: Find all references to a symbol with Shift + F12 (Windows/Linux/macOS).

10. **Comment and Uncomment**: Comment or uncomment a selected block of code with Ctrl + / (Windows/Linux) or Cmd + / (macOS).

11. **Toggle Full Screen**: Toggle full-screen mode with F11 (Windows/Linux/macOS).

12. **Zoom In and Out**: Increase or decrease the text editor's font size using Ctrl + = (Windows/Linux) or Cmd + = (macOS) to zoom in and Ctrl + - (Windows/Linux) or Cmd + - (macOS) to zoom out.

13. **Toggle Word Wrap**: Turn word wrap on or off with Alt + Z (Windows/Linux) or Option + Z (macOS).

14. **Toggle Line Numbers**: Show or hide line numbers with Ctrl + G (Windows/Linux) or Cmd + G (macOS), followed by typing Line: and the line number you want to navigate to.

15. **Close Tab**: Close the current file tab with Ctrl + F4 (Windows/Linux) or Cmd + W (macOS).

These are just a few of the many keyboard shortcuts available in Visual Studio Code. Learning and using these shortcuts can significantly boost your efficiency and make your coding experience more enjoyable. To discover more shortcuts or customize them to your liking, you can explore the "Keyboard Shortcuts" settings in Visual Studio Code.

Section 13.3: Customizing Shortcuts

Visual Studio Code's flexibility extends to keyboard shortcuts, allowing you to customize them to match your preferences or replicate shortcuts from other code editors you are familiar with. This level of customization enhances your productivity by letting you work in a way that feels most comfortable. In this section, we'll explore how to customize keyboard shortcuts in Visual Studio Code.

Accessing Keyboard Shortcuts

To access and customize keyboard shortcuts in Visual Studio Code, follow these steps:

1. Open the Command Palette by pressing Ctrl + Shift + P (Windows/Linux) or Cmd + Shift + P (macOS).

2. Type "Preferences: Open Keyboard Shortcuts" and select it from the dropdown list. Alternatively, you can directly press Ctrl + K Ctrl + S (Windows/Linux) or Cmd + K Cmd + S (macOS).

Viewing and Searching Keyboard Shortcuts

Once you've accessed the Keyboard Shortcuts settings, you can view and search for specific keyboard shortcuts. The settings panel displays a list of available keyboard shortcuts and their associated commands. You can use the search bar at the top to find a particular shortcut or command quickly.

Customizing Keyboard Shortcuts

To customize a keyboard shortcut, follow these steps:

1. Find the shortcut you want to customize by searching or scrolling through the list.

2. Hover over the shortcut, and you'll see an "Edit Keybinding" pencil icon appear on the left side. Click on it.

3. A text input field will appear, allowing you to enter your desired key combination for the shortcut. You can use common keyboard modifiers like Ctrl, Shift, Alt, or Cmd (macOS) in combination with other keys.

4. After entering the key combination, press Enter. If the combination you entered conflicts with an existing shortcut, you'll be notified. In such cases, consider modifying your key combination to avoid conflicts.

5. Your customized keyboard shortcut will now replace the default one.

Resetting Customized Shortcuts

If you want to revert a customized shortcut back to its default, follow these steps:

1. In the Keyboard Shortcuts settings, find the customized shortcut you wish to reset.

2. Hover over it, and the "Reset Keybinding" trashcan icon will appear on the right side. Click on it.

3. The shortcut will be reset to its default state.

Exporting and Importing Keybindings

Visual Studio Code allows you to export and import your customized keyboard shortcuts, making it easy to transfer your preferences across different installations or share them with colleagues. To do this:

1. In the Keyboard Shortcuts settings, click the gear icon in the top-right corner and select "Export Keybindings."

2. Choose a location to save the JSON file containing your customized keybindings.

3. To import keybindings, click the gear icon again and select "Import Keybindings." Locate and select the JSON file you want to import.

Advanced Customization

For more advanced customization, you can edit the keybindings.json file directly. To access it, click the "Edit Keybindings (JSON)" link at the top-right corner of the Keyboard Shortcuts settings. This JSON file allows you to define custom keybindings in a more detailed manner, including specific contexts and conditions.

In conclusion, customizing keyboard shortcuts in Visual Studio Code empowers you to tailor the editor to your workflow, making you more efficient and comfortable as you work on your projects. Whether you're replicating shortcuts from other editors or creating entirely new keybindings, this flexibility is one of the strengths of Visual Studio Code's user-friendly environment.

Section 13.4: Command Line Integration

Visual Studio Code provides a seamless command-line integration that allows you to execute command-line tasks and scripts directly from the editor. This feature is particularly useful when you want to run scripts, build projects, or interact with version control systems without leaving the coding environment.

Opening the Integrated Terminal

To access the integrated terminal in Visual Studio Code, you can use the following methods:

1. **Menu Bar:** Click on "Terminal" in the menu bar at the top, and then select "New Terminal."

2. **Shortcut Key:** Press Ctrl + (backtick) on Windows/Linux or Cmd + on macOS. This key combination opens and closes the integrated terminal.

3. **Command Palette:** Open the command palette (Ctrl + Shift + P or Cmd + Shift + P) and type "View: Toggle Integrated Terminal."

Customizing the Integrated Terminal

You can customize the behavior of the integrated terminal to suit your preferences. Here are a few tips:

Terminal Shell

By default, the integrated terminal uses your system's default shell (e.g., Bash on Linux, PowerShell on Windows). However, you can change the default shell to another one if you prefer. To do this:

1. Open the settings by clicking on the gear icon in the bottom-right corner and selecting "Settings."

2. Search for "terminal › integrated › shell" in the search bar.

3. In the "Shell: Linux" and "Shell: Windows" settings, specify the path to your desired shell executable.

Terminal Location

The integrated terminal opens in the workspace's root directory by default. You can change this behavior by customizing the terminal's starting directory:

1. Open the settings.

2. Search for "terminal › integrated › cwd" in the search bar.

3. Set your preferred directory as the "Terminal > Integrated > Cwd" setting.

Terminal Profiles

Visual Studio Code allows you to create and manage multiple terminal profiles. Each profile can have its settings, shell type, and starting directory. To manage profiles:

1. Open the settings.

2. Search for "terminal › integrated › profiles" in the search bar.

3. Click "Edit in settings.json" to define your custom profiles in JSON format. Here's an example:

```
"terminal.integrated.profiles.linux": {
    "myProfile": {
        "path": "/bin/bash",
        "args": [],
        "cwd": "${workspaceFolder}",
        "env": {},
        "icon": "terminal",
        "colorScheme": "Dark",
        "fontSize": 12,
        "fontFamily": "Menlo, Monaco, 'Courier New', monospace"
    }
}
```

Running Commands in the Integrated Terminal

Once you have the integrated terminal customized to your liking, you can use it to run various command-line tasks. Here are some common scenarios:

Running Scripts

If you're working on a project with script files (e.g., Python, Node.js), you can execute scripts directly from the terminal. Navigate to the directory containing your script and run it by typing python script.py (for Python) or node script.js (for Node.js).

Building Projects

Many programming projects require build commands to compile code or assets. You can execute build commands in the integrated terminal by navigating to your project's root directory and running the appropriate build command (e.g., `npm run build`, `make`, or `mvn clean install`).

Version Control

If your project uses Git for version control, you can run Git commands in the terminal. Common Git commands include `git clone`, `git pull`, `git commit`, and `git push`.

Package Managers

Package managers like npm (Node Package Manager) and pip (Python Package Index) can be used through the integrated terminal. For example, you can install Node.js packages using `npm install package-name` or Python packages using `pip install package-name`.

Running Tests

To execute tests for your project, you can use testing frameworks like Jest, pytest, or JUnit. Navigate to the directory where your tests are located and run the corresponding test command (e.g., `npm test`, `pytest`, or `mvn test`).

Output and Debugging

The integrated terminal displays the output of your commands, making it easy to review the results or debug any issues that may arise during execution. If you encounter errors or unexpected behavior, you can analyze the terminal output to identify the problem and take corrective actions.

In summary, the integrated terminal in Visual Studio Code streamlines command-line tasks, allowing you to work efficiently without leaving the editor. By customizing the terminal settings, you can tailor it to your specific needs and integrate it seamlessly into your development workflow. Whether you're running scripts, building projects, managing version control, or performing other command-line operations, the integrated terminal is a valuable tool in your coding arsenal.

Section 13.5: Efficiency Tips and Tricks

As you become more proficient with Visual Studio Code, there are several efficiency tips and tricks you can apply to streamline your workflow and make coding tasks more manageable. In this section, we'll explore some valuable techniques to boost your productivity.

1. Multiple Cursors and Selections

Visual Studio Code allows you to place multiple cursors in your code simultaneously. To do this, hold down the `Alt` key (or `Option` key on macOS) and click in the desired locations. You can also use `Ctrl + Alt + Down` to add cursors below the current line and `Ctrl + Alt`

+ Up to add cursors above it. This feature is handy for making simultaneous edits or selections.

2. Emmet Abbreviations

Emmet is a powerful tool for generating HTML and CSS code quickly. You can use Emmet abbreviations to create HTML elements and CSS properties with minimal keystrokes. For example, typing div.container>ul>li*5 and then pressing Tab will generate a nested HTML structure with five list items.

3. Fuzzy Search in Command Palette

The Command Palette (Ctrl + Shift + P or Cmd + Shift + P) is your gateway to various actions in Visual Studio Code. It supports fuzzy search, which means you can type a few letters of a command or feature you're looking for, and it will suggest relevant options. This can save you time when navigating menus or executing commands.

4. Snippets

Code snippets are predefined templates for common code patterns. Visual Studio Code includes a variety of built-in snippets, and you can create your custom ones. To use a snippet, type its associated abbreviation and press Tab or Enter to expand it. Snippets are especially useful for repetitive coding tasks.

5. Zen Mode

When you need to focus entirely on your code, Zen Mode (Ctrl + K Z or Cmd + K Z) can help. It maximizes your code editor's space and hides most UI elements, providing a distraction-free environment for coding.

6. Peek Definition and Go to Definition

You can quickly view the definition of a function or variable without leaving your current file by using "Peek Definition" (Alt + F12 or Option + F12 on macOS). "Go to Definition" (F12) takes you directly to the definition location in the codebase. These features are beneficial for code navigation.

7. Code Folding

Code folding allows you to collapse sections of code to keep your editor clean and organized. You can fold and unfold sections by clicking the small triangles or using keyboard shortcuts like Ctrl + [(fold) and Ctrl +] (unfold).

8. Custom Keybindings

Visual Studio Code lets you define custom keybindings for various commands and actions. If there are tasks you frequently perform, consider assigning keybindings to speed up your workflow. You can access the keybindings settings by searching for "keybindings" in the settings.

9. Automatic Code Formatting

Configure your code editor to automatically format your code according to your project's coding style guidelines. This helps maintain consistent code formatting and saves you from manual formatting tasks. Extensions like Prettier and ESLint can assist with code formatting.

10. Version Control Integration

If your project uses Git or other version control systems, make use of Visual Studio Code's built-in version control features. You can stage, commit, and push changes directly from the editor, which simplifies version control tasks.

11. Explore Extensions

Visual Studio Code has a vast extension ecosystem. Periodically explore the Visual Studio Code Marketplace to discover extensions that can enhance your development experience. Extensions are available for various languages, frameworks, and tools.

12. Intelligent Code Suggestions

Leverage Visual Studio Code's intelligent code completion and suggestion features. As you type, the editor offers auto-completions and relevant suggestions, saving you from typing repetitive code manually.

13. Customizing Themes and Fonts

Tailor the editor's appearance to your liking by customizing themes, fonts, and color schemes. A comfortable and visually pleasing coding environment can boost your productivity.

In conclusion, Visual Studio Code is a versatile code editor that offers numerous features and customization options to make your coding experience efficient and enjoyable. By mastering these efficiency tips and tricks, you can take full advantage of the editor's capabilities and become a more productive developer.

Chapter 14: Integrating with Other Tools and Services

Section 14.1: Connecting with Cloud Services

In modern software development, cloud services play a pivotal role in various aspects of the development lifecycle. Visual Studio Code offers integrations and extensions that enable seamless interaction with popular cloud platforms and services. This section explores how you can connect Visual Studio Code to cloud services and leverage their capabilities.

Azure Cloud Integration

Microsoft Azure is a widely used cloud platform, and Visual Studio Code provides a range of extensions to enhance your Azure development workflow. The "Azure Functions" extension, for example, allows you to create, debug, and deploy serverless functions directly from the editor. You can access Azure services, such as Azure Storage and Azure App Service, using these extensions.

To get started with Azure integration, you'll need an Azure account and the Azure CLI installed. Visual Studio Code can seamlessly connect to your Azure account, allowing you to manage resources, view logs, and deploy applications with ease.

AWS Integration

If you work with Amazon Web Services (AWS), Visual Studio Code offers extensions like the "AWS Toolkit" to simplify AWS development tasks. With this toolkit, you can manage AWS resources, interact with AWS Lambda functions, and deploy applications to AWS Elastic Beanstalk.

To use the AWS Toolkit, you'll need to configure your AWS credentials using the AWS Command Line Interface (CLI) or the AWS Toolkit itself. Once configured, you can access AWS services directly from Visual Studio Code.

Google Cloud Platform (GCP) Integration

For GCP users, the "Cloud Code" extension for Visual Studio Code streamlines the development and deployment of applications on Google Cloud Platform. It provides features like Kubernetes and Cloud Run deployment, debugging, and managing GCP resources.

To use Cloud Code, you'll need a Google Cloud account and the Google Cloud SDK installed. You can authenticate your Google Cloud account within Visual Studio Code, making it convenient to work with GCP services and deploy applications to Google Cloud.

Other Cloud Services

Apart from major cloud providers like Azure, AWS, and GCP, Visual Studio Code supports various extensions for connecting to other cloud services and platforms. These extensions cater to specific cloud-based development needs, such as integrating with Firebase for mobile and web development or working with cloud databases and IoT platforms.

Cloud-Based IDEs

In addition to cloud service integrations, Visual Studio Code supports cloud-based integrated development environments (IDEs) like GitHub Codespaces and Gitpod. These platforms allow you to develop, test, and collaborate on projects entirely in the cloud. Visual Studio Code can connect to these environments, providing a familiar coding experience with all the advantages of cloud-based development.

Key Benefits of Cloud Service Integration

1. **Seamless Development**: Integrating Visual Studio Code with cloud services streamlines development tasks, reducing the need to switch between different tools and platforms.

2. **Efficient Resource Management**: You can manage cloud resources, monitor services, and deploy applications without leaving your code editor.

3. **Debugging Capabilities**: Debugging cloud-hosted applications becomes more accessible, with tools for setting breakpoints, inspecting variables, and viewing logs directly within Visual Studio Code.

4. **Collaboration and Teamwork**: Cloud service integrations facilitate collaboration among team members, allowing them to work on shared codebases and environments.

5. **Cloud-Native Development**: With cloud integration, you can build and test applications in environments that closely resemble production settings, ensuring smoother deployment and scaling.

In conclusion, integrating Visual Studio Code with cloud services extends the capabilities of the code editor, making it a powerful tool for modern software development. Whether you're developing serverless functions, deploying applications to the cloud, or collaborating with teammates in cloud-based IDEs, Visual Studio Code offers a versatile and efficient development experience.

Section 14.2: Using Docker in Visual Studio Code

Docker has revolutionized the way applications are developed, shipped, and deployed. It provides a containerization platform that allows you to package applications and their dependencies into lightweight, portable containers. Visual Studio Code offers robust Docker integration, making it easier for developers to work with containers directly from their code editor.

Docker Extension

To begin using Docker in Visual Studio Code, you need to install the "Docker" extension from the Visual Studio Code marketplace. This extension provides a suite of Docker-related functionalities, such as managing containers, images, and Docker Compose files.

Once installed, you can access the Docker extension from the sidebar, where you'll find several Docker-related views, including a list of running containers, images, and a Docker Compose explorer.

Container Management

With the Docker extension, you can easily manage containers. You can start, stop, restart, and remove containers right from Visual Studio Code. This streamlines the development and testing process, as you can quickly spin up containerized development environments for your applications.

For example, if you're developing a web application using Node.js, you can run a Node.js container with a specific version and dependencies directly from Visual Studio Code. This ensures that your development environment matches your production environment, reducing the "it works on my machine" problem.

Docker Compose Support

Docker Compose is a tool for defining and running multi-container Docker applications. Visual Studio Code provides excellent support for Docker Compose, allowing you to define and manage complex application stacks with ease.

You can create and edit Docker Compose files (.yml) within Visual Studio Code, and the Docker extension provides autocompletion and validation for these files. This ensures that your Compose configurations are accurate and free of errors.

Debugging Containers

One of the powerful features of Visual Studio Code's Docker integration is the ability to debug applications running in containers. By configuring launch.json for your project, you can attach a debugger to a running container. This enables you to set breakpoints, inspect variables, and step through your code as if it were running locally.

Container Registry Integration

Visual Studio Code also supports various container registries, including Docker Hub, Azure Container Registry, and Amazon Elastic Container Registry. You can easily log in to your preferred registry and push or pull container images directly from the editor. This simplifies the process of sharing container images and deploying them to cloud platforms.

Key Benefits of Docker Integration

1. **Consistency**: Docker ensures that your development, testing, and production environments are consistent, reducing the chances of environment-related issues.

2. **Isolation**: Containers isolate applications and their dependencies, preventing conflicts between different projects or versions.

3. **Efficient Resource Usage**: Containers are lightweight and share the host OS kernel, optimizing resource usage and allowing you to run multiple containers on a single machine.

4. **Scalability**: Docker makes it easy to scale applications horizontally by replicating containers to handle increased loads.

5. **Easy Collaboration**: Sharing Docker Compose configurations and container images simplifies collaboration among developers and DevOps teams.

In conclusion, Docker integration in Visual Studio Code empowers developers to work with containers effortlessly. Whether you're managing containers, defining complex application stacks with Docker Compose, debugging applications in containers, or pushing images to container registries, Visual Studio Code provides a comprehensive development environment for containerized applications. This integration is particularly valuable for building, testing, and deploying microservices-based applications and other containerized workloads.

Section 14.3: Integration with Database Tools

Visual Studio Code is a versatile code editor that extends its capabilities beyond just writing code. Developers often need to interact with databases as part of their workflow. Fortunately, Visual Studio Code provides excellent integration with various database tools and extensions, making database development and management more convenient.

Database Extensions

To work with databases in Visual Studio Code, you can install database-specific extensions. There are extensions available for popular databases like Microsoft SQL Server, MySQL, PostgreSQL, MongoDB, and more. These extensions provide functionalities such as connecting to databases, running queries, managing schemas, and viewing data.

For example, if you're working with SQL Server, you can install the "SQL Server (mssql)" extension, which allows you to connect to SQL Server instances, execute SQL queries, and even debug stored procedures.

Connection Management

Database extensions typically offer a dedicated sidebar view that allows you to manage database connections. You can configure connection profiles, including server details, authentication methods, and connection parameters. Once configured, you can easily connect to databases with a single click.

Connecting to databases through Visual Studio Code provides the advantage of keeping your database-related tasks within the same editor where you're writing code. This streamlines your development process and eliminates the need to switch between different tools.

Query Execution

One of the key features of database extensions is the ability to execute SQL queries directly from Visual Studio Code. You can open SQL files, write queries, and execute them against your connected databases. The results are displayed in a dedicated output window, making it easy to review query results and error messages.

Schema Exploration

Database extensions also offer schema exploration capabilities. You can navigate through database schemas, view tables, indexes, stored procedures, and other database objects. This is especially helpful when you need to understand the structure of a database or make changes to it.

IntelliSense and Code Assistance

Just like with code editing, Visual Studio Code provides IntelliSense and code assistance features when working with databases. As you write SQL queries, you'll get suggestions for table names, column names, and SQL keywords. This helps reduce syntax errors and improves query writing efficiency.

Version Control Integration

If your database schema is versioned using version control systems like Git, Visual Studio Code can seamlessly integrate database changes into your version control workflow. You can track and commit changes to your database schema, ensuring that your database changes are also properly versioned and documented.

Database-specific Features

Different database extensions offer various features specific to the database system they target. For example, extensions for document-oriented databases like MongoDB may provide tools for working with JSON documents and collections. Extensions for relational databases may offer tools for generating entity-relationship diagrams (ERDs) or managing indexes.

In conclusion, Visual Studio Code's integration with database tools and extensions makes it a powerful choice for developers who need to work with databases alongside their code. Whether you're writing SQL queries, managing database schemas, or exploring database structures, Visual Studio Code provides a unified and efficient environment for database-related tasks. This integration simplifies the development process and enhances productivity, making it an excellent choice for database-driven application development.

Section 14.4: Working with REST APIs and Postman

In modern software development, interacting with RESTful APIs (Representational State Transfer Application Programming Interfaces) is a common requirement. Whether you're building web applications, mobile apps, or any software that communicates over the internet, Visual Studio Code provides tools and extensions that make working with REST APIs efficient and straightforward.

REST Client Extension

Visual Studio Code offers a powerful extension known as the "REST Client" extension, which simplifies the process of sending HTTP requests to REST APIs and inspecting the responses. This extension is widely used by developers for tasks such as testing APIs, debugging, and exploring endpoints.

To get started with the REST Client extension, you need to create a .http or .rest file in your project. These files contain HTTP requests written in a simple and intuitive syntax. For example:

```
GET https://jsonplaceholder.typicode.com/posts/1
```

By adding requests like this to your file, you can execute them directly from Visual Studio Code. The extension sends the request, displays the HTTP response, and even allows you to save and organize your request files.

Request Syntax

The REST Client extension supports various HTTP methods such as GET, POST, PUT, DELETE, and more. You can include headers, query parameters, request bodies, and authentication details in your requests. Here's an example of a POST request with JSON data:

```
POST https://jsonplaceholder.typicode.com/posts
Content-Type: application/json

{
  "title": "New Post",
  "body": "This is the body of the new post.",
  "userId": 1
}
```

You can also use environment variables and snippets to streamline your request writing process. This makes it easy to create and reuse requests for different APIs and endpoints.

Response Inspection

Once you execute a request, the REST Client extension displays the HTTP response directly within Visual Studio Code. You can view response headers, status codes, and the response

167

body. The extension also supports syntax highlighting for JSON and XML responses, making it easier to read and understand the data.

Collections and Environments

The REST Client extension allows you to organize your requests into collections and define environments. Collections help you group related requests together, while environments allow you to manage variables and settings for different development or production environments. This feature is especially useful when working on projects with multiple API endpoints or configurations.

Debugging and Testing

Visual Studio Code's debugging capabilities can be combined with the REST Client extension to troubleshoot API-related issues. You can set breakpoints in your request files and step through the request-response cycle, making it easier to identify problems in your API interactions.

Integration with Postman

If you're already using Postman, a popular API testing and development tool, you'll be pleased to know that the REST Client extension can import Postman collections. This allows you to migrate your existing API tests and requests to Visual Studio Code seamlessly. You can also export requests from Visual Studio Code to Postman if needed.

Version Control and Collaboration

Just like any other code file, your .http or .rest files can be versioned using Git or other version control systems. This means you can track changes to your API requests, collaborate with team members, and ensure that your API interactions are well-documented and maintained.

In conclusion, Visual Studio Code's REST Client extension enhances your productivity when working with RESTful APIs. It provides an efficient and integrated environment for sending HTTP requests, inspecting responses, debugging, and organizing your API-related tasks. Whether you're a web developer, mobile app developer, or backend engineer, this extension simplifies the process of interacting with REST APIs and contributes to a smoother development workflow.

Section 14.5: Combining with Other Development Tools

In the world of software development, it's common to work with a variety of tools and services that complement your primary development environment. Visual Studio Code's flexibility and extensibility make it an excellent choice for integrating with other development tools seamlessly.

Shell Integration

Visual Studio Code allows you to integrate with the command line or terminal shell of your choice. You can open an integrated terminal within the editor, which is preconfigured to run the same shell you use outside of Visual Studio Code. This is particularly useful for executing build scripts, running server processes, or interacting with version control systems through the command line.

The integrated terminal provides a unified experience where you can execute shell commands, PowerShell scripts, or even Node.js scripts directly from the editor. This eliminates the need to switch between different applications, streamlining your development workflow.

Git and Version Control

Version control is a fundamental aspect of software development, and Visual Studio Code provides built-in Git integration. You can manage your Git repositories, stage and commit changes, create and switch branches, and perform other Git operations without leaving the editor. The Source Control panel allows you to visualize the status of your files and commits.

Additionally, Visual Studio Code supports other version control systems, such as Mercurial and Subversion, through extensions. This ensures that you can use your preferred version control system within the same development environment.

Docker Integration

Docker is a popular platform for containerization, and Visual Studio Code offers extensions for Docker integration. With these extensions, you can manage Docker containers, build Docker images, and even debug applications running inside containers directly from the editor.

The Docker extension provides a graphical interface for managing containers and images, making it easier to work with containerized applications. You can also define Docker Compose configurations and orchestrate multi-container applications seamlessly.

Database Tools

Developers often need to interact with databases while working on applications. Visual Studio Code supports various database extensions that enable you to connect to and query databases directly from the editor. Whether you're using MySQL, PostgreSQL, MongoDB, or other database systems, there are extensions available to enhance your database-related tasks.

These extensions provide features like database schema visualization, query execution, and result visualization. You can even write and run database scripts within Visual Studio Code, making it a versatile tool for database development and management.

Cloud Services

Many applications rely on cloud services and APIs for various functionalities. Visual Studio Code allows you to integrate with popular cloud platforms like Microsoft Azure, AWS, and Google Cloud through extensions. These extensions provide features like deploying applications to the cloud, managing cloud resources, and interacting with cloud services directly from the editor.

You can develop, test, and deploy cloud-based applications with ease, thanks to the integration of cloud tools into Visual Studio Code. This streamlines the development and deployment process for cloud-native applications.

Collaboration Tools

Collaboration is essential in software development, and Visual Studio Code offers extensions for team collaboration and code review. Tools like Live Share enable real-time collaboration with teammates, allowing multiple developers to edit and debug code together in a shared session.

Additionally, code review extensions integrate with popular code review platforms like GitHub and Azure DevOps, making it convenient to review and comment on pull requests directly within the editor.

In conclusion, Visual Studio Code's extensibility and integration capabilities make it a versatile choice for developers who work with a wide range of development tools and services. Whether you need to interact with the command line, manage version control, work with containers, access databases, utilize cloud services, or collaborate with team members, Visual Studio Code provides the flexibility and extensions to enhance your development experience. This integration contributes to a more efficient and productive development workflow, allowing you to focus on writing high-quality code.

Chapter 15: Mobile and Web Development

Section 15.1: Setting Up for Web Development

Web development is a dynamic and ever-evolving field, and Visual Studio Code is an excellent choice for web developers due to its extensive features and a vast ecosystem of extensions. Before you dive into web development using Visual Studio Code, it's essential to set up your development environment properly.

Installing Node.js and npm

Node.js and npm (Node Package Manager) are fundamental tools for web development. Node.js allows you to execute JavaScript code outside the browser, which is crucial for server-side scripting and build processes. npm is a package manager that simplifies the installation and management of JavaScript libraries and tools.

You can download Node.js from the official website (https://nodejs.org/) and install it on your system. npm is included with Node.js, so once you've installed Node.js, you'll also have npm available in your terminal.

To verify that Node.js and npm are installed correctly, open a terminal and run the following commands:

```
node -v
npm -v
```

These commands should display the installed Node.js and npm versions, confirming that they are ready for use.

Setting Up a Code Editor

If you haven't already installed Visual Studio Code, you can download it from the official website (https://code.visualstudio.com/) and install it on your system. Visual Studio Code is available for Windows, macOS, and Linux, making it a versatile choice for web development on different platforms.

Installing Extensions

Visual Studio Code's strength lies in its extensions, and for web development, there are numerous extensions available that enhance your workflow. Some essential extensions for web development include:

- **HTML CSS Support**: This extension provides autocompletion and linting for HTML and CSS, making it easier to write clean and error-free code.

- **JavaScript (ES6) Code Snippets**: A collection of JavaScript code snippets for common tasks, helping you write JavaScript code faster and more efficiently.

- **Live Server**: This extension allows you to launch a local development server with live reloading, making it convenient to preview your web pages as you make changes.

- **ESLint**: If you're using ESLint for JavaScript linting, this extension integrates ESLint into Visual Studio Code, providing real-time feedback on your code quality.

- **Debugger for Chrome**: If you're developing web applications using Google Chrome, this extension enables debugging JavaScript code within the Chrome browser directly from Visual Studio Code.

You can install these extensions and more by navigating to the Extensions view in Visual Studio Code (Ctrl+Shift+X) and searching for the desired extensions. Click the Install button next to each extension to add it to your development environment.

Creating a Workspace

A workspace in Visual Studio Code is a collection of folders and settings for a specific project. It allows you to organize your code and configurations efficiently. To create a workspace, follow these steps:

1. Open Visual Studio Code.

2. Click on "File" in the top menu, then select "Add Folder to Workspace."

3. Choose the folder containing your web project files and click "Add."

4. Save the workspace by selecting "File" > "Save Workspace As" and providing a name for your workspace file (with a .code-workspace extension).

By creating a workspace, you can manage your project's files, extensions, and settings more effectively.

Conclusion

Setting up your development environment for web development in Visual Studio Code is a crucial initial step. By installing Node.js, setting up the code editor, installing essential extensions, and creating a workspace, you lay the foundation for a productive web development workflow. With the right tools and configurations in place, you can start building web applications, websites, and web services efficiently and effectively using Visual Studio Code.

Section 15.2: Mobile Development with React Native and Flutter

Mobile app development is a highly sought-after skill, and Visual Studio Code provides excellent support for building mobile applications. In this section, we'll explore two popular frameworks for mobile development: React Native and Flutter.

React Native

Setting Up React Native

React Native is a JavaScript framework for building mobile apps using React. To get started with React Native development in Visual Studio Code, follow these steps:

1. **Install Node.js and npm**: Ensure you have Node.js and npm installed, as React Native relies on these tools for package management and execution.

2. **Install Expo CLI**: Expo is a set of tools that simplifies React Native development. You can install Expo CLI globally using npm:

   ```
   npm install -g expo-cli
   ```

3. **Create a New React Native Project**: Use Expo CLI to create a new React Native project:

   ```
   expo init MyReactNativeApp
   ```

   Follow the prompts to choose a project template. Expo provides a variety of project templates to kickstart your development.

4. **Open the Project in Visual Studio Code**: Navigate to the project folder and open it in Visual Studio Code using the code command:

   ```
   cd MyReactNativeApp
   code .
   ```

Developing with React Native

Visual Studio Code offers features that enhance your React Native development experience. You can take advantage of features like IntelliSense for JavaScript and React, debugging with breakpoints, and the React Native extension, which provides tools for managing the app's state and debugging.

To run your React Native app, use the following command within the project folder:

```
expo start
```

This command will start the Expo development server, and you can choose to run your app on an emulator/simulator or a physical device using the Expo Go app.

Setting Up Flutter

Flutter is Google's UI toolkit for building natively compiled applications for mobile, web, and desktop from a single codebase. To begin Flutter development in Visual Studio Code, follow these steps:

1. **Install Flutter**: Download and install the Flutter SDK from the official website (https://flutter.dev/docs/get-started/install). Ensure that you add the Flutter bin directory to your system's PATH.

2. **Install Dart**: Flutter uses the Dart programming language. Download and install Dart from the Dart website (https://dart.dev/get-dart).

3. **Install Flutter Extension**: Open Visual Studio Code and install the "Flutter" extension, which provides tools and features for Flutter development.

4. **Create a New Flutter Project**: Use the Flutter CLI to create a new Flutter project:

    ```
    flutter create MyFlutterApp
    ```

5. **Open the Project in Visual Studio Code**: Navigate to the project folder and open it in Visual Studio Code using the code command:

    ```
    cd MyFlutterApp
    code .
    ```

Developing with Flutter

Visual Studio Code offers extensive support for Flutter development. The Flutter extension provides features such as Flutter IntelliSense, widget inspection, and debugging capabilities.

To run your Flutter app, use the following command within the project folder:

```
flutter run
```

This command will build and run your Flutter app on an emulator/simulator or a physical device connected to your computer.

Conclusion

Visual Studio Code is a versatile choice for mobile app development, whether you're building apps with React Native or Flutter. By following the setup instructions and using the available extensions, you can streamline your mobile development workflow and create high-quality mobile applications for iOS and Android platforms.

Section 15.3: Responsive Design and Cross-Browser Testing

Responsive web design is a critical aspect of modern web development, ensuring that websites look and function well across various devices and screen sizes. Visual Studio Code provides tools and extensions to help you create responsive web applications and perform cross-browser testing effectively.

Understanding Responsive Design

Responsive design involves designing web pages that adapt to different screen sizes, from large desktop monitors to small mobile devices. This approach ensures that users have a consistent and user-friendly experience regardless of the device they're using.

Media Queries

Media queries are a fundamental technique in responsive design. They allow you to apply different styles and layouts based on the characteristics of the user's device, such as screen width and height, device orientation, and more. Here's an example of a simple media query in CSS:

```css
@media (max-width: 768px) {
  /* Styles for screens with a maximum width of 768px */
  .header {
    font-size: 16px;
  }
}
```

This media query adjusts the font size for screens with a maximum width of 768 pixels.

Visual Studio Code for Responsive Design

Visual Studio Code provides several features and extensions to assist you in creating responsive web designs:

1. Live Server

The Live Server extension is a popular choice for live reloading and testing your web applications. It allows you to see real-time updates as you make changes to your code, making it easier to test responsiveness. To use it, simply install the extension and right-click on your HTML file to open it with Live Server.

2. Browser Preview

The Browser Preview extension enables you to preview your web pages in various browsers directly from Visual Studio Code. This helps you ensure that your website looks and functions consistently across different browsers. You can install this extension and access it from the status bar or the command palette.

Several extensions specifically cater to responsive web design, providing tools to visualize breakpoints, test on different device sizes, and more. Extensions like "Prettier" and "Beautify" can also help format your HTML, CSS, and JavaScript code for better readability and maintainability.

Cross-Browser Testing

Cross-browser testing is essential to ensure that your web application works as expected in different browsers. While Visual Studio Code doesn't perform testing directly, it integrates with various testing tools and services to streamline the process.

1. BrowserStack and Sauce Labs

Services like BrowserStack and Sauce Labs allow you to test your web application on a wide range of browsers and devices without the need for physical hardware. Both services offer integrations with Visual Studio Code, making it easier to run tests and debug issues across browsers.

2. Selenium WebDriver

Selenium WebDriver is a popular testing framework that can be used with Visual Studio Code. You can write test scripts in languages like JavaScript, Python, or Java and execute them to automate browser testing on multiple browsers and platforms.

Conclusion

Responsive design and cross-browser testing are crucial aspects of web development. Visual Studio Code, with its extensions and integrations, simplifies the process of creating responsive web applications and ensures that your websites function seamlessly across various devices and browsers. Incorporate these practices into your web development workflow to deliver a better user experience to your audience.

Section 15.4: JavaScript Frameworks: Angular, Vue.js, and More

In the world of web development, JavaScript frameworks play a pivotal role in simplifying and accelerating the development of complex web applications. In this section, we will explore some popular JavaScript frameworks, including Angular, Vue.js, and others, and discuss how Visual Studio Code can be used effectively with these frameworks.

The Importance of JavaScript Frameworks

JavaScript frameworks are collections of pre-written JavaScript code that provide a structured way to build web applications. They offer a range of features and tools that help developers create interactive and dynamic web experiences efficiently. Here are some key benefits of using JavaScript frameworks:

- **Structured Development**: Frameworks enforce a structured development approach, making it easier to organize code and maintain large-scale applications.

- **Reusable Components**: Many frameworks offer reusable components that can be used across different parts of your application, reducing duplication of code.

- **Efficient Data Binding**: Frameworks often provide data binding capabilities, allowing automatic synchronization of data between the UI and the underlying data model.

- **Community Support**: Popular frameworks have active and vibrant communities, providing access to a wealth of resources, libraries, and plugins.

Angular

Angular, developed and maintained by Google, is one of the most widely used JavaScript frameworks for building web applications. It employs a component-based architecture and uses TypeScript as its primary programming language. Here's how you can get started with Angular in Visual Studio Code:

1. **Install Angular CLI**: Angular CLI is a command-line tool that simplifies Angular development. You can install it globally using npm (Node Package Manager) with the following command:

   ```
   npm install -g @angular/cli
   ```

2. **Create a New Angular Application**: You can use the Angular CLI to create a new Angular application. Navigate to your project directory and run the following command:

   ```
   ng new my-angular-app
   ```

   This command will generate a new Angular project structure.

3. **Open the Project in Visual Studio Code**: Launch Visual Studio Code and open your Angular project folder using the `File > Open Folder` menu.

4. **Install Angular Extensions**: Visual Studio Code offers various extensions that enhance the Angular development experience. Some popular extensions include "Angular Language Service" for better code completion and "Angular Snippets" for code snippets. You can install these extensions from the Visual Studio Code Marketplace.

Vue.js

Vue.js is a progressive JavaScript framework for building user interfaces. It is known for its simplicity and flexibility, making it an excellent choice for both small and large-scale projects. Vue.js can be seamlessly integrated into Visual Studio Code for efficient development. Here's a brief overview of working with Vue.js in Visual Studio Code:

1. **Create a Vue.js Project**: You can start a new Vue.js project using the Vue CLI. Install it globally with the following command:

   ```
   npm install -g @vue/cli
   ```

2. **Generate a New Vue Project**: Create a new Vue.js project by running the following command:

   ```
   vue create my-vue-app
   ```

   The Vue CLI will guide you through project configuration.

3. **Open the Project in Visual Studio Code**: Launch Visual Studio Code and open your Vue.js project folder.

4. **Install Vue.js Extensions**: Visual Studio Code offers extensions such as "Vetur" and "Vue 3 Snippets" that enhance Vue.js development. Install these extensions from the Visual Studio Code Marketplace.

React and Other Frameworks

Visual Studio Code is a versatile editor that supports a wide range of JavaScript frameworks, including React, Ember.js, and more. To work with these frameworks, you can follow similar steps as outlined for Angular and Vue.js. Install the relevant CLI tools, create projects, and open them in Visual Studio Code for a seamless development experience.

Conclusion

JavaScript frameworks have revolutionized web development by providing powerful tools and structures to build modern web applications. Visual Studio Code's extensibility and support for various frameworks make it an excellent choice for developers working with JavaScript-based technologies. Whether you prefer Angular, Vue.js, React, or another framework, Visual Studio Code can accommodate your needs and streamline your development workflow.

Section 15.5: Building Progressive Web Apps

Progressive Web Apps (PWAs) represent a modern approach to building web applications that combine the best of web and mobile app experiences. In this section, we'll explore what PWAs are, their key features, and how you can build them using Visual Studio Code.

PWAs are web applications that provide a native app-like experience to users while still being accessed through a web browser. They are designed to be reliable, fast, and engaging. PWAs have several defining characteristics:

- **Progressive Enhancement**: PWAs should work for all users, regardless of the browser or device they use. They progressively enhance the user experience by taking advantage of modern web technologies when available.

- **Offline Capabilities**: One of the standout features of PWAs is their ability to work offline or in low-network conditions. This is achieved through caching strategies and service workers.

- **Responsive Design**: PWAs are built with responsive design principles, ensuring that they adapt and work well on various screen sizes and orientations.

- **App-Like Experience**: PWAs provide an app-like experience with smooth animations, navigation, and interactions. Users can even add PWAs to their device's home screen.

- **Safety and Security**: PWAs are served over HTTPS, ensuring data privacy and security. They also benefit from browser security mechanisms.

Building PWAs with Visual Studio Code

Visual Studio Code is a powerful tool for building Progressive Web Apps, thanks to its support for modern web technologies and extensions. Here are the steps to create a PWA using Visual Studio Code:

1. **Setup a Web Project**: Start by setting up a new web project in Visual Studio Code. You can create a simple HTML, CSS, and JavaScript project or use a web framework like React, Angular, or Vue.js.

2. **Ensure HTTPS**: PWAs must be served over HTTPS to ensure data security. You can use development tools like ngrok or localtunnel to create secure tunnels for testing your PWA locally.

3. **Service Workers**: Service workers are a critical component of PWAs, as they enable offline capabilities. You can create a service worker file and register it in your project. Visual Studio Code provides extensions like "Service Worker Precache" to help automate this process.

4. **Manifest File**: PWAs have a manifest file (usually named manifest.json) that provides metadata about the app, such as its name, icons, and theme colors. Create and configure this file in your project.

5. **App Shell**: To enhance performance, create an app shell that loads quickly and contains the basic structure of your app. This shell can be cached by the service worker and displayed even when offline.

6. **Responsive Design**: Ensure that your PWA is responsive and works well on various devices and screen sizes. Visual Studio Code's live server extension can be handy for testing responsiveness during development.

7. **Testing and Debugging**: Use the built-in debugging tools in Visual Studio Code to test and debug your PWA. You can also use browser developer tools to inspect and diagnose issues.

8. **Deploy and Host**: Once your PWA is ready, deploy it to a web server with HTTPS support. There are various hosting providers that offer PWA-friendly services. Ensure that your site's manifest file is discoverable.

9. **Promote Your PWA**: Encourage users to install your PWA on their devices. You can provide installation prompts on your website, and users can add your PWA to their home screen with a single click.

10. **Monitor and Update**: Regularly monitor the performance and usage of your PWA. Use tools like Google Lighthouse to assess its quality. Update your PWA with new features and improvements based on user feedback.

Conclusion

Progressive Web Apps offer a compelling way to deliver high-quality web experiences to users across various platforms and devices. With Visual Studio Code's support for web development and the use of modern web technologies, you can create PWAs that are reliable, fast, and engaging. Building PWAs is not only a technical challenge but also an opportunity to improve user satisfaction and expand your app's reach.

Chapter 16: Scripting and Automation

Section 16.1: Automating Repetitive Tasks

In this section, we'll explore the power of scripting and automation in Visual Studio Code. Scripting allows you to automate repetitive tasks, saving you time and reducing the chance of errors. We'll discuss the basics of scripting, introduce you to popular scripting languages, and show you how to create your own scripts to streamline your workflow.

Why Automation Matters

Repetitive tasks are a common part of software development. These tasks can range from simple file operations to complex build and deployment processes. Manually performing these tasks is not only time-consuming but also error-prone. Automation solves this problem by allowing you to define a series of steps that a computer can execute quickly and accurately.

Scripting Languages

Visual Studio Code supports a wide range of scripting languages that you can use for automation. Some of the popular scripting languages include:

- **JavaScript/Node.js**: If you're already familiar with JavaScript, you can leverage it for scripting within Visual Studio Code. Node.js provides access to a vast ecosystem of packages and modules.

- **Python**: Python is known for its simplicity and readability, making it an excellent choice for scripting. Visual Studio Code offers excellent support for Python development.

- **Bash**: Bash is the default shell on most Unix-based systems, and it's perfect for scripting tasks on those platforms. Visual Studio Code provides an integrated terminal where you can execute Bash scripts.

- **PowerShell**: PowerShell is a powerful scripting language for Windows systems. It's designed to automate administrative tasks and manage system configurations.

- **TypeScript**: TypeScript is a statically typed superset of JavaScript that can be transpiled into JavaScript. It's a strong choice for scripting, especially if you're working with TypeScript in your projects.

Creating Your First Script

Let's create a simple script to get started. We'll use JavaScript as our scripting language.

1. Open Visual Studio Code and create a new file with the `.js` extension, e.g., `myscript.js`.

2. In the file, you can write your script. For example, let's create a script that prints "Hello, Visual Studio Code!" to the console:

```
console.log("Hello, Visual Studio Code!");
```

3. Save the file.

4. Open the integrated terminal in Visual Studio Code by pressing Ctrl+ (backtick key) or navigating to View -> Terminal.

5. Navigate to the directory where your script is located using the cd command.

6. Execute the script by running node myscript.js.

You should see the output "Hello, Visual Studio Code!" printed in the terminal.

Automation Ideas

Automation possibilities are virtually endless. Here are some ideas for tasks you can automate using scripting in Visual Studio Code:

- **File operations**: Copying, moving, or renaming files and directories.

- **Build and deployment**: Automate the build and deployment process of your projects.

- **Version control**: Automate common Git tasks, such as committing and pushing changes.

- **Data processing**: Perform data transformations and manipulations.

- **Testing**: Automate running tests and generating reports.

- **Code generation**: Generate repetitive code snippets or boilerplate code.

As you become more familiar with scripting and automation, you'll find that you can optimize and streamline many aspects of your development workflow.

In the next sections, we'll explore more advanced scripting topics and delve into specific use cases for scripting in Visual Studio Code.

Section 16.2: Building and Running Scripts

In this section, we'll dive deeper into scripting in Visual Studio Code. You'll learn how to build and run scripts effectively, handle command-line arguments, and leverage external libraries and modules to extend the capabilities of your scripts.

Building Scripts

When building more complex scripts, it's essential to keep your code organized and maintainable. Here are some best practices for scripting in Visual Studio Code:

- **Modularize Your Code**: Break your script into smaller functions or modules. This promotes reusability and readability.

- **Use Comments**: Add comments to explain your code's logic, especially if the script is complex or intended for others to use.

- **Error Handling**: Implement error handling to gracefully handle unexpected issues during script execution.

- **Version Control**: Consider using version control systems like Git to track changes to your scripts.

- **Testing**: Write tests for your scripts to ensure they work as expected, especially for critical automation tasks.

Handling Command-Line Arguments

Many scripts require input from the command line. You can access command-line arguments in your script using the process.argv array in Node.js (for JavaScript and TypeScript scripts) or the sys.argv list in Python.

Here's an example of a JavaScript script that accepts command-line arguments:

```javascript
// myscript.js
const args = process.argv.slice(2); // Exclude the first two arguments (node and script name)

if (args.length === 0) {
  console.log("Usage: node myscript.js <name>");
} else
```

Chapter 16: Scripting and Automation

Section 16.1: Automating Repetitive Tasks

In this section, we'll explore the power of scripting and automation in Visual Studio Code. Scripting allows you to automate repetitive tasks, saving you time and reducing the chance of errors. We'll discuss the basics of scripting, introduce you to popular scripting languages, and show you how to create your own scripts to streamline your workflow.

Why Automation Matters

Repetitive tasks are a common part of software development. These tasks can range from simple file operations to complex build and deployment processes. Manually performing these tasks is not only time-consuming but also error-prone. Automation solves this problem by allowing you to define a series of steps that a computer can execute quickly and accurately.

Scripting Languages

Visual Studio Code supports a wide range of scripting languages that you can use for automation. Some of the popular scripting languages include:

- **JavaScript/Node.js:** If you're already familiar with JavaScript, you can leverage it for scripting within Visual Studio Code. Node.js provides access to a vast ecosystem of packages and modules.

- **Python:** Python is known for its simplicity and readability, making it an excellent choice for scripting. Visual Studio Code offers excellent support for Python development.

- **Bash:** Bash is the default shell on most Unix-based systems, and it's perfect for scripting tasks on those platforms. Visual Studio Code provides an integrated terminal where you can execute Bash scripts.

- **PowerShell:** PowerShell is a powerful scripting language for Windows systems. It's designed to automate administrative tasks and manage system configurations.

- **TypeScript:** TypeScript is a statically typed superset of JavaScript that can be transpiled into JavaScript. It's a strong choice for scripting, especially if you're working with TypeScript in your projects.

Creating Your First Script

Let's create a simple script to get started. We'll use JavaScript as our scripting language.

1. Open Visual Studio Code and create a new file with the `.js` extension, e.g., `myscript.js`.

2. In the file, you can write your script. For example, let's create a script that prints "Hello, Visual Studio Code!" to the console:

```
console.log("Hello, Visual Studio Code!");
```

3. Save the file.

4. Open the integrated terminal in Visual Studio Code by pressing Ctrl+ (backtick key) or navigating to View -> Terminal.

5. Navigate to the directory where your script is located using the cd command.

6. Execute the script by running node myscript.js.

You should see the output "Hello, Visual Studio Code!" printed in the terminal.

Automation Ideas

Automation possibilities are virtually endless. Here are some ideas for tasks you can automate using scripting in Visual Studio Code:

• **File operations**: Copying, moving, or renaming files and directories.

• **Build and deployment**: Automate the build and deployment process of your projects.

• **Version control**: Automate common Git tasks, such as committing and pushing changes.

• **Data processing**: Perform data transformations and manipulations.

• **Testing**: Automate running tests and generating reports.

• **Code generation**: Generate repetitive code snippets or boilerplate code.

As you become more familiar with scripting and automation, you'll find that you can optimize and streamline many aspects of your development workflow.

In the next sections, we'll explore more advanced scripting topics and delve into specific use cases for scripting in Visual Studio Code.

Section 16.2: Building and Running Scripts

In this section, we'll dive deeper into scripting and automation in Visual Studio Code. Building on what we learned in the previous section, we'll explore more advanced scripting concepts, including creating and running scripts for various tasks. We'll also discuss how to manage dependencies, handle script execution, and optimize your scripts for better performance.

Creating and Organizing Scripts

When working with scripts in Visual Studio Code, it's essential to organize your scripts effectively. You can store your scripts in a dedicated directory within your project or create a shared location for scripts that are used across multiple projects. Organizing your scripts helps maintain clarity and ensures that scripts are easily accessible.

Let's create a directory called `scripts` in your project and place your scripts there. This makes it easier to manage and execute them when needed.

```
my-project/
├── scripts/
│   ├── script1.js
│   ├── script2.py
│   └── ...
├── src/
│   ├── ...
├── package.json
└── ...
```

Managing Dependencies

Scripts often rely on external libraries or modules to perform specific tasks. Depending on the scripting language you're using, you may need to manage these dependencies. For instance, in Node.js, you can use npm (Node Package Manager) to manage dependencies for JavaScript and Node.js-based scripts.

1. To create a `package.json` file for managing dependencies, navigate to the `scripts` directory and run:

    ```
    npm init -y
    ```

    This command creates a basic `package.json` file.

2. Install any required packages using `npm install <package-name>`. For example:

    ```
    npm install axios
    ```

    This installs the "axios" package, which is a popular library for making HTTP requests.

3. In your script, you can import and use the installed package:

    ```
    const axios = require("axios");

    // Now you can use axios in your script
    axios.get("https://api.example.com/data")
      .then((response) => {
        console.log(response.data);
      })
      .catch((error) => {
    ```

```
    console.error(error);
});
```

Remember to document dependencies in your scripts so that others who work with your code know what packages are required.

Script Execution

Visual Studio Code provides various ways to execute scripts:

1. **Integrated Terminal**: You can open the integrated terminal (`View -> Terminal`) and navigate to the script's directory to run it using the appropriate command for your scripting language (e.g., `node script.js` for JavaScript/Node.js or `python script.py` for Python).

2. **Run and Debug**: Visual Studio Code offers a "Run and Debug" feature that allows you to create and run debugging configurations for your scripts. This is especially useful when you need to debug your scripts.

3. **Task Runner**: You can set up tasks in Visual Studio Code's `tasks.json` file to automate script execution. This is helpful for running scripts with specific parameters or as part of a larger workflow.

4. **Extensions**: Depending on your scripting language, you can find extensions in the Visual Studio Code Marketplace that provide additional features for script execution and debugging.

Optimizing Scripts

Optimizing scripts is crucial, especially when they are part of a larger automation workflow. Here are some tips for optimizing your scripts:

- **Error Handling**: Implement robust error handling to gracefully handle exceptions and failures.

- **Logging**: Use proper logging techniques to capture important information and debug your scripts.

- **Performance**: Profile your scripts to identify performance bottlenecks and optimize them.

- **Testing**: Create unit tests for your scripts to ensure their correctness and reliability.

- **Version Control**: Include your scripts in version control to track changes and collaborate with others effectively.

As you become more proficient in scripting and automation, you'll find that you can save significant time and effort by automating repetitive tasks and creating efficient workflows. In the following sections, we'll explore task runners, custom automation workflows, and how to use Visual Studio Code for DevOps purposes.

Section 16.3: Task Runners and Build Tools

Task runners and build tools play a significant role in automating repetitive tasks and streamlining development workflows in Visual Studio Code. In this section, we'll explore the use of task runners and build tools to automate various processes such as compiling code, running tests, and performing code quality checks.

What Are Task Runners and Build Tools?

Task runners and build tools are utilities that help you automate tasks in your development environment. These tasks can include:

- **Compiling Code**: Transpiling or compiling code from one language to another (e.g., TypeScript to JavaScript, SASS to CSS).

- **Running Tests**: Executing unit tests, integration tests, or end-to-end tests for your application.

- **Linting and Code Formatting**: Enforcing coding style and standards by analyzing and formatting code.

- **Minification and Bundling**: Reducing the size of files (e.g., JavaScript or CSS) for production deployment.

- **Deployment**: Uploading files to a server, deploying to a cloud service, or building distributable packages.

Visual Studio Code provides built-in support for configuring and running tasks, making it a powerful tool for task automation.

Configuring Tasks in Visual Studio Code

You can configure tasks in Visual Studio Code by creating a `tasks.json` file in your workspace. This file defines various tasks and their configurations. To create a `tasks.json` file:

1. Open the command palette by pressing `Ctrl+Shift+P` (Windows/Linux) or `Cmd+Shift+P` (macOS).

2. Type "Tasks: Configure Task" and select it from the list. Choose whether you want to configure tasks for the entire workspace or a specific folder.

3. Select a task template (e.g., "Others") or create a custom task.

4. Customize the task's configuration, including its command, arguments, working directory, and more.

Here's an example of a simple `tasks.json` configuration for compiling TypeScript files:

```json
{
  "version": "2.0.0",
  "tasks": [
    {
      "label": "Compile TypeScript",
      "type": "shell",
      "command": "tsc",
      "args": [],
      "group": {
        "kind": "build",
        "isDefault": true
      }
    }
  ]
}
```

In this example, we define a task named "Compile TypeScript" that runs the TypeScript Compiler (`tsc`) with no additional arguments. We mark it as the default build task.

Running Tasks

Once you've configured tasks, you can run them using the following methods:

- Open the integrated terminal (`View -> Terminal`) and use the `Tasks: Run Task` command to select and run a task.

- Use the shortcut `Ctrl+Shift+B` (Windows/Linux) or `Cmd+Shift+B` (macOS) to run the default build task.

- Access tasks through the command palette (`Ctrl+Shift+P` or `Cmd+Shift+P`) by typing "Tasks: Run Task" and selecting the desired task.

Common Use Cases for Task Runners and Build Tools

Task runners and build tools can address various development needs:

- **Building Web Applications**: Automate the compilation of JavaScript, CSS, and HTML assets, as well as bundling and minification for deployment.

- **Continuous Integration**: Set up tasks to run unit tests, lint code, and build artifacts as part of a CI/CD pipeline.

- **Code Quality Assurance**: Use tasks for code analysis, formatting, and code style enforcement to maintain code quality.

- **Server-Side Development**: Automate tasks like compiling and packaging server code or running server processes.

- **Script Execution**: Create tasks to run custom scripts for data processing, automation, or DevOps workflows.

In the next section, we'll explore custom automation workflows in more detail, showing how you can orchestrate multiple tasks to create complex automation scenarios.

Section 16.4: Custom Automation Workflows

In Visual Studio Code, you can create custom automation workflows by orchestrating multiple tasks and build tools. These workflows enable you to automate complex processes and streamline your development tasks. In this section, we'll explore how to build custom automation workflows using tasks, extensions, and scripts.

Defining Custom Workflows

Custom automation workflows are designed to address specific development needs. These can include:

- **Building and Deploying Applications**: Automate the build process, run tests, and deploy to various environments, such as development, staging, and production.

- **Continuous Integration (CI)**: Set up a CI pipeline with tasks for building, testing, and deploying your code whenever changes are pushed to a repository.

- **Code Quality Checks**: Run code analysis, linting, and code formatting tasks to ensure code quality and consistency.

- **Complex Script Execution**: Automate data processing, database migrations, or other custom scripts as part of your development workflow.

To create these workflows, you can utilize the following components:

1. Tasks: Use the built-in task runner to define and run tasks for various actions, such as compiling code, running tests, and deploying applications. Tasks are configured in the tasks.json file.

2. Extensions: Visual Studio Code has a rich ecosystem of extensions that can be integrated into your automation workflows. Extensions can provide additional functionality and customization options.

3. Scripts: Incorporate custom scripts (e.g., shell scripts, PowerShell scripts, or Node.js scripts) into your automation workflows. These scripts can execute specific tasks or perform advanced operations.

Example Custom Workflow

Let's consider an example custom workflow for a web application development project. The workflow involves building a web application, running tests, and deploying it to a development server:

1. **Task Configuration**: Create tasks in the `tasks.json` file to define the following actions:

    -   Building the application using a task runner like Webpack or Gulp.
    -   Running unit tests using a testing framework like Jest or Mocha.
    -   Deploying the application to a development server using a deployment script.

2. **Extensions**: Install extensions that enhance the workflow, such as the "Live Server" extension for launching a local development server or the "Deploy" extension for streamlined deployment.

3. **Script Integration**: Use custom scripts to automate tasks like starting the development server, performing database migrations, or sending notifications.

4. **Orchestration**: Combine these tasks and scripts in a sequence to create the complete workflow. For example:

    -   First, build the application.
    -   Second, run unit tests to ensure code quality.
    -   Finally, deploy the application to the development server.

5. **Execution**: Trigger the workflow using Visual Studio Code's task runner, the integrated terminal, or even external CI/CD systems.

Custom automation workflows allow you to save time, reduce manual errors, and ensure consistency in your development processes. By tailoring your workflows to your project's specific requirements, you can optimize your development experience in Visual Studio Code.

In the next section, we'll explore the use of Visual Studio Code for DevOps, where you can integrate development and operations tasks to streamline your software delivery pipeline.

Section 16.5: Using Visual Studio Code for DevOps

Visual Studio Code (VS Code) is not just a code editor; it can also be a powerful tool for DevOps, enabling you to integrate development and operations tasks seamlessly. In this section, we'll explore how you can leverage VS Code for various aspects of DevOps, from source control and automation to continuous integration and delivery (CI/CD).

Source Control Integration

One of the fundamental aspects of DevOps is source control management, and VS Code offers excellent integration with popular version control systems like Git. You can perform the following DevOps-related tasks within VS Code:

- **Cloning Repositories**: Use VS Code to clone Git repositories and start working on code.

- **Branch Management**: Create, switch between, and merge branches directly within the editor.

- **Commit and Push**: Stage changes, commit them, and push to remote repositories, making it easy to collaborate with your team.

- **Resolve Conflicts**: VS Code provides a user-friendly interface for resolving merge conflicts.

Task Automation

VS Code's task runner allows you to automate various tasks related to your DevOps workflow. You can define tasks in the `tasks.json` file and execute them effortlessly. Here are some examples:

- **Build Automation**: Define tasks for building your application, running tests, and creating deployable artifacts.

- **Script Execution**: Automate scripts for tasks like database migrations, environment setup, or deployment.

- **CI/CD Pipelines**: Integrate your DevOps pipeline by defining CI/CD tasks and scripts.

Continuous Integration and Delivery (CI/CD)

You can set up CI/CD pipelines in VS Code using extensions or by integrating with popular CI/CD platforms. Here's how:

- **Extensions**: Install CI/CD extensions like Azure Pipelines or GitHub Actions to create and manage your pipelines directly within VS Code.

- **Configuration Files**: Define CI/CD pipeline configurations using YAML or JSON files that are recognized by your chosen CI/CD platform. You can edit these files in VS Code.

- **Pipeline Execution**: Trigger pipeline runs, monitor progress, and view build and deployment logs without leaving the editor.

Containerization and Docker

If your DevOps workflow involves containerization using Docker, VS Code offers seamless integration:

- **Docker Extension**: Install the Docker extension to manage Docker containers, images, and Docker Compose files.

- **Dockerfile Support**: Write and edit Dockerfiles with syntax highlighting and validation.

- **Container Debugging**: Debug applications running in Docker containers directly from VS Code.

Infrastructure as Code (IaC)

For managing infrastructure as code (IaC), VS Code supports various IaC tools like Terraform, AWS CloudFormation, and Azure Resource Manager templates. You can:

- Write, edit, and validate IaC templates with the help of extensions.
- Use source control for versioning your IaC code.
- Collaborate with team members on IaC development.

Monitoring and Logging

Although VS Code is primarily a code editor, you can integrate it with monitoring and logging tools through extensions and scripts. This allows you to:

- Monitor application performance and logs.
- Set up alerts and notifications.
- Access monitoring dashboards and metrics.

Collaboration and Communication

Collaboration is a key aspect of DevOps, and VS Code provides tools to facilitate collaboration:

- **Live Share**: Collaborate with team members in real-time, share your development environment, and work together on code, debugging, and troubleshooting.

- **Chat Extensions**: Integrate chat and communication tools like Slack, Microsoft Teams, or Discord using extensions to keep your team informed and connected.

In summary, Visual Studio Code can be a central hub for your DevOps activities, offering source control integration, task automation, CI/CD support, containerization, IaC, monitoring, collaboration, and communication capabilities. By leveraging its extensibility and integrations, you can streamline and optimize your DevOps workflows, making them more efficient and productive.

Section 17.1: Setting Up for Data Science Workflows

Data science is a rapidly growing field that leverages data to extract valuable insights and make informed decisions. Visual Studio Code (VS Code) can serve as an excellent platform for data science workflows, providing a versatile environment for data analysis, modeling, and visualization. In this section, we will explore how to set up VS Code for data science tasks and introduce key extensions and configurations.

1. Installing Python and Anaconda

Python is one of the most popular programming languages for data science, and Anaconda is a widely used distribution that simplifies package management and environment creation. To get started with data science in VS Code:

- Install Python: Download and install Python from the official website (https://www.python.org/downloads/).

- Install Anaconda: Optionally, you can install Anaconda, which includes Python and popular data science packages like NumPy, Pandas, Matplotlib, and more. Visit the Anaconda website (https://www.anaconda.com/products/individual) to download and install Anaconda.

2. Installing VS Code and Python Extensions

Next, you'll need to install Visual Studio Code if you haven't already. Once VS Code is installed, you can enhance it with data science-related extensions:

- Install VS Code: Download and install Visual Studio Code from the official website (https://code.visualstudio.com/).

- Install Python Extension: In VS Code, go to the Extensions view (Ctrl+Shift+X), search for "Python," and install the Python extension provided by Microsoft. This extension provides code linting, debugging, and Jupyter Notebook support.

- Install Jupyter Extension: If you plan to use Jupyter Notebooks for interactive data analysis, install the "Jupyter" extension in VS Code.

3. Creating a Python Environment

It's good practice to create a separate Python environment for your data science projects. Anaconda makes this process straightforward:

- Open Anaconda Navigator (if installed) or use the Anaconda command-line interface (CLI) to create a new environment. For example, you can create an environment named "datascience" by running:

```
conda create --name datascience python=3.8
```

- Activate the environment:

```
conda activate datascience
```

194

4. Managing Packages

With your environment activated, you can install additional Python packages for data science using conda or pip. For example, you can install popular data science libraries like NumPy, Pandas, and Matplotlib:

```
conda install numpy pandas matplotlib
```

5. Jupyter Notebooks

Jupyter Notebooks provide an interactive and visual environment for data exploration and analysis. You can create and open Jupyter Notebooks in VS Code with the installed Jupyter extension.

- Launch a Jupyter Notebook in VS Code by clicking the "New Jupyter Notebook" button or opening an existing .ipynb file.

- Use Markdown cells for documentation and code cells for data analysis and visualization. Execute cells one at a time to see immediate results.

6. Data Visualization

VS Code supports various data visualization libraries like Matplotlib and Plotly. You can create and customize plots within Jupyter Notebooks or directly in Python scripts.

7. Data Science Extensions

Explore other VS Code extensions tailored for data science, such as the "Pandas" extension for exploring and visualizing Pandas DataFrames or the "Data Preview" extension for previewing data files.

By following these steps and configurations, you can set up Visual Studio Code as a powerful environment for data science workflows. Whether you're analyzing data, building machine learning models, or creating data visualizations, VS Code offers a flexible and integrated platform to streamline your data science projects.

Section 17.2: Python and R Integration

Data science often involves working with multiple programming languages, depending on the specific requirements of the task. In addition to Python, R is another popular language for statistical analysis and data visualization. Visual Studio Code (VS Code) supports both Python and R seamlessly, making it a versatile choice for data scientists who need to work with multiple languages within a single environment. In this section, we'll explore how to set up and use Python and R in VS Code for data science tasks.

1. Python Integration

Visual Studio Code offers robust support for Python, making it an excellent choice for Python-based data science tasks. Here's how to set up Python integration in VS Code:

- Install Python: Ensure that you have Python installed on your system. You can download Python from the official website (https://www.python.org/downloads/).

- Install Python Extension: In VS Code, navigate to the Extensions view (Ctrl+Shift+X), search for "Python," and install the Python extension provided by Microsoft. This extension provides code linting, debugging, and Jupyter Notebook support for Python.

- Create Python Environments: You can create isolated Python environments using tools like virtualenv or conda. VS Code allows you to select a specific Python interpreter for your project, ensuring compatibility and dependency management.

- Jupyter Notebook Support: VS Code's Python extension seamlessly integrates with Jupyter Notebooks. You can create, edit, and run Jupyter Notebooks directly within the VS Code interface.

- Code Editing: VS Code offers features like code completion, syntax highlighting, and code formatting for Python. It also supports popular Python libraries used in data science, such as NumPy, Pandas, and Matplotlib.

2. R Integration

Visual Studio Code also provides support for the R programming language. Here's how to set up R integration in VS Code:

- Install R: Ensure that you have R installed on your system. You can download R from the official website (https://cran.r-project.org/).

- Install R Extension: In VS Code, navigate to the Extensions view (Ctrl+Shift+X), search for "R Language," and install the "R Language" extension. This extension provides R-specific features and support.

- R Interactive Console: You can open an R interactive console within VS Code, allowing you to execute R code and see the results in real-time.

- R Markdown Support: VS Code provides excellent support for R Markdown documents, allowing you to create documents that combine narrative text, R code, and visualizations. You can render R Markdown documents to various formats, such as HTML or PDF.

- Code Editing: VS Code offers code editing features for R, including syntax highlighting, code completion, and code formatting.

3. Combining Python and R

One of the strengths of using VS Code for data science is the ability to seamlessly combine Python and R in your projects. You can create Jupyter Notebooks that contain both Python and R code cells, allowing you to leverage the strengths of both languages within a single document. This is particularly useful when you want to use specific R packages or libraries alongside your Python analysis.

In conclusion, Visual Studio Code provides excellent support for both Python and R, making it a versatile choice for data scientists who need to work with multiple languages. Whether you're analyzing data with Python's Pandas, creating interactive visualizations with R, or combining both languages in your data science workflows, VS Code offers a flexible and integrated environment.

Section 17.3: Working with Jupyter Notebooks

Jupyter Notebooks have become an integral part of data science and machine learning workflows due to their interactive and collaborative nature. Visual Studio Code (VS Code) provides excellent support for working with Jupyter Notebooks, making it a powerful tool for data scientists and analysts. In this section, we'll explore how to create, edit, and run Jupyter Notebooks within the VS Code environment.

1. Installing Jupyter

Before working with Jupyter Notebooks in VS Code, you need to ensure that Jupyter is installed on your system. You can install Jupyter using Python's package manager, pip, by running the following command in your terminal:

```
pip install jupyter
```

2. Creating a New Jupyter Notebook

In VS Code, you can create a new Jupyter Notebook by following these steps:

- Open VS Code and select the Python interpreter you want to use for your notebook.

- Click on the "New File" icon in the upper-left corner of the editor.

- Type the file name with the ".ipynb" extension (e.g., "my_notebook.ipynb") and press Enter. VS Code recognizes the ".ipynb" extension and creates a new Jupyter Notebook file.

- You'll see a new tab with your Jupyter Notebook. You can start adding cells for code, text, or visualizations.

3. Working with Cells

Jupyter Notebooks are organized into cells, which can contain code or Markdown text. Here's how you can work with cells in VS Code:

- Adding Cells: To add a new cell, click the "+" button that appears when you hover between cells. You can choose to add a code cell or a Markdown cell.

- Editing Cells: Double-click on a cell to edit its content. For code cells, you can write Python or R code, and for Markdown cells, you can add formatted text, headings, and images.

- Running Cells: To execute a code cell, select it and click the "Run Cell" button (►□) that appears in the cell's top-left corner. You can also use the keyboard shortcut Shift+Enter.

- Cell Types: You can change a cell's type to either code or Markdown using the dropdown menu in the toolbar.

4. Code Execution

When working with code cells, VS Code provides features like code completion, syntax highlighting, and inline code execution. It also displays the output of code cells directly below them, making it easy to view results and visualizations.

5. Markdown Support

For Markdown cells, you can create rich text documents with headings, lists, tables, and images. VS Code offers a preview mode that allows you to see how your Markdown will be rendered as you work on it.

6. Kernel Selection

You can switch between different Python or R kernels if you have multiple language environments installed. This allows you to work with different versions or packages of Python or R within the same notebook.

7. Saving and Sharing Notebooks

VS Code allows you to save your Jupyter Notebooks like regular files. You can also export notebooks to various formats, including HTML or PDF, for sharing with others.

8. Jupyter Extensions

VS Code supports Jupyter extensions, which can enhance your notebook experience by providing additional functionality and visualizations.

In summary, Visual Studio Code provides robust support for Jupyter Notebooks, making it a versatile tool for data scientists and analysts. You can create, edit, and run notebooks with ease, combining code, text, and visualizations in an interactive and collaborative environment. This integration streamlines the data science workflow and enhances the productivity of professionals working with Jupyter Notebooks.

Section 17.4: Visualization Tools and Libraries

Data visualization is a crucial aspect of data science and machine learning. Visualizing data helps in understanding patterns, trends, and insights that might not be apparent from raw data alone. Visual Studio Code (VS Code) provides support for various data visualization tools and libraries, allowing data scientists to create informative and visually appealing plots and charts directly within their development environment.

Here, we'll explore some of the popular data visualization libraries and tools that you can seamlessly integrate into VS Code for your data science projects.

1. Matplotlib

Matplotlib is one of the most widely used Python libraries for creating static, animated, and interactive plots. You can easily use Matplotlib within VS Code to generate a wide range of visualizations, from simple line plots to complex heatmaps.

To get started with Matplotlib in VS Code, you need to have it installed. You can install it using pip:

```
pip install matplotlib
```

Once installed, you can import Matplotlib and start creating visualizations in your Python scripts or Jupyter Notebooks within VS Code. Here's a basic example of creating a line plot using Matplotlib:

```python
import matplotlib.pyplot as plt

# Sample data
x = [1, 2, 3, 4, 5]
y = [10, 15, 13, 18, 20]

# Create a line plot
plt.plot(x, y)

# Add labels and a title
plt.xlabel('X-axis')
plt.ylabel('Y-axis')
plt.title('Sample Line Plot')

# Display the plot
plt.show()
```

2. Seaborn

Seaborn is built on top of Matplotlib and provides a high-level interface for creating attractive and informative statistical graphics. It simplifies the process of creating complex visualizations and comes with built-in themes and color palettes.

You can install Seaborn using pip:

```
pip install seaborn
```

Once installed, you can import Seaborn and start using its functions to create various types of plots. For example, you can create a histogram with Seaborn like this:

```python
import seaborn as sns

# Sample data
data = [10, 15, 13, 18, 20, 12, 17, 14, 16, 19]

# Create a histogram
sns.histplot(data, bins=5, kde=True)

# Add labels and a title
plt.xlabel('Value')
plt.ylabel('Frequency')
plt.title('Histogram with KDE')

# Display the plot
plt.show()
```

3. Plotly

Plotly is a versatile library for creating interactive and web-based visualizations. It supports a wide range of chart types, and you can use it to create interactive dashboards and reports.

To use Plotly in VS Code, you need to install the Plotly library:

```
pip install plotly
```

Here's a simple example of creating a scatter plot with Plotly:

```python
import plotly.express as px

# Sample data
data = {'X': [1, 2, 3, 4, 5], 'Y': [10, 15, 13, 18, 20]}

# Create a scatter plot
fig = px.scatter(data, x='X', y='Y', title='Sample Scatter Plot')

# Show the plot
fig.show()
```

4. Interactive Widgets

VS Code also supports interactive widgets through Jupyter Notebooks. You can use libraries like ipywidgets to create interactive elements such as sliders, buttons, and dropdowns to enhance your data visualizations and allow for user interaction within your notebooks.

In conclusion, Visual Studio Code offers excellent support for various data visualization libraries and tools, enabling data scientists to create insightful and visually appealing plots and charts. Whether you prefer Matplotlib for traditional plots, Seaborn for statistical graphics, Plotly for interactive visualizations, or interactive widgets for Jupyter Notebooks, VS Code provides a versatile environment for all your data visualization needs.

Section 17.5: Machine Learning Model Development

Machine learning (ML) has become a fundamental part of data science and software development. Visual Studio Code (VS Code) offers a robust ecosystem for developing, training, and deploying machine learning models efficiently. In this section, we'll explore the tools, libraries, and workflows that make ML model development seamless within the VS Code environment.

Setting Up Your ML Environment

Before diving into ML model development, you need to set up your development environment. VS Code simplifies this process with its support for various ML frameworks, including TensorFlow, PyTorch, and scikit-learn. You can set up your environment using virtual environments or containers, ensuring that your dependencies are isolated and manageable.

Here's an example of setting up a Python virtual environment for ML development:

```
# Create a new Python virtual environment
python -m venv my_ml_env

# Activate the virtual environment
source my_ml_env/bin/activate   # On Windows: my_ml_env\Scripts\activate

# Install required packages
pip install tensorflow scikit-learn
```

Exploratory Data Analysis (EDA)

EDA is a crucial step in ML model development, and VS Code provides a range of extensions and tools for data exploration. Jupyter Notebooks, integrated directly into VS Code, are ideal for conducting EDA. You can visualize data, generate summary statistics, and explore correlations within your dataset.

```
# Example of EDA in a Jupyter Notebook cell
import pandas as pd
import seaborn as sns
import matplotlib.pyplot as plt

# Load your dataset
```

```python
df = pd.read_csv('data.csv')

# Generate a pair plot to explore relationships
sns.pairplot(df, hue='target_variable')
plt.show()
```

Model Development and Training

VS Code's support for ML libraries like TensorFlow and PyTorch simplifies model development. You can create, train, and evaluate ML models using these frameworks directly within your code files or Jupyter Notebooks. Code completion and intelligent suggestions enhance your productivity during this phase.

Here's a simple example of building a neural network with TensorFlow in VS Code:

```python
import tensorflow as tf
from tensorflow import keras

# Define a sequential model
model = keras.Sequential([
    keras.layers.Flatten(input_shape=(28, 28)),
    keras.layers.Dense(128, activation='relu'),
    keras.layers.Dropout(0.2),
    keras.layers.Dense(10)
])

# Compile the model
model.compile(optimizer='adam',
              loss=tf.losses.SparseCategoricalCrossentropy(from_logits=True),
              metrics=['accuracy'])

# Train the model
model.fit(train_images, train_labels, epochs=10)
```

Model Evaluation and Hyperparameter Tuning

VS Code's integrated debugging and variable inspection tools are invaluable for model evaluation and hyperparameter tuning. You can monitor metrics, visualize training progress, and make necessary adjustments to optimize your models.

```python
# Evaluate the model
test_loss, test_acc = model.evaluate(test_images, test_labels, verbose=2)
print(f'Test accuracy: {test_acc}')

# Perform hyperparameter tuning
# Adjust model architecture, learning rate, batch size, etc.
```

Model Deployment and Serving

Once you've trained and fine-tuned your ML model, VS Code allows for seamless model deployment. You can deploy models as REST APIs, Docker containers, or cloud services. Extensions and integrations with platforms like Azure ML and AWS SageMaker simplify the deployment process.

```python
# Example of serving a model with Flask in VS Code
from flask import Flask, request, jsonify
import tensorflow as tf

app = Flask(__name__)

# Load the pre-trained model
model = tf.keras.models.load_model('my_model.h5')

@app.route('/predict', methods=['POST'])
def predict():
    data = request.json
    prediction = model.predict(data['input'])
    return jsonify({'prediction': prediction.tolist()})

if __name__ == '__main__':
    app.run(debug=True)
```

In conclusion, Visual Studio Code provides a comprehensive environment for machine learning model development, from setting up your ML environment to EDA, model development, evaluation, tuning, and deployment. Its integration with popular ML libraries and tools, combined with features like Jupyter Notebooks and debugging, makes it a powerful choice for data scientists and machine learning practitioners.

Chapter 18: Security and Version Control

Section 18.1: Ensuring Code Security

Code security is a critical aspect of software development, and Visual Studio Code (VS Code) provides several features and extensions to help you write secure code. In this section, we'll explore various practices, tools, and extensions to ensure the security of your codebase.

Code Analysis and Linting

One of the first steps in code security is ensuring that your code adheres to best practices and coding standards. VS Code supports numerous extensions for code analysis and linting. For example, the ESLint extension for JavaScript and TypeScript or the Pylint extension for Python can automatically identify and highlight potential security vulnerabilities and coding errors in your code.

Static Code Analysis

Static code analysis tools can scan your codebase for security vulnerabilities, such as common programming mistakes, insecure configurations, or potential code injection points. Extensions like SonarLint for VS Code can provide real-time feedback on security issues as you write code.

Dependency Scanning

Managing dependencies is a crucial part of code security. Vulnerabilities in third-party libraries can expose your application to various risks. Tools like the "npm Security" extension for JavaScript or the "safety" extension for Python can help you identify known security vulnerabilities in your project's dependencies and suggest updates.

Code Reviews and Collaboration

Collaboration and code reviews are essential for security. VS Code offers extensions like GitHub Pull Requests and Azure DevOps for seamless collaboration with your team. During code reviews, team members can identify security issues and suggest improvements to ensure secure coding practices.

Secure Coding Guidelines

Adhering to secure coding guidelines is vital for minimizing security risks. VS Code allows you to integrate coding guidelines and security best practices directly into your development process. You can create custom code snippets, templates, and documentation to help developers follow secure coding practices consistently.

Security Testing and Vulnerability Scanning

In addition to static analysis, security testing is essential to identify runtime vulnerabilities. VS Code can be integrated with security testing tools and frameworks. For web applications, you can use extensions like OWASP ZAP for automated security scanning during development.

Encryption and Authentication

VS Code provides extensions for handling encryption and authentication. You can find extensions for managing secrets, certificates, and cryptographic operations securely. These extensions help you implement secure authentication and data encryption in your applications.

Compliance and Security Standards

Many industries and organizations have specific security standards and compliance requirements. VS Code can be configured to support these standards. Extensions like the "OWASP Cheat Sheet Series" provide quick references for secure coding practices in various languages and frameworks.

Continuous Security Monitoring

Security is an ongoing process. VS Code can be integrated with continuous security monitoring tools and platforms to ensure that your code remains secure throughout its lifecycle. These tools can automatically detect and respond to security threats and vulnerabilities.

In conclusion, Visual Studio Code offers a range of features, extensions, and integrations that help you ensure the security of your codebase. By following secure coding practices, conducting thorough code reviews, and leveraging security-focused extensions and tools, you can significantly reduce the risk of security vulnerabilities in your software projects.

Section 18.2: Managing Dependencies and Security Updates

Managing dependencies is a crucial aspect of code security. Dependencies are third-party libraries or modules that your application relies on to function correctly. These dependencies can introduce security vulnerabilities, and it's essential to keep them up to date to mitigate potential risks.

Dependency Management Tools

Visual Studio Code (VS Code) integrates with various dependency management tools and extensions to help you manage your project's dependencies efficiently. One of the most popular tools is the Node Package Manager (npm) for JavaScript and Node.js projects. You can use the integrated terminal in VS Code to run npm commands, such as installing, updating, or removing dependencies.

For Python projects, you can use pip, the Python package manager, to manage dependencies. VS Code also supports the integrated terminal for running pip commands.

Dependency Scanning Extensions

To enhance your dependency management and security, you can install extensions that provide dependency scanning capabilities. These extensions can identify known vulnerabilities in your project's dependencies and suggest updates.

For JavaScript and npm projects, the "npm Security" extension is a valuable tool. It can analyze your project's dependencies and display any known security issues. The extension can also recommend updates to resolve these vulnerabilities.

For Python projects, the "safety" extension is a helpful choice. It integrates with the Safety CLI, which scans your Python requirements files and informs you of any security vulnerabilities found in your project's dependencies.

Automating Dependency Updates

Keeping dependencies up to date can be time-consuming, especially in projects with numerous dependencies. VS Code offers extensions like "npm Outdated" and "Python: Update All Dependencies" that automate the process of checking for and applying updates to your dependencies.

These extensions provide a convenient way to review the current versions of your dependencies and update them to the latest compatible versions. This helps ensure that you're using the most secure versions of third-party libraries.

Security Notifications

VS Code can be configured to provide notifications about security updates for your dependencies. These notifications can alert you when new versions of your project's dependencies are available, along with information about the security vulnerabilities they address.

Extensions like "Version Lens" for npm and "Python: Update All Dependencies" for Python can help you stay informed about security updates. By keeping your dependencies current, you reduce the risk of security vulnerabilities in your codebase.

Security Best Practices

In addition to keeping dependencies up to date, following security best practices when selecting and using third-party libraries is essential. Before adding a new dependency to your project, consider the following:

1. **Popularity**: Choose well-maintained and widely used libraries with an active developer community. Popular libraries are more likely to receive prompt security updates.

2. **Security Reviews**: Check if the library has undergone security reviews or audits. Many open-source projects publish security reports or have dedicated security teams.

3. **Version History**: Investigate the library's version history and release notes. Look for any security-related fixes or updates in recent versions.

4. **License**: Ensure that the library's license is compatible with your project's requirements and that it doesn't introduce legal issues.

5. **Documentation**: Review the library's documentation and usage examples to ensure that it meets your project's needs and follows secure coding practices.

6. **Community Support**: Check if the library has an active and responsive community that can help with issues and security concerns.

By following these practices and using the tools and extensions available in VS Code, you can effectively manage your project's dependencies, stay informed about security updates, and reduce the risk of security vulnerabilities in your code.

Section 18.3: Working with Version Control Systems

Version control systems (VCS) play a fundamental role in managing and tracking changes to your codebase. They enable collaboration, provide a history of changes, and offer a safety net for your project. Visual Studio Code (VS Code) seamlessly integrates with various VCS tools, making it easy to work with Git, Subversion, and other popular version control systems. This section explores how to effectively use VCS within VS Code.

Initializing a Repository

To start using version control in your project, you first need to initialize a repository. If you're using Git, navigate to your project's root directory in the integrated terminal and run the following command:

```
git init
```

This command initializes a new Git repository, creating a hidden `.git` directory where Git stores metadata about your project's history.

Cloning a Repository

If you're collaborating on an existing project hosted on a remote repository (e.g., GitHub, GitLab, or Bitbucket), you can clone it into your local workspace using VS Code. Open VS Code and follow these steps:

1. Click on the "Source Control" icon in the left sidebar (it looks like a branch).
2. Click the "Clone Repository" button.
3. Enter the URL of the remote repository.
4. Choose a local directory where you want to clone the repository.
5. Click "Clone."

VS Code will automatically clone the repository, and you'll have access to the project's history and branches.

Tracking Changes

Once your repository is initialized or cloned, you can start tracking changes to your code. VS Code provides a user-friendly interface for staging, committing, and viewing changes. Here's a typical workflow:

1. Make changes to your code files.
2. Open the Source Control view.
3. You'll see a list of modified files. Click the "+" icon next to a file to stage it for commit.
4. Enter a commit message describing your changes.
5. Click the checkmark icon to commit the changes.

Branching and Merging

Branching is a powerful feature that allows you to work on new features or bug fixes without affecting the main codebase. You can create branches in VS Code and switch between them seamlessly.

1. Open the Source Control view.
2. Click the "Create a new branch" button.
3. Enter a branch name and choose the base branch (usually "main" or "master").
4. Click "Create Branch."

You can now make changes on the new branch. To merge changes back into the main branch, follow these steps:

1. Switch to the main branch.
2. Open the Source Control view.
3. Click the "..." (ellipsis) menu and select "Merge Branch."
4. Choose the branch you want to merge and confirm.

Resolving Merge Conflicts

In collaborative environments, conflicts may arise when multiple contributors modify the same code. VS Code provides excellent support for resolving merge conflicts. When a conflict occurs, follow these steps:

1. Open the file with conflicts.
2. VS Code displays conflict markers (<<<<<<<, =======, and >>>>>>>) where conflicts exist.
3. Manually edit the file to resolve conflicts.
4. Save the file.

VS Code will automatically detect the conflict resolution and allow you to commit the resolved file.

Working with Remote Repositories

VS Code allows you to interact with remote repositories directly from the editor. You can push your changes to a remote repository, pull changes from it, and even create and manage pull requests on platforms like GitHub, GitLab, or Bitbucket.

To push your changes to a remote repository, use the "Publish" action in the Source Control view. To pull changes, use the "Pull" action. For creating pull requests, extensions like "GitHub Pull Requests" make the process seamless.

Commit History and Diffs

VS Code provides a powerful commit history view that lets you explore the history of your project. You can view commit messages, authors, and changes introduced in each commit. Additionally, you can compare file differences between commits to understand code changes.

VCS Extensions

VS Code's extensibility allows you to enhance your version control workflow further. Various VCS-specific extensions are available, offering advanced features and integrations with popular VCS providers.

In conclusion, working with version control systems in Visual Studio Code is a streamlined process. Whether you're using Git, Subversion, or another VCS, VS Code provides a feature-rich environment for tracking changes, collaborating with others, and managing your codebase effectively.

Section 18.4: Best Practices for Secure Coding

Security is a critical aspect of software development, and writing secure code should be a priority for every developer. Visual Studio Code (VS Code) provides a conducive environment for implementing best practices for secure coding. In this section, we'll explore some essential security guidelines to follow while using VS Code.

1. Keep Software Up-to-Date

VS Code itself, as well as its extensions and plugins, regularly receive updates that may include security patches. It's essential to keep both VS Code and your extensions up-to-date to ensure you're protected against known vulnerabilities.

You can easily check for updates in VS Code by clicking on the gear icon in the bottom-left corner and selecting "Check for Updates."

2. Use Secure Extensions

When installing extensions, make sure they come from reputable sources. Extensions with a significant user base and regular updates are more likely to be secure. Always read reviews and check for any security-related issues in the extension's repository or issue tracker.

3. Configure Security Settings

VS Code allows you to customize its settings, including security-related configurations. Consider configuring settings that enhance your code's security, such as enabling automatic code formatting and linting to catch potential security issues early.

4. Secure Your Development Environment

Ensure that your development environment is secure. This includes keeping your operating system, web browsers, and other development tools up-to-date with the latest security patches.

5. Avoid Storing Sensitive Data

Never store sensitive data, such as API keys, passwords, or encryption keys, directly in your code files. Use environment variables or a secure secrets management system to store and retrieve sensitive information.

6. Implement Proper Authentication and Authorization

When developing web applications, ensure that proper authentication and authorization mechanisms are in place. Use libraries and frameworks that have built-in security features to prevent common vulnerabilities like SQL injection and cross-site scripting (XSS) attacks.

7. Regularly Test for Vulnerabilities

Perform regular security testing, including code reviews, penetration testing, and vulnerability scanning, to identify and mitigate potential security weaknesses in your codebase.

8. Follow the Principle of Least Privilege

Grant the minimum required permissions to users, processes, and components in your application. Avoid using elevated privileges unnecessarily, as it can increase the attack surface.

9. Encrypt Data in Transit and at Rest

When dealing with sensitive data, ensure that it is encrypted both in transit and at rest. Use secure communication protocols (e.g., HTTPS) for transmitting data over networks and encrypt data stored on disk or in databases.

10. Handle Errors Securely

Avoid revealing sensitive information in error messages presented to users. Customize error messages to be generic and avoid leaking details about the application's internal structure.

11. Keep an Eye on Security Advisories

Stay informed about security advisories and vulnerabilities related to the programming languages, libraries, and frameworks you use. Subscribe to security mailing lists and regularly check for updates and patches.

12. Educate Your Development Team

Security is a team effort. Ensure that your development team is aware of security best practices and provides training and resources to help them write secure code.

By following these best practices for secure coding in Visual Studio Code, you can significantly reduce the risk of security vulnerabilities and protect your applications and data from potential threats. Security should be an integral part of your development process, and VS Code provides the tools and flexibility to support your security efforts effectively.

Section 18.5: Handling Sensitive Data and Credentials

Handling sensitive data and credentials is a crucial aspect of secure coding and application development. In this section, we will discuss best practices for managing sensitive information within your Visual Studio Code projects.

1. Use Environment Variables

One of the fundamental principles of secure coding is to avoid hardcoding sensitive data, such as API keys, passwords, or access tokens, directly into your source code. Instead, rely on environment variables to store and retrieve these sensitive values.

VS Code allows you to set environment variables in various ways. You can define them in your system environment variables or use extensions like "dotenv" to load environment variables from a .env file within your project.

```
# .env file
SECRET_KEY=mysecretkey
API_KEY=yourapikey
```

In your code, access these variables as follows:

```
const secretKey = process.env.SECRET_KEY;
const apiKey = process.env.API_KEY;
```

2. Use a Secrets Manager

For more advanced scenarios and when working on larger projects, consider using a secrets manager or a dedicated secrets management service. Services like AWS Secrets Manager, HashiCorp Vault, or Azure Key Vault provide a secure way to store and retrieve sensitive information.

These services often provide features like automatic rotation of credentials and fine-grained access control, enhancing the overall security of your application.

3. Secure Credential Storage

If your application requires storing user credentials, use secure storage mechanisms provided by your platform or framework. Avoid storing plain text passwords and consider using hashing algorithms (e.g., bcrypt) to securely store and validate passwords.

4. Encrypt Sensitive Data

When transmitting sensitive data over networks or storing it in databases, use encryption to protect the data both in transit and at rest. HTTPS should be used for web applications to encrypt data transmitted between the client and the server. For data at rest, consider encrypting data within your database.

5. Implement Access Controls

Implement proper access controls and authorization mechanisms to ensure that only authorized users and components can access sensitive data. Use role-based access control (RBAC) or similar strategies to manage permissions effectively.

6. Audit and Monitor Access

Implement logging and monitoring to track access to sensitive data. In case of a security breach or unauthorized access, having detailed logs can help identify the source and scope of the incident.

7. Regularly Rotate Credentials

Rotate sensitive credentials, such as API keys and access tokens, on a regular basis. Many third-party services and identity providers offer automated credential rotation features. This practice reduces the risk associated with long-lived credentials.

8. Educate Your Team

Security is a shared responsibility, and all team members should be aware of the importance of handling sensitive data securely. Provide training and guidelines on secure coding practices, and conduct regular security assessments of your codebase.

9. Use Encryption Libraries

When working with encryption and decryption, rely on established encryption libraries and algorithms provided by your programming language or framework. Avoid implementing encryption from scratch, as it can introduce vulnerabilities.

Handling sensitive data and credentials in your Visual Studio Code projects requires careful consideration and adherence to best practices. By using environment variables, secrets managers, encryption, access controls, and proper education, you can significantly reduce the risk of security breaches and protect sensitive information in your applications. Always stay updated on the latest security threats and mitigation strategies to maintain the highest level of security in your projects.

Chapter 19: Tailoring Visual Studio Code for Enterprise Use

In this chapter, we will explore strategies and best practices for tailoring Visual Studio Code (VS Code) for enterprise-level usage. Large organizations have unique requirements and challenges when it comes to code development and management, and VS Code can be customized and scaled to meet these demands effectively.

Section 19.1: Large-Scale Deployment Strategies

Large enterprises often deal with the deployment of software tools at a scale that demands careful planning and execution. Deploying VS Code across numerous development teams and ensuring consistency can be a complex task. Here are some strategies to consider:

1. **Standardized Installation Packages:** Create standardized installation packages for VS Code tailored to your organization's requirements. This ensures that every

developer has the same set of extensions, settings, and configurations, providing consistency in the development environment.

2. **Automated Deployment:** Implement automated deployment mechanisms, such as configuration management tools like Ansible, Puppet, or Chef, to distribute and update VS Code installations across your organization. This reduces manual intervention and minimizes configuration drift.

3. **Centralized Extension Management:** Use tools like Visual Studio Code's "Visual Studio Code Extensions" extension or private extension registries to centrally manage and distribute custom extensions and packages to your development teams. This allows you to maintain control over the extensions used within your organization.

4. **User Profiles and Workspaces:** Define standard user profiles and workspaces that align with your organization's development practices. Provide templates for different types of projects and encourage developers to use them, ensuring consistency and compliance with coding standards.

5. **Configuration as Code:** Store VS Code settings, extensions, and configurations as code in version control systems like Git. This allows you to version and track changes to development environments, making it easier to manage configurations at scale.

6. **User Training and Onboarding:** Develop training programs and documentation to onboard new developers and educate existing ones about best practices and standard workflows with VS Code. This ensures that everyone in your organization is aware of the prescribed processes and tools.

7. **Feedback Mechanism:** Establish a feedback mechanism for developers to report issues, suggest improvements, and request new features related to VS Code customizations. Act on this feedback to continually refine and enhance the development environment.

8. **Scalable Licensing:** Ensure that your organization has proper licensing agreements in place for VS Code, especially if you are using the Visual Studio Code - Insiders edition or extensions that require licensing. Track and manage licenses centrally to remain compliant.

9. **Integration with Existing Tools:** Integrate VS Code seamlessly with your existing development, CI/CD, and collaboration tools. This may involve connecting with issue trackers, build systems, and code repositories to create a unified development ecosystem.

10. **Security and Compliance:** Implement security measures and compliance checks to safeguard sensitive data and ensure that your customized VS Code environment adheres to industry standards and regulatory requirements.

Scaling VS Code for enterprise use requires careful planning, automation, and governance. By following these strategies, you can tailor VS Code to meet the specific needs of your organization, streamline development processes, and maintain a consistent and secure coding environment across large development teams.

Section 19.2: Managing Licenses and Compliance

In the context of enterprise-level usage of Visual Studio Code (VS Code), managing licenses and ensuring compliance is of paramount importance. Licensing issues can lead to legal consequences and negatively impact your organization's reputation. Here, we'll explore strategies to effectively manage licenses and maintain compliance when using VS Code in an enterprise environment.

1. **License Tracking:** Start by maintaining a comprehensive inventory of all software licenses, including those for VS Code and any extensions or plugins used within your organization. This inventory should include details such as license type, expiration dates, and the number of licenses purchased.

2. **License Agreements:** Review and understand the terms and conditions of the licenses for VS Code and any related extensions. Different extensions may have varying licensing models, so it's crucial to ensure compliance with each one.

3. **Volume Licensing:** Consider volume licensing agreements provided by Microsoft for VS Code if your organization requires a large number of licenses. These agreements often offer cost savings and simplify license management.

4. **License Audits:** Periodically conduct internal license audits to verify that the number of VS Code installations matches the number of licenses purchased. This helps identify any potential compliance issues proactively.

5. **License Enforcement:** Utilize license management tools and policies to enforce compliance. These tools can help restrict access to VS Code and extensions if valid licenses are not detected.

6. **Extension Licensing:** Keep a close eye on the licensing requirements of extensions used within your organization. Some extensions may be free for personal use but require commercial licenses for enterprise usage.

7. **License Renewal:** Establish a process for renewing and updating licenses before they expire. This prevents interruptions in development workflows due to expired licenses.

8. **Compliance Documentation:** Maintain documentation that demonstrates compliance with VS Code and extension licenses. This documentation should be readily available in case of audits or inquiries.

9. **Employee Training:** Educate your development teams about the importance of license compliance and the potential consequences of using unlicensed software. Encourage responsible use of VS Code and its extensions.

10. **License Reclamation:** Implement a process for reclaiming licenses from employees who no longer require access to VS Code or specific extensions. This helps optimize license usage and reduce costs.

11. **Open Source and Free Extensions:** While many extensions for VS Code are open source or free, it's essential to review their licenses carefully. Some open source licenses, such as the GNU GPL, have specific requirements that organizations must adhere to.

12. **Legal Consultation:** If your organization has complex licensing needs or concerns, consider seeking legal advice to ensure full compliance with software licenses.

Remember that maintaining license compliance is not only a legal requirement but also an ethical practice that supports the developers and organizations behind the software. By implementing robust license management processes, your enterprise can effectively use VS Code while staying compliant with licensing agreements and regulations.

Section 19.3: Enterprise-Level Customizations

Customizing Visual Studio Code (VS Code) at an enterprise level can significantly enhance productivity, streamline workflows, and ensure consistency across development teams. In this section, we'll explore various customization options and best practices for tailoring VS Code to your organization's specific needs.

1. **Extensions Management:** As an enterprise, you may want to standardize the use of specific extensions or provide a curated set of extensions for your development teams. To achieve this, consider creating an extension pack that bundles essential extensions, making it easier for team members to install the required tools.

2. **Custom Extensions:** In addition to leveraging existing extensions, your organization might have unique requirements that warrant the development of custom extensions. Custom extensions can add functionality specific to your projects, processes, or coding standards.

3. **Workspace Settings:** VS Code allows you to define workspace-specific settings in a settings.json file within your project directory. This is particularly useful for enforcing coding conventions, linting rules, and other project-specific configurations.

4. **User and Workspace Snippets:** Create and share code snippets that align with your organization's coding standards and best practices. These snippets can be distributed to all team members to streamline code writing.

5. **Custom Keybindings:** Define custom keybindings that facilitate common tasks or invoke specific commands within your organization. By providing a consistent set of keybindings, you can improve efficiency and reduce cognitive load for developers.

6. **Themes and Color Schemes:** Customize the appearance of VS Code to match your corporate branding or create a comfortable coding environment. You can develop custom themes or choose from existing ones that align with your organization's aesthetic preferences.

7. **Branding:** Apply your organization's branding elements, such as logos or custom icons, to VS Code's user interface. This helps create a cohesive and recognizable development environment.

8. **Productivity Features:** Leverage VS Code's productivity features, such as code snippets, IntelliSense, and code folding, to enhance development speed and consistency across projects.

9. **Version Control Integration:** Integrate VS Code with your organization's preferred version control system (e.g., Git, SVN) and define workflows that align with your version control policies.

10. **Remote Development Containers:** Consider using remote development containers to create a standardized development environment that can be replicated across teams. This ensures that all developers work in consistent development environments with the required tools and dependencies.

11. **Accessibility:** Pay attention to accessibility considerations to ensure that VS Code is usable by all team members, including those with disabilities. Customize the editor's accessibility features to meet your organization's inclusivity goals.

12. **Automated Setup:** Develop scripts or tools to automate the setup and configuration of VS Code for new team members. This ensures that developers start with a standardized development environment, reducing setup time and potential configuration errors.

13. **Documentation:** Document your customization guidelines and best practices for VS Code within your organization. This documentation should cover how to set up, configure, and use the customized environment effectively.

14. **Training and Support:** Offer training sessions and support resources to help developers become proficient in using the customized VS Code environment. Ensure that your development teams are aware of the available customizations and how to leverage them.

15. **Feedback Loop:** Establish a feedback mechanism for developers to provide input on the customized environment. This helps identify areas for improvement and ensures that the customization aligns with developers' needs and preferences.

By implementing these enterprise-level customizations, you can create a development environment in Visual Studio Code that not only enhances productivity but also aligns with your organization's unique requirements and coding standards. Customizations should be periodically reviewed and updated to adapt to changing needs and technologies.

Section 19.4: Security in an Enterprise Environment

Ensuring the security of your development environment within an enterprise is paramount to safeguard sensitive code, data, and infrastructure. In this section, we'll explore security considerations and best practices for using Visual Studio Code (VS Code) in an enterprise environment.

1. **Extension Security:** As an enterprise, it's crucial to vet and manage the extensions used within your organization. Ensure that the extensions you install are from trusted sources and regularly update them to patch any security vulnerabilities. Consider using an extension management solution to control which extensions are allowed within your organization.

2. **Integrity Verification:** Implement measures to verify the integrity of VS Code and its extensions. You can use cryptographic hashes to verify that the VS Code installation and extensions have not been tampered with. Many extensions provide checksums or signatures for this purpose.

3. **Update Management:** Keep VS Code and its extensions up to date with the latest security patches and bug fixes. Create a process for regularly reviewing and applying updates to minimize the risk of security vulnerabilities.

4. **Code Scanning and Analysis:** Integrate code scanning and analysis tools into your CI/CD pipeline to identify security vulnerabilities, code smells, and other issues early in the development process. Popular tools like SonarQube and Snyk can help with this.

5. **Static Code Analysis:** Perform static code analysis to identify potential security vulnerabilities and code quality issues. Tools like ESLint, TSLint, and SonarLint can be used to enforce coding standards and security best practices.

6. **Authentication and Authorization:** Implement strong authentication mechanisms for accessing VS Code and your development environment. Use Single Sign-On (SSO) solutions or other identity providers to ensure that only authorized personnel can access your codebase.

7. **Role-Based Access Control (RBAC):** Utilize RBAC to assign specific roles and permissions to users within VS Code and your development tools. Ensure that team members have access only to the resources and functionality required for their roles.

8. **Data Encryption:** Ensure that data transmitted between VS Code and remote servers, version control systems, and other services is encrypted using secure protocols (e.g., HTTPS, SSH). Encrypt sensitive data, such as configuration files and credentials, when stored locally.

9. **Secure Development Practices:** Educate your development teams about secure coding practices. Train developers to avoid common security pitfalls, such as code injection, cross-site scripting (XSS), and SQL injection.

10. **Dependency Scanning:** Regularly scan for known security vulnerabilities in the dependencies used in your projects. Tools like OWASP Dependency-Check can automatically identify vulnerable libraries.

11. **Incident Response Plan:** Develop an incident response plan that outlines steps to follow in the event of a security breach. Ensure that your team knows how to respond quickly and effectively to mitigate the impact of security incidents.

12. **Security Audits and Reviews:** Conduct regular security audits and code reviews to identify and remediate potential vulnerabilities. Peer reviews and automated code analysis tools can help in this regard.

13. **Secure Configuration:** Ensure that VS Code and its extensions are configured securely. Disable unnecessary features, enable security-related settings, and adhere to security best practices provided by the VS Code documentation.

14. **Monitoring and Logging:** Implement monitoring and logging solutions to track user activities and detect suspicious behavior. Monitor authentication attempts, access to sensitive resources, and changes to code repositories.

15. **Compliance and Regulations:** Stay informed about industry-specific security regulations and compliance requirements. Ensure that your development practices align with these standards, especially if your organization deals with sensitive customer data.

16. **Regular Training:** Continuously educate your development teams about emerging security threats and best practices. Security training and awareness programs can help team members stay vigilant.

17. **Third-Party Integrations:** If your organization uses third-party services or APIs in conjunction with VS Code, ensure that these integrations meet security standards and are regularly reviewed for vulnerabilities.

By incorporating these security practices into your enterprise's use of Visual Studio Code, you can significantly reduce the risk of security breaches and protect your sensitive code and data. Security should be an ongoing concern, and regular assessments and updates are essential to maintaining a secure development environment.

Section 19.5: Training and Support for Teams

In an enterprise environment, providing training and support for development teams is crucial to ensure efficient and secure use of Visual Studio Code (VS Code). This section explores strategies for training and supporting your teams effectively.

1. **Onboarding and Orientation:** When new developers join your organization, offer an onboarding process that includes an introduction to VS Code. Provide them with resources like documentation, tutorials, and best practice guidelines specific to your organization's workflows and coding standards.

2. **Customized Training:** Tailor training programs to meet the needs of different teams and roles within your organization. For example, front-end developers may require different training from back-end developers. Consider offering specialized training sessions or resources.

3. **Online Resources:** Create an online repository of resources, including documentation, video tutorials, and FAQs, that team members can access at any time. Ensure that these resources are kept up to date with the latest information.

4. **In-House Experts:** Identify and designate VS Code experts within your organization who can serve as go-to resources for team members. These experts can help troubleshoot issues, answer questions, and provide guidance on best practices.

5. **Peer Learning:** Encourage knowledge sharing and peer learning among team members. Host regular meetings or workshops where developers can share tips, tricks, and experiences with VS Code. This fosters a culture of continuous improvement.

6. **Mentorship Programs:** Establish mentorship programs where experienced developers can mentor newer team members. This can be particularly beneficial for junior developers looking to enhance their VS Code skills.

7. **Troubleshooting and Support:** Provide channels for team members to seek help when encountering issues with VS Code. Whether through a dedicated Slack channel, email support, or an internal helpdesk, ensure that support is readily available.

8. **Feedback Mechanisms:** Create feedback loops for developers to report bugs, suggest improvements, or request features related to VS Code or any custom extensions your organization may use. Regularly review and act upon this feedback.

9. **Certifications:** Consider offering certifications or badges for developers who demonstrate proficiency in using VS Code and adhering to your organization's coding standards. This can motivate team members to invest in their VS Code skills.

10. **Regular Updates:** Keep your teams informed about updates and changes related to VS Code, extensions, and any custom configurations. Share release notes and highlight new features that can improve productivity.

11. **Security Training:** Include security training as part of your support and training program. Teach developers about common security threats, best practices for secure coding, and how to use VS Code securely within the enterprise context.

12. **Scalability:** Plan for the scalability of your training and support programs as your organization grows. Ensure that new team members can access the same level of training and support as existing members.

13. **Documentation Review:** Periodically review and update your organization's documentation to ensure that it remains relevant and accurate. Make it easy for developers to find the information they need.

14. **User Communities:** Encourage your development teams to participate in VS Code user communities, forums, and online groups. These communities can provide additional insights, solutions to common problems, and networking opportunities.

15. **Evaluation and Improvement:** Continuously evaluate the effectiveness of your training and support programs. Collect feedback from developers and use metrics to identify areas for improvement.

16. **Flexibility:** Recognize that different developers have varying learning preferences. Offer a mix of training formats, such as written documentation, video tutorials, interactive workshops, and one-on-one coaching, to accommodate diverse learning styles.

By investing in training and support for your development teams, you empower them to make the most of VS Code's capabilities and contribute to a more efficient and secure development environment within your enterprise. Regular updates and a focus on continuous improvement will help your organization stay at the forefront of VS Code usage.

Chapter 20: The Future of Visual Studio Code

Section 20.1: Emerging Trends in Development

The world of software development is constantly evolving, and Visual Studio Code (VS Code) is no exception. In this section, we'll explore some emerging trends in the development landscape and how they might influence the future of VS Code.

1. **Cloud Development:** Cloud-native development is on the rise, and many developers are moving their workloads to the cloud. VS Code has been quick to adapt with extensions and tools that integrate seamlessly with various cloud providers. The future may see even deeper integration, allowing developers to build, test, and deploy applications directly from VS Code to the cloud.

2. **Remote Work:** The shift to remote work has accelerated due to recent global events. VS Code's remote development capabilities, such as Remote Containers and Remote SSH, have become essential tools for remote collaboration. In the future, we can expect further improvements and innovations in this area to enhance the remote development experience.

3. **Machine Learning and AI:** AI and machine learning are becoming integral to software development. VS Code may incorporate AI-driven features, such as code completion suggestions based on context, code refactoring recommendations, and automated error detection.

4. **Low-Code/No-Code Development:** Low-code and no-code platforms are gaining popularity, enabling individuals with limited coding experience to build applications. VS Code could explore ways to support these platforms, making it a versatile tool for both professional developers and citizen developers.

5. **Serverless Computing:** Serverless architecture simplifies application deployment and scaling. Future VS Code extensions may streamline the development and deployment of serverless applications, providing templates and debugging tools for various serverless platforms.

6. **Containerization and Kubernetes:** Containerization and orchestration technologies like Docker and Kubernetes are widely used in modern development. VS Code will likely continue improving its container support, making it easier for developers to work with containerized applications.

7. **Progressive Web Apps (PWAs):** As PWAs gain traction, VS Code might offer enhanced features for developing and testing these web applications. This includes tools for service worker development, offline testing, and performance optimization.

8. **Enhanced Collaboration:** Collaborative coding tools have become essential for teams working remotely. Future VS Code updates may further enhance live

collaboration features, enabling real-time co-editing, instant feedback, and seamless integration with team communication platforms.

9. **Security by Design:** Security is a top concern in software development. Future VS Code versions may include built-in security analysis tools, code scanning, and integration with security testing platforms to help developers identify and address security vulnerabilities early in the development process.

10. **Multi-Platform Development:** The demand for cross-platform and multi-device applications is growing. VS Code will likely continue to support a wide range of programming languages and frameworks, making it a go-to choice for multi-platform development.

11. **Voice and Natural Language Interfaces:** With advancements in voice and natural language processing, VS Code could incorporate voice commands and natural language interfaces to boost developer productivity and accessibility.

12. **Quantum Computing:** While quantum computing is still in its infancy, it holds great promise for solving complex problems. Future versions of VS Code might include extensions for quantum programming languages and simulators to facilitate quantum development.

13. **Community and Open Source:** The vibrant VS Code community is likely to remain a driving force behind its evolution. Open source contributions and community-driven extensions will continue to enrich the ecosystem.

In conclusion, the future of Visual Studio Code is bright, with exciting developments on the horizon. It will adapt to emerging trends in development, empowering developers to work more efficiently, securely, and collaboratively in an ever-changing technological landscape. As a developer, staying informed about these trends and exploring how VS Code can align with them will be key to your success.

Section 20.2: Visual Studio Code in the Next Decade

As we look ahead to the next decade, Visual Studio Code (VS Code) is poised to continue its remarkable journey as one of the most popular and versatile code editors. In this section, we'll explore what the future might hold for VS Code and how it could evolve to meet the changing needs of developers.

1. **Enhanced Language Support:** VS Code has always excelled in providing support for a wide range of programming languages. In the coming years, we can expect even deeper language integration, with improved syntax highlighting, intelligent code completion, and built-in support for new and emerging languages.

2. **AI-Driven Productivity:** Artificial intelligence (AI) and machine learning are transforming software development. VS Code could leverage AI to offer smarter code suggestions, automated code refactoring, and predictive debugging. Imagine a code editor that understands your coding style and helps you write better code with fewer errors.

3. **Seamless Collaboration:** Remote work and distributed teams are becoming the norm. VS Code's remote development capabilities will likely see further enhancements, making it even easier for developers to collaborate in real-time, no matter where they are located.

4. **Cloud Development:** The cloud is central to modern software development. VS Code may continue to integrate with cloud platforms, enabling developers to build, test, and deploy cloud-native applications effortlessly.

5. **Containerization and Kubernetes:** Containerization technologies like Docker and orchestration platforms like Kubernetes are widely used. VS Code could provide even better support for containerized development, with features for managing containers, debugging inside containers, and deploying containerized applications.

6. **Mobile and Web Development:** As the demand for mobile and web applications grows, VS Code may introduce more specialized tools and extensions for mobile app development, responsive web design, and progressive web apps (PWAs).

7. **Code Quality and Security:** Ensuring code quality and security is paramount. Future VS Code versions might incorporate advanced static code analysis tools, vulnerability scanning, and automated security checks to help developers write safer and more reliable code.

8. **Enhanced Extension Ecosystem:** The VS Code extension marketplace is already vast, but it will continue to expand. We can anticipate new extensions for niche development tasks, as well as improved extension management and discoverability features.

9. **Accessibility and Inclusivity:** Accessibility is a priority in modern software development. VS Code may focus on improving accessibility features, making the editor more inclusive for developers with disabilities.

10. **Performance Optimization:** Developers always appreciate a faster, more responsive code editor. VS Code will likely continue its efforts to optimize performance, reduce startup times, and minimize resource usage.

11. **Community Contributions:** The VS Code community is a driving force behind its success. Open source contributions, user feedback, and collaborative development will continue to shape the editor's future.

12. **Integration with Emerging Technologies:** As new technologies emerge, VS Code will adapt. This includes integrating with quantum computing platforms, augmented and virtual reality development environments, and other cutting-edge technologies.

13. **Education and Learning:** VS Code is widely used in education. Future versions may include enhanced features for teaching programming, with built-in tutorials, coding challenges, and interactive learning tools.

14. **Cross-Platform Dominance:** VS Code's cross-platform compatibility is one of its strengths. It will maintain its status as a top choice for developers on Windows, macOS, and Linux.

15. **Sustainability:** Software development has an environmental impact. VS Code may incorporate sustainability features, such as code analysis for energy efficiency and tools to reduce carbon footprint.

In summary, Visual Studio Code's journey in the next decade will be marked by continued innovation, adaptability to emerging trends, and a commitment to empowering developers worldwide. Whether you're a seasoned developer or just starting your coding journey, VS Code will remain a valuable and ever-evolving companion in your development endeavors. Stay curious, keep exploring, and embrace the exciting future of software development with VS Code.

Section 20.3: Community and Open Source Contributions

One of the key strengths of Visual Studio Code (VS Code) is its vibrant and active community, coupled with its open-source nature. In this section, we'll delve into the significance of community contributions and open source in shaping the past, present, and future of VS Code.

Open Source Foundation

VS Code is built on an open-source foundation that allows developers worldwide to collaborate, contribute, and customize the editor. This open-source approach has several notable benefits:

1. *Rapid Development: Open source accelerates the development process. Thousands of developers from different backgrounds contribute code, bug fixes, and new features, resulting in a faster release cycle.*

2. *Diverse Perspectives: An open-source project like VS Code benefits from diverse perspectives and ideas. Developers from around the globe bring their unique insights, leading to innovative solutions and improved usability.*

3. *Transparency: The source code of VS Code is available for scrutiny by anyone. This transparency fosters trust and ensures that the software is free from hidden vulnerabilities or backdoors.*

4. *Extensibility: The extensibility of VS Code is a direct result of its open-source nature. Anyone can create extensions, enhancing the editor's functionality for specific use cases.*

5. *Community Ownership: The community actively shapes the direction of VS Code. User feedback, feature requests, and bug reports play a vital role in prioritizing development efforts.*

The Extension Marketplace

The VS Code extension marketplace is a testament to the power of community-driven development. Here's why it's so crucial:

1. *Diverse Ecosystem: The marketplace boasts thousands of extensions catering to various programming languages, frameworks, and development workflows. This diversity ensures that VS Code remains relevant to a wide range of developers.*

2. *Constant Innovation: Extension developers are continually pushing the boundaries of what VS Code can do. They introduce new tools, integrations, and enhancements that keep the editor at the forefront of technology.*

3. *Customization: Extensions allow developers to tailor VS Code to their specific needs. Whether it's adding support for a niche language or integrating with a cloud service, extensions empower users to make VS Code their own.*

4. *Collaboration: Many extensions are the result of collaboration between developers within the community. These joint efforts lead to high-quality, feature-rich extensions that benefit everyone.*

5. *User Ratings and Feedback: The marketplace includes user ratings and reviews, helping developers discover the best extensions. Users can provide feedback and report issues, fostering a sense of community involvement.*

Collaboration Beyond Borders

VS Code's global user base means that it's not bound by geographical constraints. Developers from different time zones and cultures collaborate seamlessly. This global collaboration results in:

1. 24/7 Development: The distributed nature of the community means that development and support can happen around the clock. This ensures quick issue resolution and continuous improvement.

2. Diverse Use Cases: Developers worldwide use VS Code for various purposes, from web development to data science. This diversity leads to a more versatile and adaptable code editor.

3. Multilingual Support: Language localization and internationalization efforts make VS Code accessible to developers who speak different languages.

A Culture of Giving Back

Contributing to open source is a way for developers to give back to the community. Many successful developers started by contributing to projects like VS Code. The act of giving back includes:

1. Code Contributions: Developers can contribute to the VS Code core by submitting code changes, bug fixes, or improvements.

2. Extension Development: Creating and sharing extensions is another way to contribute. It allows developers to address specific needs and share their solutions with others.

3. Documentation and Tutorials: Clear and comprehensive documentation is essential. Contributing to documentation or creating tutorials helps new users and enhances the learning experience.

4. Community Support: Active community members often help answer questions, troubleshoot issues, and offer guidance to fellow developers.

5. Evangelism: Spreading the word about VS Code and its capabilities is a valuable contribution. Advocating for the editor helps grow the user base and foster new collaborations.

The Future of Community and Open Source

As VS Code continues to evolve, the role of the community and open source remains pivotal. The future promises even more collaborative efforts, innovative extensions, and user-driven improvements. Developers, whether seasoned veterans or newcomers, will find opportunities to shape the editor's trajectory. The community-driven spirit of VS Code ensures that it will remain a tool built by developers, for developers, for years to come.

Section 20.4: Integrating AI and Machine Learning Tools

The integration of Artificial Intelligence (AI) and Machine Learning (ML) tools is becoming increasingly important in the development landscape. Visual Studio Code (VS Code) recognizes this trend and offers a range of extensions and features to support developers in leveraging AI and ML capabilities within their development workflows.

AI-Powered Code Assistance

One of the significant advantages of AI in development is its ability to assist developers in writing better code. VS Code provides AI-powered code assistance through various extensions and features:

1. Code Completion: AI-driven code completion suggests code snippets and auto-completes code as you type. It can predict what you intend to write, saving time and reducing errors.

```
// AI-powered code completion
function calculateSum(arr) {
    return arr.reduce((acc, val) => acc + val, 0);
}

const numbers = [1, 2, 3, 4, 5];
calculateSum(numbers). // AI suggests methods like 'toFixed', 'toString', etc
```

2. Code Linting: AI-based code linters can analyze your code for common mistakes, code style violations, and potential bugs. They offer suggestions for improving code quality.

```
# AI-powered code linting in Python
def divide(a, b):
    if b == 0:
        return "Division by zero"
    else:
        return a / b

result = divide(10, 0)  # AI-based linter detects potential division by zero.
```

3. Intelligent Refactoring: AI-driven refactoring tools can suggest and automate code refactoring, making your code more readable and maintainable.

```
// AI-assisted refactoring in Java
public class Calculator {
    public int add(int a, int b) {
        return a + b;
    }
}

// AI suggests renaming the 'add' method to 'sum' for better readability.
```

ML-Powered Predictive Analysis

Machine Learning can be harnessed for predictive analysis, helping developers make data-driven decisions within VS Code:

1. Data Exploration: VS Code extensions can integrate with ML libraries to provide data exploration capabilities, allowing developers to visualize and analyze data.

```python
# ML-powered data exploration in Jupyter Notebook within VS Code
import pandas as pd
import matplotlib.pyplot as plt

# Load a dataset
data = pd.read_csv('data.csv')

# Visualize data using ML-powered plotting libraries
plt.scatter(data['X'], data['Y'])
plt.xlabel('X')
plt.ylabel('Y')
plt.title('Scatter Plot')
plt.show()
```

2. Predictive Modeling: ML models can be trained and deployed within VS Code to make predictions based on historical data. This can be valuable for various applications, from forecasting to recommendation systems.

```python
# ML-powered predictive modeling in VS Code
from sklearn.linear_model import LinearRegression

# Load training data
X_train, y_train = load_training_data()

# Train a machine learning model
model = LinearRegression()
model.fit(X_train, y_train)

# Make predictions
predictions = model.predict(X_test)
```

AI-Enhanced Testing

AI can play a significant role in optimizing testing processes within VS Code:

1. Test Automation: AI-driven test automation tools can automatically generate test cases, execute them, and analyze the results to identify potential issues.

```javascript
// AI-driven test automation in VS Code
const { AI_TestRunner } = require('ai-test-runner');

const tests = AI_TestRunner.generateTestCases('myApp.js');
AI_TestRunner.executeTests(tests);

// AI analyzes test results and reports issues.
```

2. Test Data Generation: ML algorithms can assist in generating diverse and comprehensive test data, ensuring thorough test coverage.

```
// ML-powered test data generation in VS Code
import mlTestDataGenerator from 'ml-test-data-generator';

const testData = mlTestDataGenerator.generateTestData('testConfig.json');
runTests(testData);
```

Future Possibilities

As AI and ML continue to advance, their integration into VS Code will likely expand. This may include more sophisticated code generation, AI-driven bug detection, and enhanced collaboration tools. Developers can look forward to an ecosystem where AI and ML are seamlessly woven into their daily development tasks, making them more productive and efficient. The future of development with VS Code promises exciting possibilities at the intersection of AI and coding.

Section 20.5: Staying Ahead with Visual Studio Code

Staying ahead in the world of software development means continuously adapting to new technologies, tools, and best practices. Visual Studio Code (VS Code) is no exception, as it evolves to meet the changing needs of developers. In this section, we'll explore strategies and resources to help you stay up-to-date and make the most of VS Code's capabilities.

1. Keep VS Code Updated

The first step in staying ahead with VS Code is ensuring you're using the latest version. Microsoft regularly releases updates with bug fixes, performance improvements, and new features. You can set VS Code to update automatically or manually check for updates through the menu.

```
VS Code Menu > Help > Check for Updates
```

2. Explore New Extensions

The VS Code extension marketplace is a treasure trove of productivity-enhancing tools. Periodically browse the marketplace to discover new extensions that can streamline your workflow or provide new capabilities. Look for extensions related to your programming languages, frameworks, or development tasks.

```
VS Code Menu > Extensions (Ctrl+Shift+X)
```

3. Join the Community

The VS Code community is vibrant and active. Engage with other developers, share your knowledge, and learn from others through forums, discussion groups, and social media. The official VS Code website and GitHub repository are excellent places to start.

4. Attend Webinars and Conferences

Stay informed about VS Code and broader software development trends by attending webinars, virtual conferences, and meetups. These events often feature presentations by VS Code team members and experienced developers who share their insights and best practices.

5. Learn Keyboard Shortcuts

Mastering keyboard shortcuts can significantly boost your productivity in VS Code. Take the time to learn and practice useful shortcuts for navigation, editing, and other common tasks. VS Code provides a built-in Keyboard Shortcuts Reference for easy reference.

```
VS Code Menu > File > Preferences > Keyboard Shortcuts (Ctrl+K Ctrl+S)
```

6. Explore Insider Builds

If you're eager to test bleeding-edge features and improvements, consider using the VS Code Insider build. It provides early access to upcoming changes and allows you to provide feedback to shape the future of VS Code.

7. Embrace AI-Powered Tools

As AI and machine learning become more integrated into development tools, stay open to AI-powered features in VS Code. These tools can assist with code completion, debugging, and even writing unit tests. Regularly check for extensions that harness AI for coding assistance.

8. Experiment with Remote Development

VS Code offers remote development extensions that enable you to code on remote servers, containers, or even in the cloud. Experiment with remote development to stay agile and adapt to changing project requirements.

9. Contribute to Open Source

If you're passionate about VS Code and have the skills, consider contributing to its development. Microsoft welcomes contributions from the community, including bug reports, code contributions, and documentation improvements.

10. Explore Emerging Trends

Stay informed about emerging trends in software development, such as cloud-native development, serverless computing, and microservices architecture. VS Code continues to evolve to support these trends, so being aware of them can help you make informed decisions.

In conclusion, staying ahead with Visual Studio Code involves a commitment to continuous learning, exploration, and community engagement. By keeping your tools and skills up-to-date, you can remain a proficient and innovative developer in the ever-evolving world of software development.